Emigration and the Chinese Lineage

This volume is sponsored by the
Center for Chinese Studies,
University of California, Berkeley

THE CENTER FOR CHINESE STUDIES
at the University of California, Berkeley, supported by the Ford Foundation,
the Institute of International Studies (University of California, Berkeley),
and the State of California, is the unifying organization for social science
and interdisciplinary research on contemporary China.

RECENT PUBLICATIONS:

LOWELL DITTMER
Liu Shao-ch'i and the Chinese Cultural Revolution:
The Politics of Mass Criticism

TETSUYA KATAOKA
Resistance and Revolution in China:
The Communists and the Second United Front

ILPYONG J. KIM
The Politics of Chinese Communism:
Kiangsi under the Soviets

EDWARD E. RICE
Mao's Way

FREDERIC WAKEMAN, JR.
History and Will:
Philosophical Perspectives of Mao Tse-tung's Thought

Emigration and the Chinese Lineage

The Mans in Hong Kong and London

JAMES L. WATSON

UNIVERSITY OF CALIFORNIA PRESS
Berkeley, Los Angeles, London

University of California Press

Berkeley and Los Angeles, California

University of California Press, Ltd.

London, England

Copyright © 1975, by
The Regents of the University of California

ISBN 0-520-02647-0

Library of Congress Catalog Card Number: 73-90654

Printed in the United States of America

For My Parents
R. R. and D. B. WATSON

CONTENTS

MAPS

FIGURE

TABLES

CHINESE TERMS AND NAMES

Unless otherwise noted, Chinese terms in the text are in Mandarin (standard Wade-Giles Romanization system). A few specialized terms are in Cantonese (Yale Romanization system) and are marked (c). For example: (c) *san nguk.* Separate glossaries for Mandarin and Cantonese terms are provided at the end of this study.

Place names in Hong Kong follow the general usage as set out by the Hong Kong Government in its *Gazetteer of Place Names in Hong Kong, Kowloon and the New Territories* (1969 re-issue), Hong Kong Government Press.

Except for historical figures, all personal names used in this study are pseudonyms.

TABLE OF MEASURES

1 catty	1.33 lbs.
1 picul	100 catties
1 tou	1/6 acre (approx.)

CURRENCY

1HK$	US$0.16 (1970)
1 £	US$2.40 (1970)

ACKNOWLEDGMENTS

I WOULD like to express my gratitude to a number of people who helped make this study possible. Jack M. Potter served as my graduate advisor at Berkeley and first encouraged me to work in Hong Kong. I was fortunate indeed to have such a conscientious thesis director. Professor Potter's comments on earlier drafts of this book have been extremely helpful and I offer him my sincerest thanks. I am also indebted to Professors Burton Benedict, Chalmers A. Johnson, George M. Foster, and Wolfram Eberhard (all of Berkeley) for their valuable comments on this study; and I would like to thank them for the help and encouragement they have given me over the years.

Rubie S. Watson shared the field experience with me in San Tin and contributed a great deal to the success of the project. Even though she was busy with her own research, she still managed to help with the analysis of Hong Kong Government records pertaining to emigration. She also read the manuscript at every stage and acted as my severest—and most constructive —critic.

In addition to the people mentioned above, I would like to thank several others for reading and commenting on various parts of this study: Armando da Silva, Elizabeth L. Johnson, Graham E. Johnson, George W. Lovelace, Henry P. Lundsgaarde, Lindy Li Mark, Patty Jo Watson, and Richard A. Watson. The Social Science Research Institute (University of Hawaii) subsidized the typing of the manuscript; and my colleagues in the Department of Anthropology at the University of Hawaii provided a congenial atmosphere in which to write.

My wife and I were extremely fortunate to have had Mr. Stanley S. Y. Wong serve as our research assistant while we lived in San Tin. It is impossible to thank all of the villagers who helped us, but my debt to our landlord, Mr. Man Tso-chuen, is very great indeed. In writing this book I have made a special effort to protect the identity of key informants who were instrumental in San Tin's conversion to emigration. At the same time, however, I feel a strong obligation to record the life histories of the ex-sailors and the retired farmers who spent many long afternoons helping me reconstruct the history of their remarkable community.

The Foreign Area Fellowship Program (SSRC-ACLS) generously supported my field research and was kind enough to give me a six month write-up grant after returning to the States. The Center for Chinese Studies, University of California at Berkeley, also sponsored my research with a timely grant that made the London phase of this study possible. I would like to take this opportunity to thank the Center for supporting me through two years of graduate school and for providing me with a place to work on several occasions.

The field research itself would have been more difficult had it not been for the existence of the Universities Service Centre in Hong Kong. My wife and I made frequent use of the USC's facilities and benefited greatly from our contacts with the staff and the other resident scholars. The Centre of Asian Studies at the University of Hong Kong opened its doors to us and allowed us to use its special collection of local research materials. I would like to thank Dr. Marjorie Topley of the HKU Centre for her help and advice during the early stages of my research. The staff members of the Yuen Long District Office in Hong Kong's New Territories were exceptionally helpful and cooperative throughout my stay in San Tin. I would also like to thank the Hong Kong Government's Immigration Department for providing the unpublished emigration data used in Chapter Four.

A special note of thanks is due to Dale and Judy Bratton for the hospitality they showed us while we were living in the village (their bathtub was always a welcome sight).

In London, the Hong Kong Government Office took a genuine interest in my research and arranged for me to meet leaders of the Chinese restaurant trade. Mr. S. A. Webb-Johnson, HKGO Liaison Officer, was especially helpful during this phase of the study. I also benefited from a series of conversations with Hugh D. R. Baker, Maurice Freedman, Howard G. H. Nelson, Ng Kwee-choo, and Barbara E. Ward regarding the Chinese community in Britain. My wife and I both made extensive use of the Reading Room of the British Museum and the library of the Institute of Race Relations in London.

The following publishers and institutions have kindly allowed me to use copyrighted materials in this book: The Institute of Race Relations, London (for a quotation from page 42 of Ng Kwee-choo's *The Chinese in London*); The University of British Columbia Press and *Pacific Affairs* (for use of a table from page 260 of Chen Ta's *Emigrant Communities in South China*); The MIT Press (for a quotation from page 180 of C. K. Yang's *A Chinese Village in Early Communist Transition*); and the Hong Kong Government, Public Works Department, Crown Lands and Survey Office (for use of their survey sheet no. 75-NW-B, Map of San Tin Village).

None of the institutions or individuals mentioned above bears any responsibility for the conclusions or the interpretations presented in this book.

J. L. W.
London, 1974

Chapter One

INTRODUCTION

THIS study focuses on a particular type of peasant village known as an "emigrant community." Perhaps the best known definition is one offered by the Chinese sociologist Chen Ta in his 1939 book on the subject: "An emigrant community . . . means a community from which considerable numbers of persons have for some time emigrated, and continue to emigrate. . . ; a non-emigrant community is one from which such emigration is rare" (Chen Ta 1939:4, note 3). In order to avoid confusion, it is best to reserve the term "emigrant community" for villages that have a high rate of *international* emigration as opposed to internal or rural-urban migration. Emigrants from this type of specialized community retain close ties to the kinsmen they leave behind, even after many years of settlement abroad. Emigrant communites as defined here are found most notably in societies with well-established traditions of labor out-migration, such as Ireland, Lebanon, India, and China.

The present study deals with the emigration of peasants from one Chinese village. The research was carried out for 20 months between 1969 and 1971, and was divided into two phases: (1) an intensive investigation of the village of San Tin, the largest emigrant community in rural Hong Kong, and (2) a brief follow-up survey of San Tin emigrants working in London. This is a reversal of the usual approach to the study of peasant migration movements. Most anthropologists who have done migration research focus on the migrants in the host society (or in the host city) and pay only secondary attention to the

1

emigrant community in the sending society.[1] The present study
is concerned with both sides of the emigration network, with
primary emphasis on the migrant's home community.

Although the following chapters touch on many problems,
a central theme throughout the study is the relation between
emigration and social change. San Tin is an ideal setting for
this kind of investigation because its emigration movement is
a relatively recent development and it is still possible to
determine the actual process of change. Until approximately
fifteen years ago, San Tin was a traditional peasant community
with an economy based on agriculture. By the early 1960s,
however, the villagers had ceased farming and San Tin was
converted into an emigrant community with an economy almost totally dependent upon remittances. Eighty-five to ninety
percent of San Tin's able-bodied men now work in Chinese
restaurants scattered throughout the United Kingdom and
other parts of Western Europe. The initial task of this study
is to reconstruct the social history of the village to determine
the most significant causes of the conversion to emigration.
The reconstruction demonstrates that the "push" of economic
necessity and the "pull" of opportunity from abroad were
equally important causal factors in the rise of out-migration
from San Tin.

As might be expected, the high rate of emigration has had
a massive impact on the economic and social life of the village.
A large section of this study is devoted to the analysis of these
recent changes, and it is found that many have had the
paradoxical effect of preserving traditional patterns of social
organization. Rather than acting as a force for "modernizing"

---

[1] There are a few important exceptions to this pattern and these will
be discussed in the concluding chapter. For other studies of emigrant
communities, see the following: Chen Ta 1939, Douglass 1970, Gonzalez
1969, Gulick 1955, R. Lewis 1968, Tannous 1942. A recent monograph by
Stuart B. Philpott, *West Indian Migration: The Montserrat Case* (1973),
is of special interest because it deals with both ends of the migration chain.
It is similar in structure to the present study.

change, emigration has allowed the residents of San Tin to maintain a way of life that is rapidly disappearing in other parts of rural Hong Kong. There is considerable evidence to suggest that this kind of traditionalism may be characteristic of emigrant communities in newly developing societies all over the world, not just the Chinese culture area (see Chapter Ten).

Another major goal of the research was to determine how peasant emigration movements are organized both at home and abroad. In most previous studies of this kind little is shown about the critical links between the home villages and the overseas communities. In order to understand fully the process of emigration, it is important to know *who* organizes the movement and *how* it is accomplished. Although the London phase of the present study was brief (three months), it was able to provide much of the information necessary for a thorough analysis of the emigration process.

CHINESE EMIGRANT COMMUNITIES

Soon after the People's Republic was established in 1949, China was closed to most foreign scholars and, except for a few isolated cases (e.g., Geddes 1963, Myrdal 1965), first-hand field research became impossible. As a partial consequence of the closure, social scientists interested in Chinese culture began to concentrate more of their work on clusters of Chinese immigrants settled permanently abroad. A great deal has subsequently been published about these overseas groups,[2] known collectively as *hua ch'iao*, or "Overseas Chinese." In comparison, relatively little is known about the emigrant communities from which the majority of Overseas Chinese originated.

---

[2] The following is a selective list of Overseas Chinese studies: Amyot 1960; Coughlin 1960; Crissman 1967; Elliott 1955; Freedman 1957, 1960; Freedman and Topley 1961; Fried 1958; Lee 1960; Newell 1962; Purcell 1965; Skinner 1957, 1958; T'ien 1953; Topley 1961; Ward 1954a; Wickberg 1965; D. Willmott 1960; W. Willmott 1964, 1967, 1970.

The most notable exception is the book by Chen Ta, *Emigrant Communities in South China* (1939), which is a loosely defined survey of emigrant districts in the southernmost provinces of Kwangtung and Fukien. An earlier contribution is Kulp's *Country Life in South China* (1925), which also happens to be one of the first community studies published on China (see Fried 1954:18). Although the village described by Kulp is an emigrant community, the problem of out-migration is not a central focus of his book. Another study that deals indirectly with the home villages of emigrants from South China is Amyot's monograph on the Chinese of Manila (1960:28-54). Some of the more recent additions to the literature on this subject are based on field research among Hakka-speaking Chinese in Hong Kong (Aijmer 1967, Bracey 1967, Pratt 1960).

Except for a few passing references in other sources, this is about the extent of the published material presently available on emigrant communities in China. Almost every book on the Overseas Chinese contains a section on the original causes of emigration, but they seldom present any significant new information on the home villages back in South China. Considering how important the phenomenon of labor out-migration had been in China prior to the Revolution, this is one of the more irritating gaps in the literature on Chinese society.

The British Colony of Hong Kong is the only place where it is still possible to investigate viable Chinese emigrant communities.[3] It seemed logical, therefore, to choose the largest

[3] Traditional emigrant communities of the kind discussed in this study are now defunct in the People's Republic. Some villagers may continue to receive remittances from relatives abroad, but the chain of emigration has stopped and the local economies have readjusted. There are reports of returned-emigrant settlements in contemporary China, but these appear to have more in common with Western "retirement communities" than with the traditional emigrant communities (see e.g., Cheng 1972:14-15). In Taiwan, emigrant communities of the classic model did not develop for historical reasons (in most cases, Taiwan was in fact the receiving society). An increasing number of Taiwanese villages are becoming dependent upon

of these few remaining villages in the Colony's rural hinterland as the site of the present study. But there was another reason for selecting this particular community: San Tin is a "single-lineage village," a closed community in which all males are direct descendants of a common founding ancestor. Lineage communities of this type have been a central feature of South China's rural landscape for centuries. Although it is generally assumed that the lineage played an important role in the great waves of emigration during the 1800s, very little is known about the actual organization of the movements. I hoped to throw some light on this old problem by choosing the lineage-based community of San Tin as the site of the present study. As outlined in later chapters, the villagers have used their traditional kinship ties so effectively that they have succeeded in converting the lineage into a kind of emigration agency.

Fortunately, a considerable amount of research had already been conducted on single-lineage villages in South China, and the baseline was well known (see e.g., Baker 1968; Freedman 1958, 1966; Potter 1968). I was able to use the excellent monographs by Jack M. Potter, *Capitalism and the Chinese Peasant: Social and Economic Change in a Hong Kong Village* (1968), and Hugh D. R. Baker, *A Chinese Lineage Village: Sheung Shui* (1968), for the purposes of controlled comparison throughout my stay in San Tin. It would have been considerably more difficult to conduct the present specialized study without the help of these two monographs.

EMIGRANTS, IMMIGRANTS, AND RURAL-URBAN MIGRANTS

There are three major kinds of migrants in rural Hong Kong: emigrants, immigrants, and rural-urban migrants. The "emi-

remittances, but the absentee workers are usually rural-urban migrants (see e.g., Speare 1971).

grants" as defined hereafter are indigenous Hong Kong Chinese (British subjects) who have migrated to Europe, where the vast majority work in Chinese restaurants. The "immigrants" are Chinese expatriates without British citizenship who have come to Hong Kong since the Chinese Revolution in 1949. Finally, there are the rural-to-urban migrants who have left their native villages in the hinterlands of the Colony to find employment in the cities. The present study touches on the relationship between the emigrants and the immigrants (see Chapter Three), but it does not present any new data on the rural-urban migrants. The absentee workers from the village of San Tin are almost exclusively international emigrants.

Most of these restaurant workers leave their families in the home village and return for holidays whenever they can afford the passage. This is a common feature of Chinese emigration movements since the beginning of the great exodus in the eighteenth and nineteenth centuries. Women rarely emigrated, and in some parts of China the local lineage councils did not allow wives to leave the village for fear of losing the entire family (Skinner 1957:126). The ideal pattern of emigration was for the males to work hard and defer material gratification while abroad in hopes of striking it rich in the shortest possible time. Successful Chinese emigrants were expected to return in triumph and retire in their home villages (see e.g., Amyot 1960:58, Chen Ta 1939:109, Freedman 1957:26). Not all of the emigrants, of course, were able to attain this ideal (see Kulp 1925:53), but whenever possible they did return to their families upon retirement. The typical sojourn abroad lasted approximately twenty years, although ideally it was broken up by a number of brief visits home. Meanwhile the emigrant supported his family as best he could by remittances. These are the basic elements of what is referred to in this study as the "classic pattern" of Chinese emigration. With certain modifications, this pattern is still characteristic of the restaurant workers from San Tin.

There have been several attempts to construct cross-cultural typologies of migrants, but few of these make adequate provision for the Chinese pattern discussed here. One of the best typologies is presented by Gonzalez in her article "Family Organization in Five Types of Migratory Wage Labor" (1961). Gonzalez reviews much of the anthropological literature on migration available at that time and isolates the following categories:

I. Seasonal Migration (family units following harvests)
II. Temporary, Nonseasonal Migration (usually young, unmarried adults)
III. Recurrent Migration (married men; families left in home communities)
IV. Continuous Migration (family units; limited to U.S.A.)
V. Permanent Removal (new residence: with or without families)

Although many of the San Tin emigrants are restaurant owners and are not strictly wage-laborers, the majority would fall into Category Three of this typology because they "make irregular journeys, of varying lengths of time, to obtain wage labor throughout their productive years" (Gonzalez 1961:1268). Recurrent migrants leave their families at home, but they return whenever possible, especially for important ceremonies and family crises (p. 1269). Only an insignificant number of emigrants from San Tin have made the transition to Category Five by choosing to settle abroad.

I do not feel, however, that "recurrent migrant" is an adequate descriptive category for the type of individual discussed in this study. The term "sojourner" is perhaps a better representation because it is closer to the emigrants' own self-image. A good definition of this kind of migrant is found in R. H. Lee's study of the Chinese in the United States: "Sociologically speaking, a sojourner is a person whose mental orientation is towards the home country ... [T]he Chinese sojourner ...

spends a major portion of his lifetime striving . . . for economic betterment and higher social status, but the full enjoyment and final achievement of his objective is to be in his place of origin" (Lee 1960:69).

As I demonstrate in later chapters, the San Tin emigrants still consider themselves to be active members of the home community. Their sojourn is conceived of as a period of temporary employment in an alien setting; it is not a prelude to a new life (see also Siu 1952). Evidence from the London phase of this study suggests that as long as the restaurant workers choose to retire in San Tin, they will continue to be "sojourners" who follow the classic pattern of Chinese emigration.

ORGANIZATION OF STUDY

This study was conceived and executed as a "community study" in the usual sense of the term, but it focuses on the central problem of emigration and social change. Chapters Two through Four trace the historical background and outline the intricate pattern of push-and-pull factors that caused San Tin's conversion to emigration. Chapters Five to Seven deal with the actual process of emigration: the organization of the movement, the arrangement of passage, and the pattern of restaurant management abroad. Chapter Six contains most of the data from the London follow-up survey and discusses the emergence of an Overseas Chinese community in the United Kingdom. The last three chapters are concerned with the effects of emigration on the traditional social structure of the village. In the concluding chapter, I discuss the role of international emigration as an agent of social change and speculate about the future of San Tin as a lineage-based community.

Chapter Two

THE SETTING

THE British Crown Colony of Hong Kong is located on the southern coast of China, forty miles east of Macao and eighty miles south of Canton. For reasons that are still not entirely clear, this anachronistic bit of Empire has survived the revolution which culminated in the formation of the Chinese People's Republic well over two decades ago. The bulk of the Colony and the key to its political future is the "New Territories," a 365-square-mile acquisition consisting of a section of the Chinese mainland and over 200 small islands. In 1898, the British Government negotiated a ninety-nine-year lease on the New Territories, ostensibly to enlarge the Colony's defensive perimeter (see Endacott 1964:260-1). This land could be reclaimed by China at any time and it is impossible to predict what will happen in 1997 when the lease expires.

Despite political uncertainties, Hong Kong has flourished since the Second World War. The Port of Hong Kong is one of the busiest harbors in Asia, and the Colony has become an important center of light industry. The cities of Kowloon and Victoria are among the most densely populated urban areas in the world, with concentrations of up to 3,000 people per acre (Davis 1964:49-50). The main reason for Hong Kong's remarkable success is an economy based on nineteenth-century principles of laissez-faire capitalism and a large, free-floating labor force (see Owen 1971:141-143). Industrial wages are low, working conditions are difficult, and unions are still in their infancy. Most of the labor necessary to support the industrial

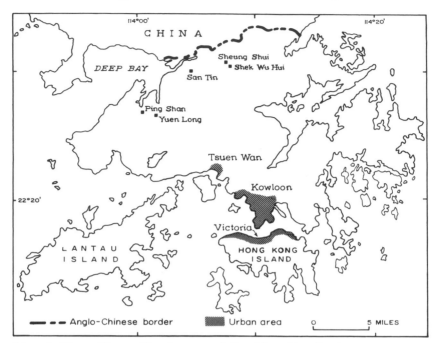

Map 1. Hong Kong, Kowloon, and the New Territories

expansion has come from China since the war. In 1945, Hong Kong had a total population of less than 600,000 but it is now over the four-million mark (Podmore 1971:26, Census and Statistics Department 1972:9).

In the seventy-five years since the signing of the New Territories lease, Hong Kong's rural hinterlands have also undergone a series of fundamental changes. The government initiated a plan to develop three new industrial towns in the New Territories beginning in the 1950s. One of these towns, Tsuen Wan, has already become a major industrial site (Johnson 1971), while the new towns of Castle Peak and Sha Tin are at present in the development stages. The old markets of Tai Po, Shek Wu Hui, and Yuen Long have been transformed into boom towns during the last decade. Even the most isolated villages in the backhills of the Colony have been affected in some way by the recent changes in Hong Kong's economy.

This does not mean, however, that the traditional peasant culture of the New Territories has disappeared. The colonial authorities have followed a social policy of noninterference with the indigenous population of the region, which has encouraged the preservation of important aspects of the original culture. Until the postwar era when Hong Kong was flooded with newcomers from all over China, three distinct ethnic groups inhabited the New Territories: Cantonese, Hakka, and boat-people. The Cantonese-speaking *pen-ti* ("native," often Romanized as *punti*) are generally thought to be descendants of the northern Chinese pioneers who gained control of the Kwangtung region by the T'ang—seventh to tenth centuries A.D. (FitzGerald 1972:xiii, xviii). The Hakka (*k'e-chia*, "guest people") speak a separate language and arrived later than the dominant *pen-ti* group (see Cohen 1968:237-251). Since they were the last to come, the Hakka settled in the less desirable, hilly areas of the New Territories. The boatpeople managed to survive in this highly competitive social environment by occupying a niche on the fringe of the dominant groups' territory. As the name implies, boatpeople are fishermen who spend most of their lives aboard the junks and boats that cluster in the Colony's typhoon shelters. Contrary to popular beliefs about this caste-like minority, the boatpeople speak Cantonese, and their culture is similar to that of the local *pen-ti* farmers (Anderson 1970:364, 1972:6-8). The land-dwelling Chinese perceive them as a separate ethnic group, however, and have discriminated against them for centuries. The boatpeople were never able to play more than a passive role in the political and economic history of the region. These three ethnic groups constitute the "indigenous" population of the New Territories.

Except for the important early work of Barbara Ward (1954b, 1959), the New Territories was largely ignored by anthropologists as a field site until the early 1960s. In the last decade, however, a considerable amount of anthropological and sociological research has been conducted in Hong Kong, most of it concentrating on the rural areas (see Topley 1969). The New Territories may now have become one of the more intensively studied areas in the world, although it does not yet rival parts of Mexico in the level of intensity. As a consequence, the social organization of this small section of Chinese countryside is well known.

THE VILLAGE OF SAN TIN

The village of San Tin is located in the northwest corner of the Colony, near the Anglo-Chinese border (see Map 1). It lies in a low coastal plain and is surrounded on three sides by the saline marshes of Deep Bay. The land in this area is devoted to highly productive vegetable fields, duck ponds, and chicken farms. In 1970, the village had a population of nearly 4,000 (including emigrants), all members of the dominant, Cantonese-speaking *pen-ti* ethnic group in the region. The urban reality of Hong Kong as an overcrowded industrial colony with its monumental social problems has little meaning to the people of this community. Many of the older residents have not even visited the city of Kowloon, which is less than two hours away by bus or train.

"San Tin" (Mandarin *hsin t'ien*, "new fields") is the generalized name for a cluster of eight hamlet-like settlements which I prefer to call subvillages. The subvillages constitute separate neighborhoods in the larger community, much like the barrio divisions in Latin American villages (Foster 1967:32, O. Lewis 1951:19-26). The boundaries between these units are so obscure that they are often defined by nothing more than a narrow alley or a row of houses. Except for slight variations of the local cultural tradition, the subvillage distinctions are of little social importance. The residents refer to themselves collectively as "people of San Tin" (c. *san tin yahn*) and sometimes have difficulty remembering the names of all the subvillages. This study concentrates most directly on the six subvillages that make up the nucleated "core" of the community: Fan Tin Tsuen, Yan Shau Wai, Tung Chan Wai, On Lung Tsuen, Wing Ping Tsuen, and San Lung Tsuen (see Map 2). The remaining two, Tsing Lung Tsuen and Shek Wu Wai, are smaller subvillages that lie a short distance outside the core settlement.

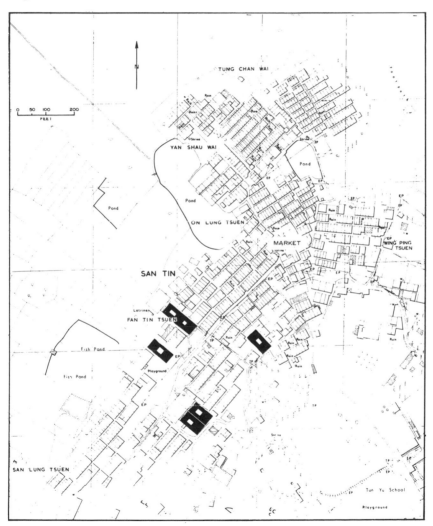

Map 2. San Tin Village (dark blocks are Ancestral Halls)

It its outward appearance, San Tin is little different from the other villages in this part of South China. The community is tightly nucleated around a central plaza containing four large ancestral halls (see page 21). The brick houses share common walls and are arranged in rows along narrow lanes. Each household claims a section of the lane nearest its dwelling as additional living space to accommodate the women, especially the older ones, who spend much of their time working and talking outdoors. The granite slab benches in these lanes are worn smooth from centuries of daily use. When not at home, the women congregate at one of the fifteen public water taps where they wash clothes, exchange news, and draw water (private houses do not have running water). Since the sexes seldom mix outside the home, the men have a separate set of gathering spots. Local teahouses that double as gambling halls are the favorite hangouts for the teenagers and the returned emigrants, while many of the elders prefer to spend their afternoons in the largest ancestral hall—which also happens to be the coolest place in the village during Hong Kong's oppressive summer. An important part of my research routine was to make the rounds of these male gathering spots every day in order to keep up with local gossip.

Since the village is obscured from the highway by a low hill, strangers rarely find their way through the maze of paths to the central market or the plaza area. If they do, their arrival is announced by the watch dogs that guard every housing compound and gated passageway in the village. These dogs are an indispensable part of San Tin's security system because they are conditioned to bark at anyone they do not recognize. Although they rarely bite, the mere sight of a snarling pack of unchained dogs in the narrow lanes is enough to discourage the most determined intruder. Even after seventeen months, there were certain isolated areas of San Tin I dared not venture into unless accompanied by a resident. At night the dogs roam at will throughout the village, and it is often dangerous to wander too far from home. During our stay in San Tin, my wife and I were adopted by a watch dog whose original master had emigrated to Holland. We kept him well fed and, in return, he served as our "protector."

Even without the dogs, San Tin's physical appearance is enough to discourage casual visitors and to make outsiders feel uncomfortable when they pass through. Everywhere one looks there are walls. The village paths wind through a labyrinth of gated passageways, some of which bear the message "Strangers Keep Out" in bold characters. One of the subvillages, Yan Shau Wai, is surrounded by a ten-foot brick wall that was built originally for protection against bandits and hostile neighboring lineages. Until the 1950s, the gate to this walled hamlet was closed at night to keep out intruders and, according to the older residents, wandering ghosts. Smaller walled compounds are found in other parts of the village, and every home is equipped with a substantial, double-bolt door. Although these security measures evolved during a time of real need, San Tin's closed appearance is also a reflection of the villagers' attitudes toward outsiders (see page 25).

This does not mean, of course, that the community is totally cut off or isolated. The people of San Tin have never been completely self-sufficient and have always relied upon the outside world for many of their essential services. This is true today even more than it was in the past. Thirty-seven shops and a daily food market now provide the ordinary necessities of life, but residents must visit the nearby market towns of Shek Wu Hui and Yuen Long to buy specialty items. Villagers take advantage of every possible excuse to make the fifteen minute bus ride to the towns because, compared to San Tin, these are colorful and exciting places. During market hours (especially in the morning),the streets of Yuen Long are overflowing with people who come from the surrounding countryside to shop or, in many cases, simply to escape the monotony of their home villages. Besides the variety of large stores and the bustling street market, the towns provide important services unavailable in San Tin (for example: photography, prostitution, banquet catering, fortune-telling, coffin-making, and banking). The villagers are also dependent on the market towns for most of their medical needs. An unlicensed, Western-style medic and two herbalists practice in San Tin, but residents with serious ailments are taken to the government clinic in Yuen Long for treatment. Similarly, since San Tin has only a primary school and three kindergartens, the few parents who desire a middle school (high school) education for their children must send them to the towns nearby.

CONTACTS ACROSS THE RIVER

Before the Chinese Revolution, San Tin depended upon a different marketing system, one surrounding the town of Sham Chun which is now in Chinese territory, only five miles across the river. At the turn of the century, Sham Chun was the largest market in Kwangtung's San On District, with sixty-one large shops and over 300 permanent hawker stalls (Groves 1969:39). The town's intermediate market met on a periodic schedule every third day and attracted large crowds of peasants from a fifteen-mile radius. Local farmers relied on this town for the sale of their produce and for most of their contacts with the outside world. The marketing "community" formed by villages that depended on the same periodic market represented the effective limits of San Tin's social universe (see Potter 1969:9-10, Skinner 1964:32-42). In 1951 the Anglo-Chinese border was closed and San Tin found itself cut off from the market town of Sham Chun. Prior to that time the political boundaries had not significantly interfered with San Tin's social networks, but the border closure disrupted the traditional marketing system and forced the villagers to orient themselves toward the growing market town of Yuen Long. This reorientation had important consequences for the local people because it made them completely dependent on the colonial economy and brought them into direct contact with the rapidly changing, Westernized society that was emerging in parts of Hong Kong.

Although the border near San Tin was officially closed, the villagers continued to have limited contact with the People's Republic until the start of the Cultural Revolution in 1966. Local women visited their natal homes in China for funerals, and village guardsmen occasionally ventured across the river to return straying water buffaloes. During the Korean War, San Tin's location made it an ideal site for smuggling vital supplies past the American blockade to the People's Liberation Army, and many villagers responded by treating this as an economic windfall. (For a discussion of the smuggling activities see Chapter Four.) Villagers also have indirect contacts with China via refugees, although San Tin is too far inland to be near any of the regular escape routes along the border. The few refugees who do manage to cross the river in this vicinity usually avoid the village because of the dogs. The only exception occurred during a mass exodus in May, 1962, when the Chinese authorities lifted all restrictions on border movements for a brief period (Immigration Report 1966-67:4, 11; Vogel 1969:293-296). Like many other border villages at that time, San Tin was inundated by people who had crossed over into British territory. Local residents fed and clothed as many of the transients as they could and helped them locate relatives living in the Colony's urban areas.

In spite of the refugees, these contacts with the People's Republic have done little to alter the traditional attitude of political neutrality in the village. Most people in San Tin are only vaguely aware of the revolutionary changes that have occurred across the river, even though they do feel a certain pride in China's achievements. The village has not been involved with Left or Right Wing political movements that are active in parts of the New Territories. Furthermore, like most people in Hong Kong, they do not identify with the colonial government and do not consider themselves to be "citizens" of the British Commonwealth. They prefer to be left alone.

In 1967, however, Hong Kong's political stability was threatened by a series of urban riots and border incidents that occurred in the wake of the Great Proletarian Cultural Revolution. Although San Tin was not directly affected by the border incidents, a bomb exploded outside the office of the government-sponsored Rural Committee during the height of the troubles, and on two occasions students from Communist middle schools in Kowloon staged revolutionary dramas in the village plaza. Rumors that hundreds of Red Guards were massing just across the river for an assault on the village terrified the older residents who had heard about youthful excesses in China. By this time, Gurkha troops from a nearby garrison had sealed off the border, and all contacts with friends or relatives in China ceased for almost two years. During our stay in the village (1969-1970) much of the tension had subsided, however, and relations between Hong Kong and China were returning to normal.

When we first arrived, I was amazed at the extent to which the people of San Tin had retained their traditional way of life, in spite of these seemingly monumental political and economic changes. The more I learned of their community, however, it became clear that there was no mystery. San Tin's resilience is due in large part to the fact that the lineage—a traditional kinship organization—still plays a dominant role in the economic and social life of the community.

THE MAN LINEAGE

Except for a handful of resident outsiders, every male in San Tin bears the surname "Man," which rhymes with "Don" as in Donald according to the local pronunciation (Mandarin *Wen*). All of the Mans in San Tin are direct lineal descendants of a common founding ancestor who settled in the Hong Kong region nearly 600 years ago. Traditionally the village was closed to outsiders, and even today the lineage permits only a few nonmembers to live inside the community. Since surname exogamy is strictly enforced in this part of China, all wives must be brought in from other villages.

The Mans claim an illustrious history dating back to the thirteenth century. According to their written genealogy, the San Tin Mans are descendants of the younger brother of the Sung patriot, General Man Tin-ch'eung (Wen T'ien-hsiang, 1267-1314), a national hero. After the General was killed by invading Mongol troops, his younger brother, Tin-shui, fled to the frontier areas of South China. A century later during the eighth generation of Tin-shui descendants, a young farmer named Man Sai-gok moved his family to the village which is now called San Tin.

According to the local oral tradition, San Tin was settled previously by two lineages, Poon and Lam, which may have been composed of earlier Chinese pioneers. There is no record of what happened to the subordinate Lam lineage, but the Poons play an important role in the origin myths of the village. One of the most common of these stories explains the Poon downfall in terms of trickery and geomantic manipulation: Man Sai-gok, the story begins, first settled near San Tin as an unwanted outsider and was persecuted by the original inhabitants for several years. Since the Poons far outnumbered the Mans, there was little he could do except use his wits and wait for an opportunity to strike back. When the Poons announced they had decided to build their first ancestral hall, ordinarily a sign of prosperity and good fortune, Man Sai-gok knew his chance had finally arrived. He sold everything he owned and bribed the geomancer in charge of the new hall to recommend a site with disastrous *feng shui*[1] ("wind and

[1] *Feng shui*, "wind and water," is an important concept in the cosmological system of South China. It refers to geomantic forces that can be either beneficial or detrimental, according to the way they flow through the landscape (see Freedman 1966:118-154, Potter 1970b).

water," geomantic influences). From that point on the Poons had nothing but bad luck, and eventually the Mans took over their property—even the original houses, according to most stories.

Besides the oral record, all that remains of San Tin's original inhabitants is an auxiliary shrine attached to the central village shrine. This tiny shrine is maintained to placate the spirit of the last Poon leader, who was driven out of the village with his remaining lineage mates in the fifteenth century. Many San Tin residents believe that the neighboring village of Poon Uk Tsuen ("Poon Home Village") is populated by the descendants of that leader.

Even by their own accounts, therefore, the Mans were relatively late arrivals in the New Territories region. Some of the other lineages nearby were established a century or more earlier (see, e.g., Potter 1968:22). By the time the Mans had arrived, the best paddy land in the region had already been claimed (Baker 1966:27-31). The Mans were forced to compete for the remaining territory, and they chose the marginal, swampy land near San Tin. The consequences of this late settlement are explored in the following chapter, but it is important to note here that the Man lineage was never as wealthy as the lineages studied by Potter (1968) and Baker (1968). In South China, lineage wealth is ordinarily associated with the control of highly productive, double-crop paddy lands. Unlike the other dominant lineages in the New Territories, the Mans subsisted for centuries on reclaimed land capable of producing only a single crop of low quality rice each year.

Counting General Man's younger brother as the first ancestor, the San Tin Mans are now in their twenty-seventh generation. The lineage grew by a process of segmentation until it became a powerful force in the northern part of the New Territories. Three of Sai-gok's five sons are the focal ancestors for the three major "branches" of the lineage (see Figure 1). Beyond this point, the lineage is divided into several dozen

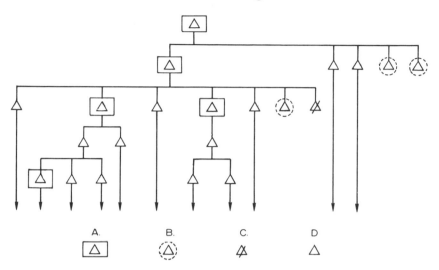

Figure 1. Structure of the Man Lineage

A. Focus of ancestral hall (actual or honorary founder).
B. Moved away.
C. Deceased before bearing descendants (and no apparent adopted heir).
D. Important founding ancestors.

"segments" composed of the descendants of each ancestor in whose name a landed estate has been set aside. The estates are held in trust as corporately-owned property and the benefits are shared among the segment members on a *per stirpes* basis. Without an estate a segment cannot exist because there would be no independent source of money to pay for the annual observances associated with the ancestor worship cult. In the present study, "segments" are defined as property-owning divisions of the lineage. Some incorporate no more than a handful of members, while others include over a thousand men. A more detailed discussion of the lineage segments is presented in Chapters Three and Ten.

In the past, some of the higher level segments of the Man lineage were wealthy enough to erect large, temple-like buildings known as ancestral halls (*tsu t'ang*). These impressive structures loom high above the surrounding dwellings and dominate the central portion of the village. As shown in Figure 1, the entire lineage belongs to the Main Hall (*ta tsu t'ang*) built to honor Sai-gok, the founding ancestor. The four other ancestral halls in San Tin, however, are the exclusive property of the major segments descending from Sai-gok's eldest son. Besides the ancestral halls, there are fifteen smaller public buildings in San Tin called "study-room halls" (*shu fang*), which are owned by lower-level segments. The study-room halls were built ostensibly as schools for the segments involved, but only a few in San Tin ever served this function. Most of these halls are used for banquets, and, hence, are sometimes referred to in the present study as "banquet halls." The primary distinction between ancestral halls and study-room halls is that the latter do not contain ancestral tablets[2] and are of less ceremonial significance (see also Baker 1968:112).

The proliferation of public halls in San Tin is symbolic of the internal rivalries that characterize the Man lineage. In the past, the more powerful segments were constantly maneuvering to gain control of the community. Occasionally these rivalries developed into open fights that threatened the unity of the lineage. In one case about forty years ago, two segments could not agree on the proper distribution of hawker fees from the local market, and a pitched battle resulted. This case is not particularly unusual because the oral tradition of the lineage abounds with stories of intersegment disputes and usurpations of property. According to a local maxim, "The rich segments (*fang*) exploit the poor, and the powerful exploit the weak."

In spite of the segmentary rivalries, the Man lineage confronts the outside world as a unified whole. This is especially true whenever the lineage is threatened by an external force. Before the British pacification, the dominant lineages in the

[2] Ancestral tablets are wooden plaques, about one foot high, bearing the carved names of the ancestor and his wives. They are kept on altars in the ancestral halls and are the focus of many ancestral rites (see Baker 1968:61-64, Freedman 1958:81-83).

New Territories fought among themselves for control of land and other resources (see Baker 1966:39-41, Groves 1969:32). The Mans were constantly at odds with other lineages, partly because they operated a protection racket[3] that encompassed nearly half of the New Territories and a large section of land just across the Sham Chun River. As a direct consequence of these irregular activities, the Mans maintain that they were drawn into three full-scale lineage wars during the seventeenth and eighteenth centuries. Because of its location, San Tin also had to deal with bandits and renegade soldiers who made occasional raids from hideouts in the nearby Canton Delta marshlands. In order to meet these threats, the Mans built up a strong lineage militia and kept at least six members of the village guard on duty at all times.

The lineage continued to be the primary mechanism of physical protection for the residents of San Tin well into the twentieth century. It was also used by individual members as a buffer in their dealings with people and institutions outside the community. In traditional times, imperial land taxes were levied on the lineage as a whole and paid every year by a group of elders who were delegated to visit the tax offices in the town of Nam Tau, now in Chinese territory (see also Hsiao 1960:339-340). Lineage leaders acted as spokesmen for ordinary members whenever they became involved in a legal suit or a criminal prosecution. Contemporary villagers still rely upon lineage intermediaries for contacts with government bureaucracies. As in the past, these intermediaries are the informal leaders of

[3] This protection racket was managed by members of the San Tin village guard. The guardsmen extorted protection fees from shopkeepers and gambling house operators all over the New Territories until the Japanese occupation forces put an end to the practice during the War. In its heyday, the guard also "protected" a number of smaller villages in the San Tin area and levied an annual tax on the tenants renting Man-owned land. The Mans had a fierce reputation in the New Territories (see e.g., Baker 1968:182), and many of their neighbors still refer to them as "The Terrible Mans."

the lineage who have attained positons of influence in the local community through personal wealth or exceptional ability. Theoretically the lineage is controlled by the lineage master (*tsu chang*), the oldest surviving member of the most senior generation, and by a council of elders (*fu lao*) consisting of all men age 61 or older. The council of elders has considerable moral authority in the community, but the informal leaders are capable of manipulating important decisions in their own favor (see Chapter Five).

Besides acting as a protective buffer, the lineage in many parts of Southeast China constituted a nearly complete social environment for the majority of its members. This is still true in San Tin, where the lineage permeates and controls the social activities of the community. Even the local voluntary associations are not alternative forms of organization because they operate within the framework of the lineage. For instance, the major function of San Tin's half dozen small religious associations is to provide an annual banquet for devotees of a particular deity; they do not serve as the focus of important community activities in San Tin as they do in many multi-lineage villages (see e.g., Brim 1970, Pasternak 1972a:95, 108-9). All of the other Man associations, including two funeral societies and a football club, bring people together for a single purpose and, as a consequence, voluntary groups do not flourish in San Tin. As one resident outsider observed rather contemptuously: "The Mans have only one association—their lineage."

It is clear that the lineage represents much more to the residents of San Tin than a formal kinship organization. The lineage has always been central to the personal identity of every (male) individual who has belonged to it. Without his lineage identity, the villager would be simply another peasant, susceptible to the arbitrary whim of powers beyond his control. The Mans may not always trust their fellow lineage mates from other segments, but they trust outsiders even less. As a consequence, the villagers view interactions with the larger society in terms of ingroup versus outgroup, or in San Tin's case, Man versus outsider.

RELATIONS WITH OUTSIDERS

The Mans refer to people who are not members of their lineage as (c) *ngoi leih yahn,* "those who come from outside." Until the early 1950s, San Tin was closed to all outsiders; even itinerant hawkers who wished to conduct business in the village were not allowed to stay inside the nucleus of subvillages after dark. The only exceptions to this rule were approximately fifteen families of hereditary servants, called *hsi min,*[4] which were attached to wealthy Man households. One family of *hsi min* still remains in San Tin. Even though they do not bear the Man surname, the members of this low-status family are considered to be local residents and are not called outsiders.

The residential restrictions against outsiders have been relaxed in the last two decades because the Mans now allow about twenty nonlineage families to live in the village. Many are recent immigrants from China who came during the 1962 exodus referred to earlier in this chapter. Outsiders perform vital services in the community and run two-thirds of the local shops (see Table 1). There are two possible explanations for the influx of resident outsiders: First, the change may have been a direct consequence of the out-migration of lineage males

[4] *Hsi min* (sometimes called *ha fu* in Cantonese) are hereditary, indentured servants who were bought and sold by their owners. Little is known about these people because the institution died out approximately forty years ago in the British Colony and there are few references to it in the literature about South China. *Hsi min* appear to have been a luxury supported only by the more powerful lineages. Potter (1968:20-22) and Baker (1968:155-160) report that *hsi min* also existed in the wealthy single-lineage villages of Ping Shan and Sheung Shui.

TABLE 1

Management of Shops in San Tin
(1970)

Type of shop	Operators*	
	Man	Outsider
Gambling/Tea house	3	4
Gambling	4	0
Gambling/General store	3	0
Teahouse (food and snacks)	0	4
General store (food, dry goods, etc.)	2	5
Medicine shop	0	2
Rice shop	0	4
Barber shop	1	2
Traditional tailor	0	1
Modern (Western-style) tailor................	1	0
Lumberyard	0	1
	14	23

* All shop premises are owned by Man landlords, but the equipment and inventory belong to the operator.

who left to take up better jobs abroad. This view is not entirely satisfactory, however, because there is evidence that outsiders tend to dominate the shops of non-emigrant, single-lineage villages as well (Potter 1968:126 and personal observations in the New Territories). A second and more feasible explanation is that outsiders gradually fill this niche in San Tin's economy because they are not hampered by kinship obligations and, thus, are more willing to assume the social burdens of doing business in a lineage-based community. Coming into the village as strangers, they are not expected to give special favors to anyone. The Man shopkeepers, on the other hand, complain bitterly that they must treat their clientele as kinsmen first and customers second. One afternoon while escaping the hot sun in a store I happened to observe an elder purchasing a mosquito net and overheard him ask the owner, a fellow lineage member, for a special wholesale price. What followed was ten minutes of nervous interchange known as "talking in circles" (the local

equivalent of "beating around the bush"), which is the villagers' favorite method of avoiding an embarrassing situation.
Finally the elder left with a gift package of cigarettes, but no
mosquito net.

The outsider shopkeepers also have problems because they
are thought to be parasites in the community, but they have
the option of selling out and leaving for another part of the
Colony. It is not surprising that there is a fairly high turnover
of shop owners in San Tin. The Mans make it difficult for
outsiders to stay because the old prejudices against them still
prevail. Those who do not live in their shops are segregated
in a small hamlet of squatter shacks on the fringe of the village.
No matter how long they may have lived in the village, the
Mans do not consider them part of the community. Outsiders
are not allowed to vote in the local elections for Village
Representatives (see Chapter Five) and are constantly under
pressure from the village guard, a lineage-controlled institution,
to pay protection fees for their shops and homes. Relations
between the lineage members and the outsiders in San Tin
appear to be more strained than in other single-lineage villages
nearby (cf. Baker 1968:162). Although the newcomers try to
remain as unobtrusive as possible, the Mans barely tolerate
their presence.

In the last decade, the countryside surrounding San Tin has
been occupied by recent immigrants from China who rent
Man-owned land for use as vegetable plots and poultry farms.
Unlike the shopkeepers and other resident outsiders, these
immigrants are perceived as a serious challenge to the hege-
mony of the lineage, even though they do not live inside the
village. The Mans have been unable to maintain their traditional sphere of influence because most of the working-age men
have emigrated to Europe, leaving only the unproductive
dependents behind. The antagonistic relationship that has
developed between these outsider farmers and the residents
of San Tin will be examined in the next chapter.

OCCUPATIONAL STRUCTURE: A VILLAGE OF EMIGRANTS

Traditionally, San Tin's economy was based on agriculture and its occupational structure was similar to that of other communities nearby (cf. Baker 1968:22-23, Potter 1968:40-56). Approximately 50 percent of the villagers were full-time farmers while another 15 percent served as part-time farm operators and part-time agricultural laborers. The remaining 35 percent were employed in a wide range of nonagricultural occupations, including laborer, hawker, merchant, policeman, and sailor.[5] Today the situation has changed completely because the village is dependent on one specialized occupation. In a 1970 sample of eighty-two working age males, seventy-one (87 percent) were employed as restaurant workers in Europe (see Table 2). One of the most striking features of the village, therefore, is the absence of men between the ages of 18 and 50. Since San Tin no longer has a productive economy, the residents subsist almost entirely on emigrant remittances.

The best indicators of the total number of emigrants from San Tin are the passport data made available to me by the Hong Kong Immigration Department. The colonial administration issued nearly 800 passports to San Tin residents between 1952 and 1970.[6] This figure is not a true representation of all the villagers abroad, however, because dependents are often included on the passport of the family head. I estimate that there are now at least 1,000 San Tin emigrants living in Europe. Approximately 600 work in the United Kingdom; another 350 live in Holland; and 50 more in West Germany and Belgium.

---

[5] These percentages are based on a census of thirty-eight households. One of the questions dealt with the occupations of working-age males and their fathers, now deceased or retired. The currently employed males are represented in Table 2, and their 38 fathers as follows: farmers 19; part-farmer/part-laborer 6; other 13.

[6] Source: Documents Section, Immigration Department, Hong Kong Government, in a special search of passport files, October 1970.

TABLE 2

Working-Age Males of San Tin, 1970
(Ages 18 to 50)
(Sample of 82 men from 38 households)

Emigrants	71*
Urban workers	6*
Market-town workers	2
Policemen	2
Government employee	1*

* Absentee workers living and working outside San Tin.

Most work in Chinese restaurants owned and operated by fellow villagers.

Although the high rate of emigration has had a profound impact on the social life of the village (see Chapters Eight and Nine), it has not changed the basic structure of San Tin as a closed-corporate community. The picture that emerges is a group of proud and exclusive people who prefer to keep the world at arm's length. The Mans depend heavily on outside remittances for their livelihood and rely upon the market towns for many of their essential services; but the traditional attitudes of suspicion toward outsiders still prevail. As will be demonstrated later, this is true even of emigrants who have had years of experience abroad. The Mans consider themselves to be members of a rural elite, represented by the powerful lineages that once controlled South China. They feel superior to their neighbors in multilineage villages and expect to be treated with deference when they visit the nearby market towns. Outsiders, in turn, often consider the Mans to be arrogant and backward, but this only reinforces the elitist attitudes in San Tin.

Without a prior knowledge of the historical and ecological factors involved, one would not expect members of a closed community like this to embrace emigration so wholeheartedly. In the next Chapter I will examine the reasons why the fiercely independent Mans chose to leave the security of their home villages and seek employment as immigrant workers in an alien society.

Chapter Three

PRELUDE TO EMIGRATION:
THE AGRICULTURAL CRISIS

DURING the 1950s, immigrant farmers from China began to rent small plots of land in the New Territories and proceeded to grow vegetables for the Hong Kong urban market. This was the beginning of a "vegetable revolution," which changed the indigenous rice-based economy of the New Territories and converted the village-oriented peasant into a market-oriented farmer. The innovative immigrants demonstrated that it was much more profitable to grow vegetables on fields originally set aside for paddy rice. For most of the land owners in the New Territories the shift to vegetables was an unexpected windfall. However, due to its ecological setting, San Tin was one of the few communities that did not benefit from these changes.

In the brief period between 1957 and 1962, San Tin changed from an agricultural village into the most striking emigrant community in the entire Colony. As late as 1955, the village economy was based on farming, with more than half of the Man households deriving the bulk of their income from rice cultivation. By 1962, however, all but a handful of the village farmers had stopped growing rice and were unable or unwilling to develop other possibilities in the local environment. The bottom had fallen out of San Tin's six-century-old economy and the Mans were forced to search for alternative means of support.

Before continuing, the reader should note that the rise of emigration and the decline of agriculture in San Tin were interdependent developments, occurring simultaneously during the 1950s and early 1960s. For the purpose of analysis, however, the two developments are treated in separate chapters which may create the impression that they were independent events. This is not the case. The present chapter is an attempt to explain the complex interplay of local, regional, and international factors which led to the collapse of San Tin's agricultural economy. Chapter Four will demonstrate why emigration was the most attractive route to employment open to members of the Man lineage and why this particular group was able to gain an early foothold in the Chinese restaurant market in Europe.

LAND RECLAMATION AND LINEAGE FORMATION

When the Mans first came to the remote, southern tip of Kwangtung Province in the thirteenth century, the region was in a late phase of pioneer development and "Sinification." Four other major lineage groups—*Tang* (Kam Tin, Ping Shan, Ha Tsuen), *Hau* (Ping Kong, Kam Tsin), *Pang* (Fan Ling), and *Liao* (Sheung Shui)—were already in control of the best paddy lands in the present day New Territories region (Baker 1966:25-30). The only land open for further exploitation at that time was an area of undesirable marshes located on the fringe of Deep Bay. The Mans chose to settle near the convergence of the Sham Chun River and the shallow marshes of Deep Bay and proceeded to make the best of a bad environmental situation. After the Mans expelled the original settlers from the chosen location (see Chapter Two), they began to convert some of the marshland into moderately productive brackish-water fields. These early reclamation efforts produced the first collectively owned property, or the "new fields," (c) *san tin*, of the Man lineage.

San Tin was built on a low peninsula surrounded on three sides by near sea-level stretches of marshes and ponds. As the

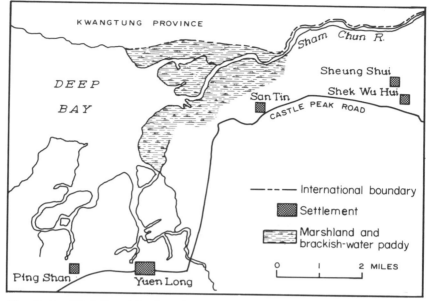

Map 3. San Tin's Local Setting

lineage reclaimed more and more land, the open waters of the river and bay receded farther from the village.[1] Yan Shau Wai, the original Man settlement (and the first of San Tin's eight subvillages), was a walled fortress that reputedly had a pier connecting it to a channel deep enough to carry river-boat traffic. Yan Shau Wai is now one-half mile from open water and faces a wide expanse of saline fields.

The topographic changes in the San Tin area were not all due to man-made reclamation efforts. Deep Bay itself is slowly filling in and new land is appearing as a result of a geological movement that is uplifting the northwest part of the New Territories (Barnett 1964:45). Near San Tin the results of this movement are greatly magnified because the bay is so shallow that the slightest uplift exposes a new expanse of land. Over the centuries, the lineage also benefited from the gradual

---

[1] A map presented by Grant (1960:fig Ic) shows that the marshes around San Tin have emerged from Deep Bay within the last 500 years.

extension of the Sham Chun River delta into the bay as a result of silt deposition. The Mans, therefore, had two major geological advantages in their fight against the sea.

The reclamation work involved the enclosure of virgin marsh land by a gradually expanding network of earthen dikes. Given the level of technology available, it was impossible to exclude all salt water from the low-lying fields. As a consequence, the dike's primary function was to retain fresh rain water and only secondarily to protect the crops from salt water flooding during the growing season. Excess water was discharged from the fields through wooden locks, or sluice gates, which were opened at low tide. These locks were skillfully manipulated to minimize the salt content of the water, thus allowing a special variety of brackish paddy rice to flourish (see page 38).

The technology of land reclamation is highly developed in South China, especially in the Canton Delta region. The Imperial government recognized the vast potential of the delta area and adopted a policy to help destitute farmers open new land as part of its famine relief program. In 1851, for instance, the Emperor authorized the Kwangtung provincial administration to release partially submerged land along the delta for reclamation (Hsiao 1960:388-9). The majority of these projects were carried out by villagers who lived along fresh-water alluvial flood plains. Perhaps the best known example of fresh-water reclamation is the "new enclosure" described by C. K. Yang in his study of Nanching village. The dominant lineage of this multi-surname community enclosed a fifteen-acre stretch of mud flats and converted it into fertile rice land (C. K. Yang 1959:24-27). Large "dike farms" for fruit and rice are also reported on the riverine islands near Canton (Feng and Yung 1931:115). From Yang's description, the technology of fresh-water enclosure appears to be quite similar to that of brackish-water reclamation.

The initial construction of the dikes near San Tin was a major cooperative effort by the Man lineage. Furthermore, the maintenance of the system demanded regular attention and an annual expenditure of labor and capital. In terms of organization and management, San Tin's reclamation projects have much in common with the large-scale irrigation systems that have been more thoroughly scrutinized in the social science literature (see e.g., Geertz 1963; Hanks 1972; Pasternak 1968b, 1972b; Wittfogel 1957).

A good deal has already been written about the close relationship between Chinese lineage formation and irrigation systems in frontier areas (e.g., Freedman 1966:160ff, Potter 1970a). According to Potter, the strongest lineages developed in double-crop rice regions that were originally frontiers far from Imperial government control (1970a:138). Here the incipient lineages were allowed free range to open new lands for irrigation and thus to expand to the limits set only by the relative strength of similar competing groups. Freedman has postulated that single-lineage communities could emerge relatively quickly in a pioneer situation (1966:164). Recently, however, Pasternak (1969, 1972a:136ff) has challenged these views with evidence from Taiwan—another Chinese pioneer region on the fringe of the Empire. Pasternak maintains that "the exigencies of the frontier initially inhibit rather than stimulate such a development, and that the concentration and elaboration of localized lineage structures in southeast China took place in spite of, rather than because of, frontier conditions" (1969:551). The point of this argument is that lineages were "second stage" developments after the frontier had already been opened and pacified (Pasternak 1969:561; see also Jordan 1972:xviii, 17-20).

In his recent book, *Kinship and Community in Two Chinese Villages,* Pasternak goes one step further and hypothesizes that single-lineage villages emerged in the New Territories region because there was little need for cooperation across agnatic lines and little competition for strategic resources during the pioneer era (1972a:18-19, 155-157). From one point of view, the

San Tin data would seem to verify this hypothesis. I have already shown that San Tin was settled relatively late in Kwangtung's frontier history. The Man lineage did not begin to expand and thus to attain a high level of internal segmentation until the late fifteenth century—well after the region had been thoroughly Sinified. Furthermore, throughout their history the Mans have been notorious for their inability to cooperate with other agnatic groups. Another part of the hypothesis may not apply to San Tin, however, because there was fierce competition for strategic resources in the New Territories when the lineage began to develop. The scramble for land was so intense that the Mans were forced to settle near a brackish swamp, and even here they had to expel the original inhabitants. Under these circumstances it was essential to form strong cooperative groups for protection; but, unlike in the Taiwanese situation, this need found expression through an elaboration of preexisting agnatic ties.

Whether or not the hypothesis is correct in all of its implications, Pasternak is certainly on the right track when he isolates the control of subsistence resources as a key factor in explaining the development of single-lineage villages (1972a:156). In San Tin's case, the lineage maintained rigorous control over the community's primary resources—the reclaimed rice fields—from their very inception.

The Man lineage reclaimed nearly 1,000 acres of land from the marshes of Deep Bay. In order to evade the Imperial tax collectors, much of this new land was never reported to the government (Lockhart 1900:15). According to the oral tradition of the village, the earliest reclamation efforts involved the whole lineage, which at that time was much smaller and probably included no more than a hundred men. The "new fields" became the property of the lineage's corporate estate, embodied in the main ancestral hall. Each participating member had a share in this hall and thus a share in the income from the reclamation project. Later, when the membership had grown to several hundred males, reclamation was undertaken by smaller groups of men or financed by richer individuals. In these cases, the new land became the property of the founder or founders, and after their deaths the property was held in trust as corporate estates by their own descendants. In this way, the lineage grew by a process of segmentation with the ancestral estates forming the organizational and material foci of the various branches of the lineage. According to the land records kept by the British in the New Territories, the Man lineage had 126 major ancestral estates in 1905. San Tin's four branch ancestral halls and fifteen lesser "study halls" are physical representations testifying to the material success of some of these ancestral estates. The land rents from the corporately-owned estates financed the construction and maintenance of halls, as well as the continuation of the yearly cycle of ancestral rites, lineage schools and welfare activities. Stronger branches (or segments) of the lineage had enough money and men to reclaim a disproportionate amount of land around San Tin and thus to reinforce their dominant positions in the lineage hierarchy.

As a partial result of the reclamation projects, approximately 65 percent of the Man land is held in trust by lineage segments as corporately-owned ancestral estates. Of course not all of the land near San Tin is owned by the lineage segments. The remaining 35 percent of the land controlled by the Man lineage is registered as private property in the Hong Kong Government land records.[2] It is important to note, however, that most of this private property is categorized by the local people as

_____

[2] This is a rough estimate based on a random survey of the land records for San Tin Sub-District held by the Yuen Long District Office. "Private property" in the sense used here designates any land registered as being owned by a single individual, i.e., someone who is not acting as an estate manager for a lineage segment. Some of this private property might have become corporately-owned by the registrants' descendants because the land records are often considerably out of date. For a full explanation of the distinction between private and corporately-owned property, see Brim 1970 and Potter 1968:95-117.

inferior varieties of dry land while the lineage segments continue to own the bulk of reclaimed paddy land.

LINEAGE WEALTH AND ECOLOGICAL VARIATIONS

San Tin has always been an unusual, if not aberrant, community. Compared to the nearby single-lineage villages studied by Baker (1968) and Potter (1968), the people of San Tin lived at a relatively modest level in traditional times. The Mans may have been more affluent than the residents of the smaller, multilineage villages that are scattered throughout the area, but their power and influence never depended exclusively on wealth. Instead, the Mans relied upon a large population and a fierce reputation to maintain their traditional sphere of control in the northern New Territories. They were always a force to be dealt with; hence, the other lineages granted them elite status in the regional power circles.

The key to understanding San Tin's historical position is its peculiar ecological adaptation: the brackish-water fields of the Mans are suitable only for a single-crop variety of red rice. The limited productivity of the Man fields prevented the accumulation of great wealth that characterized the ancestral estates of the lineages in the fertile, double-crop valleys nearby. Although the Man lineage is large and highly segmented, the variations between rich and poor seem never to have been so pronounced as those discussed by Potter in his study of the Tang lineage of Ping Shan (1968). Compared to the Tangs, the Mans of San Tin have had few wealthy landlords or leisured scholars. There has been only one person in village history who was rich enough to buy an Imperial title and to build an impressive mansion. Significantly, his wealth had nothing to do with the lineage—he is said to have found a cache of pirate gold.[3]

[3] This is the case of San Tin's *ta fu ti* (holder of a low ranking Imperial title), who built a splendid dwelling on the outskirts of the village two

The relative uniqueness of the Man lineage can be traced directly to its ecological setting, not to any major differences in social organization or cultural content. Until the advent of emigration, San Tin was quite similar to the other single-lineage villages nearby in terms of family structure, lineage segmentation, social life, religion, etc. It differed only in the kind of land available in the local environment and the variety of rice traditionally grown on that land.

RED RICE AND BRACKISH-WATER FIELDS

The brackish-water fields near Deep Bay are subjected to saltwater flooding only at times of high spring tides (Grant 1964:57). During the other months the locks are manipulated to retain rain water and to expel a certain amount of saline water so that a hardy variety of red rice can grow. This variety

---

centuries ago (see Akers-Jones 1964). Villagers tell at least eight versions of the story relating how this man, who is said to have been an ordinary peasant, discovered his gold. Even though the stories are highly mythologized, it is clear from his genealogy that he gained his wealth by unorthodox means; and, given San Tin's location on a coastal bay in the pirate infested Canton Delta region, he may indeed have found a cache of gold. Armando da Silva (personal communication) maintains that a more likely explanation is that the man in question was a salt smuggler. The salt trade was a highly profitable monopoly controlled by the Imperial Government. Although the Mans did not mention a history of salt works in the San Tin area, they may have existed at one time. Salt pans (for sea water evaporation) are often associated with brackish-water paddy fields (da Silva 1972:34-35).

Whatever means he used to acquire his wealth, the stories regarding San Tin's *ta fu ti* are typical of treasure tales found in peasant societies all over the world (Foster 1964). Fei and Chang report a case which is almost identical to the one in San Tin: After a poor family had suddenly acquired land, rumors began to spread that "the head of this family had received a mysterious revelation which led him to unearth a hoard of gold on his farm. While the rumor was undoubtedly false, it serves to illustrate the common disbelief in the possibility of accumulating wealth from farming alone" (Fei and Chang 1948:128-9).

is technically known as (c) *haahm mun*, "salty" or "brackish" (Lai 1964:81), and appears to have been used in the New Territories region for several centuries. In most parts of the world, red rice is considered to be a pest that grows as a volunteer crop in paddy fields devoted to white rice (Grist 1959:225-227). The Chinese seem to have domesticated at least two varieties of red rice—one for brackish paddy and another for dry land (see e.g., Fei and Chang 1948:208). The brackish variety is grown first in fresh water seed beds before it is transplanted into the saline fields (Grant 1960:121). The residents of San Tin call the brackish paddies (c) *haahm tin*, "salt fields," and the rice *(c) huhng mai*, "red rice," after the dull reddish hue of the harvested grain. Red rice requires a relatively long growing season of 150 days as opposed to 110 and 120 for the white rice varieties (Lai 1964:84). The long growing season and the annual flood cycle limit the brackish fields to a single crop, which is sown in mid-May, transplanted in late June, and harvested in late November.

Red rice provided relatively high yields, but there was sometimes a danger of crop failures from unexpected floods. The elders of San Tin generally agree that the average yield was between 300 and 400 catties per *tou* of brackish-paddy.[4] Fields closer to the river were less productive, and the few fields nearest the village (i.e., the least brackish) reached a maximum yield of 600 catties per *tou* in good years. These figures are close to the annual yields possible on double-crop paddy land, which are estimated at an average of between 400 and 600 catties per *tou* (Potter 1968:82). In addition to the single-crop handicap, the saline fields are unable to produce "catch crops"[5] of sweet potatoes and winter vegetables.

[4] This compares with Tregear's estimate of 250 catties per *tou* of brackish paddy (Tregear 1958:37).

[5] Catch crops, usually winter vegetables or sweet potatoes, are planted on the paddy fields when they are drained between rice crops (see Potter 1968:57). They are considered an added bonus by the rice farmers.

The red rice also brought a lower price on the market than the other varieties of paddy rice. Man farmers could generally expect to receive at least 30 percent less than the prevailing exchange rates for fresh-water rice (Grant 1964:57). For instance, in 1959 red rice brought HK$30 per picul while the market price for good quality white rice was HK$45 per picul (Grant 1960:103). Most of the unhusked rice was not actually sold; it was exchanged in the nearby market towns for inferior grades of polished (i.e., milled) rice. For every catty of fresh-water, unhusked rice the New Territories farmers brought to market, the rice mills gave them one catty of low-quality, polished rice in return (Topley 1964:182). This was known as the "catty for catty" system: it increased the local food supply by approximately 25 percent because unhusked grain is bulkier than the milled product (Chiu 1964:77). The exchange rate fluctuated, of course, but the standard for red rice was always lower than for other varieties. According to San Tin informants, red rice was less desirable because it was bitter tasting and, hence, it was used most often as a feed grain or as a basic ingredient for making wine. This contrasts unfavorably with the excellent varieties of long-grain white rice grown in the Yuen Long Valley just a few miles to the south. Yuen Long rice is highly prized and commands a good price on the market even today. It is exported all over the world to Overseas Chinese communities and is generally considered to be one of the best tasting strains of Chinese rice. During the Imperial era, some strains of exceptionally fine rice from the present-day New Territories region were sent to the Emperor as tribute (R. Ng 1964:33). The red rice of San Tin was very poor by comparison.

However, the older Man farmers always stress that there were a number of advantages to red rice. The individual farmer did not have to expend as much labor for the upkeep of salt fields as his counterpart in fresh-water paddies because the brackish hydraulic system is less complicated than ordinary irrigation works.[6] The most difficult aspect of red rice cultivation was the exceptionally deep plowing required, which meant that the Mans had to use the strongest (and, according to their own testimony, the most stubborn) variety of water buffalo available in this part of China.[7] The seedlings were placed farther apart than ordinary rice because the plants required more room to grow and produced great quantities of straw. After transplantation, however, the brackish-water fields needed comparatively little labor to bring the crop to harvest. Red rice did not need any fertilizer, and the saline fields required very little weeding or care during the growing season.

In the eyes of the Mans, these factors compensated for many of the drawbacks of growing red rice. They were reluctant to expend the labor and capital necessary for opening dry fields in the surrounding hills because the returns would have been minimal. It was only in the late 1950s, during the "vegetable revolution," that the nearby dry land was exploited successfully by energetic immigrants from China. The Mans relied heavily on their saline fields and never sold any of the reclaimed land to outsiders. Red rice certainly did not make the Mans rich, but the brackish fields were productive enough to support a large population. San Tin became the largest single-surname

[6] Unlike irrigated land, the brackish paddies were not divided into small fields with separate dikes and water works. The saline water often covered wide expanses of rice land which meant that the individual farmer had less control over the hydraulic system. The Mans have devised a unique system of surveying based on local landmarks which they used every spring to block out the field boundaries.

[7] Brackish-water paddy fields are very difficult to plow because the sea water reacts with the soil and causes it to become sticky. In order to flocculate the soil and make it penetrable, slaked lime (which is obtained by burning oyster shells) must be spread over the fields (da Silva 1972:51-53). However, even when this is done, powerful water buffaloes are still needed. Buffaloes are not required in some of the fresh-water, double-crop areas of the New Territories; instead, the farmers use light cattle for plowing (Grant 1960:85).

village in the New Territories and may have been one of the
largest single-lineage villages in Southeastern China. As one
of the Man elders put it: "We were never rich, but none of
us ever went hungry. The salt fields were fertile, and we could
always eat a lot of fish and shrimp from the river. Look at
the Tang lineage at Kam Tin! They were always rich, but their
males all died off. They had good *feng shui* [geomantic influ-
ences] for wealth, we had good *feng shui* for a large population.
What good is wealth without descendants to enjoy it?"

THE VEGETABLE REVOLUTION

The stable production of red rice and the gradual expansion
of reclaimed land sustained the Man lineage for six centuries.
Some of the villagers derived a substantial part of their income
from outside employment or business activities and from the
protection racket run by the village guard.[8] However, until the
last decade, the majority of San Tin's residents subsisted as
rice farmers with a technology little different from that of their
founding ancestors. As long as the lineage was able to support
itself by traditional agricultural production, the lifestyle of
most residents was only slightly affected by developments
outside the intermediate market town area. The rice farmers
of San Tin were very conservative and demonstrated a great
ability to keep the outside world at arm's length. They survived
the interminable rural chaos of the late Imperial era and the
British takeover of the New Territories. Later the Man farmers
recovered from the repressive Japanese occupation and with-
stood a flood of refugees from the Chinese civil war. Their

[8] The village guard activities served as an auxiliary occupation for many
of the Mans who were unable to subsist on farming or commerce alone.
At one time the protection racket run by this organization was very lucrative
because the guardsmen extorted fees from shops and gambling houses all
over the northern half of the New Territories.

survival was almost assured because the reclaimed fields were reasonably productive and there had always been a market for the red rice. However, in the 1950s and early 1960s the traditional ground rules changed and the Man farmers fell victim to a radical change in Hong Kong's agricultural economy.

The Chinese Revolution stopped at the Sham Chun River, but the events in China had a profound impact on the Colony of Hong Kong. The most dramatic effect was the massive immigration of Kwangtung peasants into the urban centers of the Colony (see page 10). Many of the newcomers were attracted to Fan Ling District (northcentral New Territories) because the lineage restrictions against outsiders were weaker in this area and they could rent land more easily than in other New Territories districts (Grant 1960:107). A high percentage of these immigrants were expert vegetable farmers who used their skills to start small-scale garden enterprises (Topley 1964:157, Potter 1968:59). Vegetables, of course, had always been grown in parts of the New Territories, but the dominant crop was rice. However, the combination of an expanding urban market and a growing demand for vegetables led to a wholesale conversion of paddy land to vegetable plots and an expansion of the new crops into hitherto uncultivated lands. Fresh vegetables are an absolute necessity for Chinese cuisine. As more and more people poured into Kowloon, the urban vegetable markets were hard pressed to meet the needs of the growing population.

Transportation of crops from field to market was the most difficult problem encountered by the early vegetable farmers. The Hong Kong Government had anticipated the difficulty and established a system of vegetable marketing cooperatives with a large fleet of trucks to help the farmers in the late 1940s (Peterson 1957, Potter 1968:59-60, Topley 1964). These cooperatives were semiautonomous and derived their incomes from commissions on the sale of members' produce. Not all of the vegetable farmers in the New Territories joined the marketing organizations (see e.g., Potter 1968:91-94), but the cooperative system was instrumental in solving the transportation problem. It also put an end to the unscrupulous practices of many truckfarming middlemen who had been exploiting the vegetable gardeners in the remoter areas of the Colony (Topley 1964:179-181). The colonial government encouraged the incipient vegetable revolution as part of its general policy to develop a self-sufficient economy in the period immediately following the Chinese Revolution. British authorities were uncertain whether the new Communist government would maintain a hostile stance and refuse to sell food to the Colony. These fears eventually proved groundless, but the Hong Kong Government continued to support and expand the cooperative marketing system.

The higher profits of truck farming were sufficient to convince a large number of indigenous New Territories farmers to switch from rice to vegetables. In 1954, 70 percent of the total agricultural land in the Colony was under paddy rice cultivation; but by 1966, this figure had fallen to 44 percent (Land Use 1968:13). Vegetable farming has so increased that is now unusual to see good quality land devoted to rice in the Colony's central valleys. After the initial expenditure of capital and labor necessary to convert paddy fields into vegetable plots, the land is much more productive. Most vegetable plots produce an average of five crops per year, but some energetic farmers are able to market up to eight.

Potter found that the profit from one *tou* of rice land was HK$107 per year for the farmers of Hang Mei village in 1961. The optimal profit from a *tou* of vegetable land was HK$2,251 on five crops per year (Potter 1968:85-86). Although these figures are based on the good quality land of the Tang lineage in the central Yuen Long Valley, the vegetable revolution had similar effects in other parts of the New Territories.[9] San Tin

[9] In 1950, before the vegetable revolution had reached its peak, the average yearly income for rice was HK$161 per *tou* in the Fan Ling area and HK$558

was the only one of the larger, single-lineage villages that did not benefit from the new crops.

The Mans had never developed a reclamation technology sophisticated enough to protect their fields from the annual spring floods of salt water, even though this has been accomplished in other parts of the New Territories.[10] One of the fundamental necessities of vegetable cultivation is a plentiful supply of fresh water. If this criterion is met, it is possible to grow hardy varieties of Chinese vegetables on land that would ordinarily appear useless. For instance, immigrant farmers have been able to convert the sandy lowlands just above the high water mark on the beaches near Lau Fau Shan (northwest New Territories) into profitable vegetable land. High salt content in the water, however, is an environmental influence that even the most resilient vegetables will not tolerate. The reclaimed fields of San Tin contain a relatively high concentration of salt throughout the year, and the flow of rain water is never sufficient to cleanse the soil when the tides are low. Even if the Mans had been willing to expend the huge amounts of capital necessary for a true reclamation

---

per *tou* for vegetables (Lin 1957:27). This Fan Ling rice production figure is close to the 1953 estimate of HK$172 per *tou* for the Colony as a whole (Ma and Szczepanik 1955:35).

   [10] There have been some commercial, nonlineage-based reclamation projects in the New Territories during recent times. For instance, around the turn of the century a private company reclaimed a large stretch of Deep Bay swamp land farther west along the coast from the San Tin area, known as the Ha Tsuen-Mong Tseng Wai reclamation project (Grant 1964:56). The technology of this reclamation is more advanced than the Man projects because the salinity is decreasing and the fields are being converted gradually into fresh-water paddy (Grant 1960:102). The conversion is possible only when salt water is completely eliminated from the ecosystem and the soil is cleansed by a leaching process: "Reclamation of saline soil involves reducing soluble salt content to a level at which the salts will not seriously interfere with plant growth. The only practical way of removing salt from soil is washing it out with water, a process commonly referred to as leaching" (Pearson and Ayers 1960:2). This usually means that the surface of a reclaimed patch of land must be covered initially by fresh-water ponds.

project, it still would have taken years for the old brackish paddy environment to be properly flushed and converted into a fresh water ecosystem.

DRY FIELDS AND OUTSIDERS

Not all of the Man land, of course, was reclaimed from the marshes of Deep Bay. Approximately 60 percent of the area controlled by the lineage was relatively low quality, dry land broken up by a series of brushy hills. Traditionally this dry area was not fully exploited because it lacked a natural supply of water and its sandy soil was not suitable for rice cultivation. Some of the dry fields produced crops of peanuts, but many were used only to grow rough brush for fuel. The villagers generally ignored this hilly land and preferred to expand their holdings of saline paddy rather than develop a dry field technology.

The Mans were aware that the sandy soil of these dry fields had the potential for high vegetable yields. In order to exploit this potential, however, they would have had to construct an elaborate new irrigation system based on well water. Much of the dry land also had to be terraced before it could be utilized for cultivation. For a variety of reasons, the Mans themselves did very little of this land development. Vegetable farming never had much appeal to the San Tin rice farmers who were accustomed to an agricultural cycle that required only two major outputs of labor every year for planting and harvest. A primary characteristic of successful Chinese vegetable farming is a continuous, year-round input of backbreaking labor. Furthermore, the development of the dry fields demanded an enormous expenditure of labor just to bring the land to a point where cultivation could begin. Since few of the Mans were interested in opening new vegetable fields, the potential remained unexploited until enough highly motivated outsiders were willing to try it themselves. Adverse conditions in China during the first years of the Revolution ensured that there was no shortage of candidates for the job.

By the late 1950s, immigrant farmers from China had rented almost all of the dry land that could possibly support a vegetable plot or a poultry farm in San Tin Sub-District. Most of the immigrants who settled near the village are Ch'ao Chou (Teochiu) farmers from the Swatow region on the coast of Kwangtung Province north of Hong Kong. These outsiders rent Man-owned fields at the low annual rate of HK$100 per *tou*, although some of the dry land draws a higher rent of up to HK$200 per *tou* if it is used for housing or poultry sheds. The newly opened vegetable fields now produce an average of five crops per year, thanks to the work of the ambitious and hard-working immigrants. Some of the newcomers have purchased their fields at the rate of HK$2 per square foot (approximately US$1500 per acre, 1970 prices), but the majority are still tenants. As a result of their highly efficient, labor-intensive farming methods the Ch'ao Chou farmers around San Tin have become moderately prosperous. The Mans are piqued by this and consider the immigrants to be pushy, rootless upstarts who are devoid of social responsibility. The view of a lineage trustee is typical: "We could have done everything they did, but it was too risky. We can't take such big chances because if we fail there is no place to go. This is our home. Those outsiders can just leave and forget about their debts and responsibilities." These opinions are not an accurate reflection of the people involved, however, because the majority of Ch'ao Chou outsiders near San Tin are honest, highly motivated farmers.

The Mans are suspicious of the hard-working outsiders, and the relations between the two groups have never been good. It is rare for the Mans to interact with the Ch'ao Chou farmers in any context other than the transaction of business between landlord and tenant. The Mans continue to view the dry fields as second class property, unworthy of serious attention. Rice cultivation came to be equated with lineage membership, responsibility, and civility; only the "vulgar" outsiders were capable of exploiting the low-status fields.

IMPORTED RICE AND A CASH ECONOMY

Despite their strong convictions about rice agriculture, the farmers of San Tin were unable to remain aloof from the vegetable revolution that was sweeping the New Territories. While other farmers were making a rapid conversion to high-profit, labor-intensive vegetable marketing, the Mans continued to produce an annual crop of red rice. By the early 1960s, the profits from brackish paddy cultivation dwindled to almost zero because the value of low quality rice remained relatively stable in the nearby market towns while the cost of production increased sharply. During this same period the rice consumption patterns of the Colony were altered radically by the influx of relatively cheap Southeast Asian rice, mostly from Thailand. The Hong Kong consumers regarded the new varieties as inferior to the white rice from the New Territories or other parts of South China, but the Thai strains looked like high quality, long-grain rice and were cheaper than the more familiar varieties. As a consequence, the indigenous rice market in Hong Kong was seriously affected. The only profitable rice paddies left in the Colony were devoted to special strains of Yuen Long rice that were consumed by the wealthy Hong Kong Chinese or exported to the Chinese communities in the West where they brought high prices. Farmers could still exchange their rice in the market towns, but the profit on low and medium quality varieties was reduced to a bare minimum. The Mans were more adversely affected than others because their rice drew the lowest price, even in the "good old days."

The Mans might have been able to eke out a bare living from their brackish fields if the influences of the outside world and the modern cash economy had not already penetrated so deeply into the New Territories. It is true that the Chinese rural economy has been affected by international monetary fluctuations for well over a century and that the peasants were quite sophisticated in their ability to handle cash (Freedman 1959), but the villagers of the New Territories were not immersed completely in a market economy until recently. They were able to fulfill many of their needs without relying on cash. In San Tin, for instance, the general stores extended long-term credit to the rice farmers who paid their bills after each year's harvest. Some of the payments, in fact, were made "in kind" (i.e., grain was used instead of money). However, a new marketing system emerged with the vegetable revolution and, for the first time, most farmers in the Colony had access to ready cash throughout the year—not just at harvest times. As a result, the traditional credit arrangements in the villages began to erode and the farmers relied more and more on cash to make daily purchases of necessities.

The people of San Tin were particularly hard hit by the rise of a cash-based economy in the New Territories because their earning ability had declined. One immediate consequence of the increased use of money was a rise in the cost of living and an inflation of wages demanded by agricultural laborers. Like many Chinese rice farmers (Fei and Chang 1948:57-63), the Man households were generally unable to harvest their rice crops without hiring outside labor. Before the vegetable revolution, the cost of this labor was acceptable and did not bite too deeply into the final profits. By 1960, however, not only had labor costs risen, but it was even difficult to find seasonal workers because the labor-intensive vegetable plots had absorbed nearly everyone available. Potter found that the average daily wage for temporary laborers around Ping Shan in 1961 was HK$7 plus meals for men and HK$5 plus meals for women (Potter 1968:77). The workers near San Tin were demanding a daily wage of up to HK$10, which was too high for most of the Man rice farmers to pay and still make a profit.

As I have demonstrated, there were many reasons for the ultimate decline of rice agriculture in San Tin. However, the farmers themselves tend to single out the labor crisis as the most important cause. In a survey of retired farmers, thirty-five out of thirty-nine cited the rising cost of labor as the major factor in their decisions to stop growing rice on Man land. This crisis was further intensified by the problems many farmers had in keeping their own sons working on the fields. The changes that accompanied the vegetable revolution made the world outside the village more attractive every year. The nearby markets of Yuen Long and Shek Wu Hui had been transformed into exciting boom towns with new stores carrying the latest imported consumer items. All of these changes made the younger Mans restless and dissatisfied with the traditional lifestyle in San Tin. In order to enjoy the benefits of the emerging consumer economy, they needed hard cash—something their fathers' rice fields could not provide.

According to my village census, the majority of Man households stopped farming between 1960 and 1962. After this period it became physically impossible to bring a good crop of red rice to harvest. The reclaimed fields were not difficult to maintain under ordinary circumstances, but once a critical number of farmers had stopped cultivation, the brackish paddy ecosystem began to change. A chain reaction of deterioration set in when approximately one-third of the fields were abandoned and left fallow. The explanation of this process offered by the more experienced farmers is that an abandoned field disturbs or impedes the flow of water through the neighboring fields. It was very difficult for even the most determined rice farmers to continue after this critical stage was reached in the decline of the brackish paddy environment. The turning point had arrived by 1960, and it caused the involuntary retirement of several stubborn old farmers.

COLLAPSE OF AGRICULTURE AND THE SEARCH
FOR ALTERNATIVE OCCUPATIONS

Although many contributing factors were involved, the immediate and most important reason for the collapse of San Tin's traditional economy was the inability of the farmers to clear a profit from their red rice. The Mans were forced to find an alternative, or several alternatives, to replace the core element of rice in their economy. Why not vegetables? What prevented the Mans from simply taking over the vegetable plots that the outsiders had developed on lineage land? For a variety of reasons, this was not an acceptable alternative.

The Mans were well aware that vegetable farming required vast amounts of continuous labor in order to be profitable. They could not afford to hire the necessary workers, and they were generally unwilling to do it themselves. In comparison to the Ch'ao Chou immigrants, the Mans as a whole were less interested in developing their dry land to its full potential because they were not convinced that the rewards would justify their efforts. In this sense, they were similar to other groups of indigenous New Territories farmers who let their marginal lands lay fallow (see e.g., C. Wong 1964:68). As noted earlier in this chapter, vegetable farming came to be associated with outsiders in the San Tin area and gained a reputation among the Mans as a low-status occupation. These attitudes are common throughout the region where rice farming is generally thought to be more "honorable" than vegetable gardening (Topley 1964:171).

Furthermore, the majority of San Tin's farmers were not skilled in the technology of vegetable cultivation. Successful vegetable farmers must be able to grow a wide range of crops, each with individual requirements of water, fertilizer, and labor. In addition, they must keep in touch with the rapid and unpredictable changes in the urban market. Many of the old men were incapable of adjusting to a form of agriculture so radically different from the familiar system of brackish paddy cultivation.

In some cases, it was legally impossible to repossess the vegetable plots. The outsiders were foresighted enough to demand long leases before they would undertake any structural improvements in the land, such as digging wells or constructing irrigation works. Leases normally run between five and eight years for Man-owned land, and they are legally binding on both parties. The income from the leased land (between HK$100-200/*tou*/year) is not sufficient in itself to maintain the lineage and its members. Although a large number of Mans might fall into the category of "landlord," in most cases the land rent does not even cover the owners' annual supply of cigarettes. In other New Territories communities, such as Ping Shan, the vegetable revolution and the urban sprawl of the market town complexes greatly increased the value of lineage land (Potter 1968:58, 100-101). The Mans, however, were again excluded from these benefits of the changing rural economy because their lands are not close to any of the booming market towns.

Vegetable farming and "landlordism" were thus eliminated as possible alternatives to rice cultivation. Similarly, the residents of San Tin were not inclined toward poultry farming or fish pond management because these also require heavy inputs of labor and capital—and they were not as attractive as the emerging emigrant occupations. Poultry farming in the New Territories is a high-risk enterprise, but it offers equally high profits. Again, however, the outsiders had already exploited this niche in the economy and were making a conspicuous success of it. There is also some evidence that Chinese rice farmers tend to regard poultry raising as a slightly disreputable occupation (e.g., Fei and Chang 1948:236). Another possibility was to convert the brackish-water paddy land into high-yield fish ponds. Periodically, field officers from the government's

Agriculture and Fisheries Department remind the villagers that the land around San Tin is ideal for this kind of pond. However, the lineage elders object to the construction of fish ponds because they would increase the danger of floods and, in the eyes of the more traditional, alter the flow of geomantic influences through the village. At any rate, there is little interest in exploiting this potential niche in the local environment. Fish ponds, like vegetable plots, are expensive to build and tedious to maintain (Mak 1964:147). Outsiders are generally afraid to build ponds on the brackish fields because the danger of entanglement in a local dispute is too great. As a result, the brackish-water expanse near San Tin is the only area in the Deep Bay flat lands without an extensive pond industry.

All of the factors outlined above helped convince the Mans not to pursue any of the other possibilities in the local environment. The most important reason for their decision, however, was the existence of a more attractive alternative. By 1960, San Tin was well on its way to becoming a full-fledged emigrant community. For the Mans, the prospects of working in restaurants abroad were much more appealing than any of the alternative occupations available in Hong Kong. They were well aware that emigrant labor was very hard and often extremely lonely, but as one young waiter in London put it: "This is better than carrying water cans in the hot sun."

Chapter Four

TRANSITION TO EMIGRATION

THE agricultural crisis described in the previous chapter was one of the most traumatic events in the recent history of the Man lineage. An entire generation of self-assured, older farmers was forced into early retirement and, for the first time in nearly 600 years, outsiders (vegetable farmers) had gained a foothold in Man territory. But that is only part of the story. Not all of the Mans stood by helplessly and allowed themselves to become victims of Hong Kong's changing economy. Half way around the world, several adventurous entrepreneurs were laying the groundwork for San Tin's economic recovery. As we shall see, it was no accident that the Mans were to become the most successful group of emigrants from Hong Kong's New Territories.

In discussing the causes of migration, it has been customary for social scientists to distinguish between the "push" of economic necessity in the sending society and the "pull" of opportunity from abroad (see e.g., Jansen 1970:12-13, Wrong 1961:88). For instance, in the present case the decline of San Tin's agricultural economy was the primary "push" factor in the conversion to emigration. There were also a number of important "pull" factors that made emigrant labor the most attractive occupation available. These included the lure of high-paying jobs and a nucleus of fellow lineage members already established abroad. However, as the following reconstruction demonstrates, not all of the critical elements in the equation can be so conveniently categorized as either "push" or "pull" factors. A complete analysis of San Tin's transition into an emigrant community must include a wide range of local and international developments that bear little apparent relation to the problem at hand, such as the rise of smuggling along the Anglo-Chinese border during the Korean War and the 1962 passage of the Commonwealth Immigrants Act in Britain.

This does not mean that the basic "push-pull" dichotomy is of little value in understanding migration phenomena.[1] The distinction can be helpful if it is used judiciously and if it is made clear from the outset that the migrants involved are not automatons reacting to forces beyond their control. The Man emigrants were free agents who made logical choices from a limited set of alternatives. The people of San Tin are not easily pushed into anything, but the collapse of their local economy forced them to look outside the community. Some of the dispossessed farmers and their sons tried to find employment other than emigrant labor, but few succeeded. They learned from bitter personal experience that they could not compete in either the rural or the urban sector of Hong Kong's changing economy—and the only logical choice under the circumstances was international emigration.

In order to avoid confusion, the term "push" is reserved for causal factors that made the range of choice within the Colony more limited for the Mans, and "pull" refers to developments in Europe that facilitated the movement of new emigrants.

[1] Attempts to explain migration phenomena by the use of the "push-pull" framework have been severely criticized in recent years. Bose argues that the earlier studies do not account for such factors as "urban push" or "push back" (1971:100-101). McGee (1971:164) and MacDonald (1956:454) have found the "push-pull" framework to be oversimplified, if not misleading, in some cases. Most of these criticisms are lodged against rural-urban migration studies that place undue emphasis on economic push. I have retained the traditional "push-pull" dichotomy because I believe it helps clarify the underlying causes of San Tin's conversion to emigration; but I do not argue that all of the decisive factors involved fit the framework. Nor do I underplay the role of individual choice among the emigrants themselves.

San Tin's rapid conversion into an emigrant community was the result of a unique combination of circumstances and events that would set this village apart from most others in the New Territories.

ALTERNATIVES TO EMIGRATION

When the Mans gave up rice farming in the early 1960s there were few employment opportunities for males around the village. San Tin had only two rattan works and four small-scale knitting enterprises, all of which preferred to employ women. A speculator from Kowloon had tried to set up a large machine-tooling plant in San Tin, but his factory was sabotaged by the residents.[2] Since he was an outsider the Mans were very suspicious of this speculator and refused to cooperate, thus eliminating a much needed source of local jobs. All of the other commercial ventures in San Tin's immediate vicinity were either too small to accommodate any new workers or were operated by immediate family members.

The nearby market towns offered mostly low status jobs such as hawker or day-laborer, neither of which appealed to the farmers from San Tin. The Mans had always felt superior to the landless workers who toiled "like stupid buffaloes" in the market towns. Furthermore, they were not interested in working as menial laborers or domestic servants in the British army camps near San Tin. In their eyes, the only acceptable jobs within reasonable commuting distance of the village were either filled or unobtainable. Because of their general lack of educa-

[2] In the mid 1960s, a rich outsider built a large plant with an office and independent power supply near the entrance of the village. The plant never produced anything, however, and is now abandoned. For a variety of reasons, the factory so incensed the Mans that they actively disrupted the speculator's plans. Although there are many sides to the story, the owner apparently would not agree to pay enough compensation to the community, causing the lineage leaders to raise a whole series of objections, which led to outright physical sabotage.

tion and training the younger Mans could not compete for the limited number of skilled jobs available in the New Territories. Nor did they have the right "connections" to land jobs as salaried workers in the Hong Kong Government's rural administration. Many of these government jobs would have been acceptable alternatives to emigration because they are relatively prestigious and offer a high degree of security—but they were not open when the Mans needed them most.

Rather than seek low status employment, it was more suited to their self-image for the Mans to approach the outside world as potential businessmen. During the transition stage from agriculture to emigration (1957-1962), a number of villagers tried to establish themselves as merchants or small-scale manufacturers in the nearby market towns of Yuen Long and Shek Wu Hui. Most of these aspiring entrepreneurs were ex-farmers who had little knowledge of business operations. Rather than starting gradually and learning through practical experience, they jumped immediately into the highly competitive world of market town commerce by investing in a knitting factory, a grocery store, a Western medicine shop, and two or three other high risk enterprises. For the men involved, success or failure in business was a matter of "luck," just as in earlier times the fate of their crops depended largely on the weather. In one typical case, three men sank their life savings into an automobile tire retread shop and set themselves up for business near the main road in Yuen Long. They soon discovered that the demand for retreads in the New Territories was limited and that the Kowloon market was controlled by underworld elements. Most of the Man business ventures in the market towns failed within two years because of a similar lack of insight and planning (cf. Potter 1968:132). Without exception, however, the unsuccessful speculators maintain that they were simply "unlucky."

Only a handful of the Man leaders was able to build up moderately successful commercial enterprises in the New Territories (e.g., land brokerage and gambling). These men are exceptional because they had prior business experience and a wide circle of interpersonal connections in the market towns predating the crisis in San Tin's local economy. More will be said about these successful leaders later (see page 68) because they served as critical links in the transition to emigration. For the majority of San Tin's residents, however, the village and the New Territories did not offer a very attractive array of occupations or business opportunities.

Although the possibilities were greater, the urban job market was also unappealing to the younger Man workers. Kowloon is approximately one and one-half hours away from San Tin by public transportation. Even though it is feasible to do so, no one in the village now commutes to work in the city (although three or four middle school students make the trip daily). In fact, only six out of a sample of eighty-two working age men from San Tin were employed in the urban areas of Hong Kong in 1970 (see Table 2), and these six were no longer living in the village. Kowloon is one of the world's most productive centers of light industry, but its factories are characterized by low wages, long working hours, and few holidays. In 1962, the average daily wage for an industrial worker in Hong Kong was HK$7.40 (see Table 3). Even if the Mans were not discouraged by the low wages and the difficult working conditions in industry, their chances of procuring a good job were not very high. As the Commissioner of Labour in Hong Kong observes: "[T]he system of personal introduction to employment favours the recruitment of candidates who are clansmen or fellow villagers of existing employees" (Labour Report 1967-8:47-48). The Mans had very few, if any, fellow lineage members working at industrial jobs during the late 1950s and early 1960s. If they had been forced to accept work in Kowloon, therefore, the men from San Tin would have had to compete for the most menial, lumpenproletarian jobs, which pay even less than the average wages shown in Table 3.

TABLE 3

Average Daily Wages for Industrial Workers in Hong Kong

1958	HK $5.50
1960	6.80
1962	7.40
1964	8.70

Source: Labour Report 1967–8: table page 91.

Rural-urban migration was not an acceptable solution to the Mans' employment problems. Only a few had succeeded as businessmen in the New Territories, and the others were unwilling to accept work as "coolies" (a term used by the Mans themselves) in the market towns or in the urban areas. The lack of good jobs open to the younger men of San Tin was another important push factor in the conversion to emigration. The Mans were forced to look outside the Colony for sustained and lucrative employment.

BRITISH PASSPORTS AND FOOTHOLDS ABROAD

Because the Mans are born in the Crown Colony of Hong Kong and are therefore British subjects, they are entitled to carry British passports.[3] The indigenous residents of the New Territories, therefore, have a definite advantage over the recently arrived outsiders who were born in China. Before the passage of the 1962 Commonwealth Immigrants Act (see page 77), New Territories emigrants were admitted to Britain without any restrictions. However, the high cost of passage and the problems of finding jobs in England meant that most British subjects in Hong Kong were unable to take advantage of this freedom to migrate. The Mans were not the only villagers

[3] There is a clear difference, however, between British passports issued in Hong Kong and those issued in the United Kingdom. This allows the immigration authorities to distinguish between people born in the United Kingdom and citizens originating from the colonies.

who were "pushed" toward emigration because of unemployment and economic depression, but they were among the few potential emigrants with the advantage of a foothold abroad.

Prior to the transitional stage in the late 1950s and the early 1960s, San Tin already had approximately sixty emigrants located in England. Some of these men were ex-sailors who had jumped ship in Europe during the Second World War. A few stayed in England after the war and established Chinese restaurants in and around London. The ex-sailors formed the crucial foothold in Britain which the Mans needed in order to initiate a successful transition to large-scale emigration.

SAILORS AND JUMPED-SHIP IMMIGRANTS

Since Hong Kong was a regular stop on most Pacific freighter routes, the New Territories became a convenient recruiting ground for European ships that employed Chinese seamen during the early part of this century. Chinese crew members would generally sign on at much lower rates than their European counterparts. But by local standards, the sailors were paid a reasonably high wage and their jobs were sought after. As a consequence, the recruiting process tended to favor people with proper connections (i.e., relatives or fellow villagers already signed aboard). The demand for Chinese seamen grew steadily until it reached a peak in the 1920s and 1930s. After World War II, however, many of the larger shipping companies, like Canadian Pacific, began to phase out some of their traffic in the Far East (New Territories Report 1948:11). A few ships continued to recruit sailors from the New Territories until the late 1940s, but the hiring finally ended when the China coast freight traffic was disrupted during the Korean War (Labour and Mines Report 1955-56:57).

One of the most surprising findings of my village census was that one-third of the households surveyed (n = 38) had a male who had worked as a sailor between 1900 and 1940. During that period San Tin's economy could not support all of the local men, and the majority of these "excess" sons found work aboard European freighters. With few exceptions, the sailors came from poor and landless families. Only one of the retired sailors I encountered in the village stated that he originally shipped out for reasons other than poverty. This man is an adventurous type who told me he left because he did not like the dull life in the village and hoped to strike it rich abroad.

It is difficult to determine when the Mans first began to send out their sons as seamen, but a number left at least as early as 1885. One 65-year-old elder now living in San Tin was born in Jamaica, where his father had jumped ship in the 1890s (see Chapter Seven, page 149). However, according to the older sailors, the Mans were not actively recruited in large numbers for European freighters until the British had thoroughly consolidated their control over the New Territories by about 1910.

The people of San Tin knew that seamen led a dangerous and difficult life, but there were few alternatives if their families could not support them. Man fathers kept their sons home on the land if at all possible because they could never be certain that a sailor would return. At least 15 percent of the sailors who left San Tin were either killed at sea or never heard from again. Besides the risk of losing a son, the family usually did not benefit from the venture because the sailors were rarely able to contribute to the household budget on a regular basis. The people of San Tin, therefore, regarded the occupation of seaman as a dead end, a convenient escape valve for the village's surplus population. Seamen contributed very little to the local economy, and in return they received little from the village except an introduction to a receptive recruiter and a place to retire if they were lucky enough to make it back.

Few of the Chinese sailors who found jobs on European freighters at that time remained active seamen for very long. With one known exception, the Mans jumped ship at the first opportunity either in the United States (usually New York) or in Europe (London and Amsterdam). The local people do not make any distinction between "sailors" and jumped-ship, illegal immigrants because it is assumed that all of the men had signed up only as a convenient means of transportation to the promised lands. Some of the Mans, in fact, served four or five separate tours as seamen and jumped ship in several ports until they found one that suited their needs. Most of them spent an average of twenty years working as illegal immigrants before they returned to San Tin.

There are now about fifty retired sailor-immigrants living out their last years in the village. I learned of their presence during my third day in San Tin when a voice with a flawless American accent startled me from behind: "Hey Buddy, wha-daya doin' here?" It was a 73-year-old ex-sailor who had jumped ship in New York City, where he spent over twenty years. Many of the old seamen speak a limited amount of English, while a few are able to converse in exotic versions of pidgin English and Dutch. They distinguish themselves in the local teahouses by drinking coffee or whiskey, instead of the usual tea or brandy. Other than that, the ex-sailors make every effort to blend in with the retired farmers. Whenever they are given a chance, however, they launch into long and highly entertaining stories of their exploits abroad. Together these men have been in nearly every port in the world, and they survived one of the most difficult occupations available during the early part of this century. Following are some brief life sketches taken from my interviews with three ex-sailors retired in San Tin.

SUCCESS AND FAILURE: THREE LIFE HISTORIES

Man Bing-sap (age 68) is now living in comfortable retirement after spending twenty-six years abroad as a jumped-ship immigrant. The youngest of three sons, he left the village when he was 22 because he was unable to find steady work and because his father could afford to rent only enough land to keep two sons occupied. He might have been able to rent a small plot of his own, but "to be a farmer at that time without any family members to help was useless." So he spoke with a maternal cousin who was a sailor from a nearby village, and soon afterward was on his way to Singapore. Bing-sap's first ship was an old coal steamer that carried freight between Southeast Asian ports, but after a year he was transferred to a second ship, which had a diesel engine. Bing-sap had worked long hours as a coal stoker on the older vessel, so his second job as an apprentice mechanic was relatively easy. When asked to compare the two types of ships, he said: "If I had worked any longer on a coal ship, I probably would have died at sea." After signing on as crewmen, most of the San Tin sailors found themselves shoveling coal in the boiler rooms—the lowest ranking job on the old ships. According to Bing-sap, a common belief among Chinese sailors was that a man could last no more than five years as a stoker—he then had to quit or die. Suicide was frequent on the tramp steamers, and many of the retired sailors in San Tin knew stokers who had leaped overboard in a final, desperate attempt to escape the heat of the boiler room. Bing-sap was lucky to have spent only a short time as a coal stoker, but he was not so fortunate when his chance came to jump ship in America.

During his second year at sea, Bing-sap's ship took him around the world to New York, the mecca for San Tin sailors at that time. Few of the Mans jumped ship in other ports until they had missed their chance in New York harbor. However, during this particular voyage, Bing-sap and his companions were unsuccessful: "As soon as we passed the 'Big Lady' [Statue of Liberty], all of us, every Chinese sailor on board including myself, wanted desperately to jump ship. But we weren't allowed to go ashore that trip. The marine police kept circling the ship day and night with searchlights, watching for ship jumpers. None of us made it that trip."

Soon afterwards, Bing-sap jumped ship in Amsterdam and spent two years working in a laundry. Just before World War II he signed on another ship in hopes of making it to New York but found himself stranded in England for the duration of the conflict. Instead of returning home after the war, he stayed in London and worked at various jobs until he had saved enough to open his own small restaurant. We will return to Bing-sap later in this chapter because he, and others like him, play an important part in our story.

Man Chuen-gan is the only sailor I met who had left the village in the early part of the century for reasons other than immediate necessity. Although his father had plenty of land, Chuen-gan did not like farming and wanted to see the world beyond the South China coast. So he shipped out at age 16 and deserted in New York during his first year at sea. After two difficult years of working in Chinese restaurants and laundries, he somehow managed to land a job as a civilian employee on an army base. Thereafter he was employed by the United States Government for nearly thirty years until, at age 48, he retired to the village. Immediately upon his return to San Tin, Chuen-gan proceeded to start his belated family by marrying a young woman who has since borne him four children. Chuen-gan is one of the few fortunate sailors who returned with a monthly pension and enough money saved up to start a small store. Most of the Man sailors returned with very little to show for their years of hard work abroad.

Man Sek-gong is typical of the unsuccessful sailors. He left San Tin in 1923 at the relatively late age of 32 after having tried to earn a living as an agricultural laborer and handyman for several years. Sek-gong had to wait until his third round-the-world voyage before he was able to jump ship in New York. He spent most of his twenty-three years abroad in New York's Chinatown, working at unremunerative odd jobs in restaurants and laundries. His only experience outside the sheltered social environment of Chinatown was a short stint as a seasonal fruit picker. Sek-gong, therefore, was never able to save much money and did not send regular remittances back to his family in San Tin. Even though he did not maintain a correspondence with his father, a "blind marriage," in which a live chicken substituted for the groom during the festivities, was arranged and carried out in his absence. Absentee marriages of this type have been noted among emigrants from other parts of China (Topley 1959:214), but in San Tin they were rare.[4] In Sek-gong's case, the blind marriage was solely for the benefit of his parents because it provided them with a daughter-in-law to help with the housework. By the time Sek-gong returned to the village, his "wife" had already died.

When Sek-gong decided to retire, he had managed to save only enough money to pay his passage home and to buy a single *tou* of salt paddy. But even this had dwindled by the time he finally reached San Tin because Sek-gong, like a number of other Man sailors, had taken out his original sea-man's credentials as a Chinese citizen. Sek-gong's papers stated that he was a native of Po An District, Kwangtung Province, which was technically correct since he was born in 1891, seven years before the New Territories came under British control. The immigration officials would not permit Sek-gong to land in Hong Kong, so he had to disembark in Canton and pay a number of bribes to the Chinese authorities before he finally made it back to San Tin. This depleted his meager savings to the point that he returned almost as poor as the day he left twenty-three years earlier.

Sek-gong's story is typical of the difficult and basically unsuccessful life histories of San Tin's sailors and jumped-ship

[4] In another mock marriage of this type in San Tin, a sailor-immigrant sent enough money for his parents to arrange a wedding in his absence. After the feast, the cock was killed and the bride drank its blood, thus sealing the union. A cock substitute is also used in "ghost marriages," which are arranged to placate the spirit of a dead person (Topley 1955). See the "mail-order bride" section of Chapter Nine for a recent variation of the absentee marriage system in San Tin.

immigrants. Most of the retired Man sailors saved only enough to buy a small plot of land or to rebuild an old-style house in the village. This initial expenditure usually exhausted their life savings; and since the sailors were often too old to work, many were forced to live on the charity of their nephews or brothers.

The success of a jumped-ship immigrant was measured by his ability to return with a pension, a steady source of income (such as an ongoing restaurant enterprise in Europe), or a lump sum sufficient to support himself and his family in relative comfort. By these standards, only about 15 percent of the Man sailors were successful. Their failure rate, in fact, was almost as high as the 90 percent figure cited by Kulp for emigrants who went to the Nan Yang ("Southern Seas"—Southeast Asia) from Phenix Village (sic) in Kwangtung (Kulp 1925:53). Although there were many similarities between the first group of San Tin emigrants and the Nan Yang emigrants described by Kulp and by Chen Ta (1939), *the Mans never jumped ship in Southeast Asian ports.* I did not find any evidence of a San Tin resident ever having lived in the Nan Yang, although people from several other New Territories villages did emigrate to parts of Southeast Asia and Australia.[5] Furthermore, the Mans did not become indentured laborers, even though Hong Kong was one of the major embarkation points for the nineteenth century "coolie" traffic (see e.g., Campbell 1923:94, Chen Ta 1923:13). The Man sailors may have been extremely poor, but they had more freedom of action than most other Chinese emigrants of that era.

[5] The Hakkas of the New Territories worked in many parts of the Nan Yang (Aijmer 1967) and in Australia (Hayes 1970:197). A number of successful emigrants who made their fortunes in Indonesia have built elaborate mansions just south of Yuen Long (John A. Young: personal communication).

THREE STAGES OF EMIGRATION

In the last century, the Man lineage has produced three relatively distinct types of emigrants: (1) the sailors who became jumped-ship immigrants, (2) the initial restaurant founders, and (3) the contemporary restaurant employees. These emigrant types correspond roughly to three generations, except that there is some overlap between the sailors and the restaurant founders.

The second stage of emigration from San Tin was initiated by the few successful sailors who had established restaurants in the United Kingdom. Man Bing-sap, whose experiences at sea were discussed earlier, was one of the five original founders of Man-owned Chinese restaurants whom I was able to trace during my research in London. Although there may have been others, the five whose life histories are known to me all spent the Second World War stranded in England, where they worked at odd jobs. After the war they stayed in the London area and saved their money until they were able to start small restaurants. These men acted as primary catalysts for the second wave of emigration from San Tin because they demonstrated the feasibility of running profitable enterprises in England, and they encouraged some of the other Mans to join them abroad.

During the early 1950s, the restaurant business began to attract some of the wealthier members of the lineage and a second type of emigrant left the village. These new emigrants benefited from the experiences of their jumped-ship predecessors and set up more restaurants in the London metropolitan area. Only two of the original sailor-founders became important restaurateurs; the others were eclipsed by lineage mates who had more business knowledge and entrepreneurial ability. In 1952-53, several of San Tin's government appointed Village

Representatives[6] resigned their Rural Committee posts in order to go to England. These local leaders formed the core of a seven-man group that was most responsible for starting the large-scale conversion to emigration. Within a few years, the seven entrepreneurs—along with the two remaining ex-sailor founders—were able to expand the Man foothold in the British restaurant market from a few "chop suey" diners to a dozen large establishments with full staffs.

The seven nonsailors who became recognized leaders in the Chinese restaurant circles abroad all shared a common background of prior entrepreneurial experience in the New Territories. By San Tin standards, these men were fairly wealthy before they made their decisions to emigrate. They had made their money through land brokerage, gambling operations, and market town business investments. Unlike previous Man emigrants, the restaurateurs were generally middle-aged men when they left the Colony for the first time.

Man Chu-leung is typical of this second group of San Tin emigrants. He was one of the few Mans whose father was able to live comfortably as a landlord, thus freeing Chu-leung from the necessity of working in the fields and allowing him to develop business connections in the surrounding countryside. Chu-leung was shrewd enough to build up a prestigious position for himself as an important leader in the northern part of the New Territories. In other activities, Chu-leung became a partner in a large gambling house in Yuen Long market and established himself as a reliable intermediary for land brokerage deals in the Yuen Long region.

In 1952, Chu-leung resigned his position in San Tin's Rural Committee and emigrated to England to start a new episode in his varied career. He had been encouraged by friends and close kinsmen to follow them abroad where the restaurant market was just beginning to expand. Chu-leung bought one

[6] See Chapter Five, page 92, for a discussion of the Rural Committee and its Village Representative leadership system.

of the first large restaurants to be managed by the Mans and staffed it with his two sons and a few other "descendants of common-grandfather" (*su-po hsiung-ti*). Even though Chu-leung eventually expanded his holdings abroad to include three large and lucrative restaurants, he did not sever his business connections in the village or in the nearby market town. His venture in the United Kingdom, in fact, seems to have been originally conceived as an extension of his New Territories operations. In the early 1950s, investments in restaurants abroad were thought to be more secure than local enterprises because of the unstable political situation in Hong Kong following the Chinese Revolution. Chu-leung stayed abroad until his restaurants were established well enough to be managed by his sons and nephews and then returned to San Tin where he resumed his pursuit of local power and prestige. Although he is now past 60 and has retired from active management of the restaurants, he still spends up to three months of every year in England escaping from Hong Kong's oppressive summers while looking after his investments.

The histories of the other original restaurant founders are similar to Chu-leung's, except for variations in background and length of stay abroad. None of these key men left San Tin with the intention of pulling up stakes and building a totally new business career abroad. Only one of the original founders, an ex-sailor, has not maintained or initiated business connections in the New Territories. Not all of the second stage emigrants, of course, were skilled entrepreneurs. Nearly one hundred cooks, waiters, and kitchen assistants also went to work in the earlier restaurants. However, these workers probably would not have left if the entrepreneurial leaders had not employed them and provided their passage money as an advance on future wages.

By 1957, the second stage of emigration had ceased and the third had begun. The changeover between stages is reflected in a sudden step-up of passport applications for San Tin residents in 1957 (see Table 4). Of the 48 Mans who filed passport applications at the Yuen Long District Office between October 1957 and April 1958, thirty-five gave their occupations as farmers and thirteen as unskilled workers.[7] None of the applications was made by a wealthy entrepreneur because these men had left earlier. The first- and second-stage emigrants, therefore, were the pioneers of the Man interests abroad, while the contemporary emigrants are largely third-generation followers.

TABLE 4

Number of Passports Issued for Mans from San Tin (1946–1970)

1946	1	1959	36
1947	2	1960	42
1948	1	1961	46
1949	0	1962	71
1950	3	1963	18
1951	0	1964	53
1952	2	1965	57
1953	10	1966	58
1954	14	1967	3*
1955	19	1968	60
1956	21	1969	85
1957	51	1970	50**
1958	55		

Source: Hong Kong Government, Immigration Department, Documents Section, in a special search of passport files.
  * This low figure may be a result of some unrecorded data in the passport files.
  ** As of July 1970.

The life-style and the business activities of the contemporary emigrants are discussed in Chapter Six, but it may be helpful at this point to make a few general comparisons of the three emigrant types. Each group is characterized by a different method of selection. For instance, the sailors emigrated because of economic necessity, while the entrepreneurs left in order to follow up an economic opportunity. The selection of the contemporary restaurant employees does not depend as heavily

[7] Source: Passport application records on file at the Yuen Long District Office.

on the push or pull factors that determined the composition of the first two groups of Man emigrants. After 1960, almost all of the able-bodied men in the Man lineage became restaurant workers. The old selective criteria of relative wealth or poverty no longer determine who will leave San Tin because *emigration has become a way of life for the Mans* (see also, Amyot 1960:56). As many of the workers themselves put it: "In some villages everyone grows rice for a living, but in San Tin we are all emigrants. That's what we do best."

The ex-sailors were initially responsible for the involvement of the Mans in the British catering trade, but they lacked the capital and expertise necessary to exploit fully the profit potential of Chinese restaurants. The second group of San Tin emigrants supplied this expertise, and the fates of war provided the opportunity to accumulate much of the capital.

SMUGGLING AND RESTAURANT CAPITAL

The American government placed an embargo on trade with China soon after the Communists came to power in 1949. In the following years, the embargo was tightened when the Chinese entered Korea to stop the American drive north. Throughout the Korean War, China had difficulty supplying its troops with certain strategic materials because of the United Nations blockade of North Korea and the American embargo of China. As a result, a number of thriving smuggling operations began along the Anglo-Chinese border in 1950. San Tin's location on the Sham Chun River made it an ideal site for smuggling, and the Mans took full advantage of the situation.

The smuggling had already started on a limited scale even before the Communists consolidated their control over Kwangtung Province. A number of Mans sold rice and petrol to the Communist forces in early 1949. The cadres with whom they dealt wore civilian clothes at first, but after Liberation the same men reappeared in People's Liberation Army (PLA) uniforms. The smuggling operations reached a peak for the Mans in 1951 and began to subside by late 1952, even though the war did not end until 1953.

The PLA bought a wide range of items from the villagers, including copper, petrol, tires, machinery, and even trucks. Most of the small-scale smuggling was undertaken by individual farmers who pretended to be working near the river while they floated the booty across the border to waiting cadres. Almost everyone in the village who could afford to purchase a gallon of petrol participated in this type of smuggling. A few of the Mans took advantage of the unique opportunity and turned their operations into big businesses.

The smuggling was a windfall for the residents of San Tin, and many of the wealthier Mans made their fortune at that time. This was also true for other villages near the border, such as Sheung Shui, where "some of the richest men of the area are said to owe their present fortune to the period when the severity of the sanctions against China was accompanied by the highest prices for embargoed goods" (Baker 1968:38).

Smuggling, therefore, provided much of the initial capital the entrepreneurs needed to expand their holdings in Europe beyond the small establishments of the ex-sailors. The village economy itself could not have generated enough capital for this purpose; and without an external source the Mans might not have gained an early foothold in the British restaurant market. The blockade could not have occurred at a more convenient time for the people of San Tin.

OTHER FACTORS IN THE TRANSITION

The restaurants established by the ex-sailors and the early emigrants were major pull factors in the conversion to emigration because they provided jobs for prospective emigrants back home in San Tin. Other pull factors, however, were equally important. The earlier restaurants formed only the initial base for future expansion and could not have supported a large influx of kinsmen without an added boost from the British economy.

The expansion phase arrived when the growing popularity of Chinese food created a restaurant boom in the late 1950s. This boom was part of a general proliferation of restaurants which began in Britain during the immediate postwar period (see K. Ng 1968:28). The number of Chinese restaurants more than doubled between 1956 and 1964 (Table 5) and the rate of emigration from Hong Kong's New Territories rose accordingly (Table 6). The Mans were well represented among these new emigrants, as is shown by the passport data in Table 4. The rate of emigration from San Tin was relatively low between 1953 and 1956, with an average of sixteen new passports issued per year. However, in response to the British restaurant boom, the number of passport applications jumped to fifty-one in 1957. Although San Tin's conversion to emigration had started earlier, these records indicate that 1957 was an important turning point. After that year, the Mans began to claim a disproportionate number of the passports issued to prospective emigrants in the New Territories. For instance, between January 1957

TABLE 5

Stages of Chinese Restaurant Expansion in Britain

Time periods	Approximate number of restaurants
Prewar (up to 1940)	30–40
Postwar (1945–1951)	100
1952–1956	300
1957–1964	800
1965–1970	1,000*

Sources: Cheung 1970 a and b; K. Ng 1968; records of the Hong Kong Government Office in London; and interviews with leaders of the Chinese community in London. The restaurant figures are only rough estimates based on the balance of information from the sources available.

* This figure is less than the 1,400 Chinese restaurants listed in the card file of the Hong Kong Government Office in London (see n. 2, Ch. 6) because it does not include small carry-out establishments or fish-and-chips shops.

TABLE 6

Number of Passports Issued to New Territories Residents for Employment
in the United Kingdom (1952–1965)

1952–3	15[a]	1959–60	927[d]
1953–4	118[a]	1960–61	1275[e]
1954–5	96[b]	1961–62	2270[f*]
1955–6	235[c]	1962–63	1138[g]
1956–7	?	1963–64	775
1957–8	?	1964–65	591[g]
1958–9	839[d]		

Sources: [a] Police Report 1953–4:46.
    [b] Police Report 1954–5:51.
    [c] Police Report 1955–6:89.
    [d] Police Report 1959–60:48.
    [e] Police Report 1960–61:43.
    [f] New Territories Report 1961–62:11.
    [g] Immigration Report 1964–5:22.

* This figure is the estimated number of emigrants entering the United Kingdom, not the number of passports issued.

and August 1958, 62 percent of the Yuen Long District's passport applications came from Man residents of San Tin[8]—a village making up only 2 percent of the District's total population.

The restaurant boom in the United Kingdom, therefore, caused a major step-up in the rate of emigration from San Tin. The Mans were able to open new establishments which, in turn, provided even more jobs for their kinsmen in the village. During the conversion period between 1957 and 1962, the rate of emigration increased steadily. As more and more villagers made the decision to leave, the inhibitions and constraints of others were overcome by a contagious feeling of optimism. Informants speak of this time in vivid terms: "Suddenly the whole village was boiling with enthusiasm. Everyone wanted to go to England!"

As soon as the new emigrants were established abroad, a portion of their high wages was remitted back to the village. This immediately improved the living standards of the workers'

[8] Source: Records on file at the Yuen Long District Office. Unfortunately, this period is the only one for which such detailed information is available.

families in San Tin and set them apart from their nonemigrant neighbors. Also, by 1960 a number of large and conspicuously expensive new houses began to go up in the village, all financed by remittances from abroad (see Chapter Eight). These developments raised the expectations of the people left home in San Tin and encouraged an even higher rate of emigration. The wages of an ordinary restaurant worker in Europe were so much higher than anything available in Hong Kong that four Man policemen quit their coveted jobs in order to emigrate. Similarly, the lure of high paying jobs abroad made it difficult for the few remaining Man farmers to keep their sons on the land.

As a further encouragement to join the restaurant workers, the advent of inexpensive commerical air traffic completely revolutionized the centuries-old emigration process. In earlier times, an emigrant left San Tin with the knowledge that he would be lucky to return in twenty years—if ever. Contemporary restaurant workers are confident that under ordinary circumstances they will be able to return for a holiday at least once every three to five years. In 1960, New Territories emigrants began to fly directly from Hong Kong to London on charter flights (New Territories Report 1960-61:27). Until this time, the workers had taken uncomfortable, month-long boat passages to Europe, and their experiences had dampened the enthusiasm of other prospective emigrants. A century earlier, the introduction of the steamship was partly responsible for a large increase in the rate of Chinese emigration to the Nan Yang (Skinner 1957:32). The charter flights acted in a similar way to encourage emigration from the New Territories.

The Mans consider the present mode of transportation so safe and reliable that many parents now encourage their only sons to emigrate. In traditional times, a San Tin family with only one son would never have permitted their potential breadwinner to risk his life on the seas. However, several of San Tin's most conservative residents, including the local Taoist priest, now have their only sons working in restaurants abroad.

The villagers almost always stress the improvement in transportation when they are asked to explain San Tin's rapid and
wholehearted conversion to emigration.

Without the cooperation of the two governments involved,
the Mans could never have left the Colony in such large
numbers. Prior to 1962, New Territories emigrant workers were
permitted to enter the United Kingdom free of restrictions
because they were British subjects. At home, the restaurant
workers also benefited from a general colonial policy that
encouraged emigration as one solution to the growing problem
of unemployment in the New Territories. Many remote areas
in the Colony suffered from a economic depression that had
persisted through the Second World War and into the mid-
1950s. The New Territories Administration tried to alleviate
the situation by finding jobs for some of the villagers with the
government and the army camps. One of the most successful
employment programs was the recruitment of New Territories
workers for the British Phosphate Works on Nauru and Ocean
Island and for the oilfields in Brunei. Several hundred villagers
were hired through the offices of the New Territories Administration and were sent off with two-year contracts to the islands
during the early 1950s (New Territories Report 1954-55:13). The
colonial government also encouraged emigration to the United
Kingdom and other parts of Western Europe as part of the
general program to ease unemployment in the New Territories.[9]
Although the Mans did not sign up for the oilfields or the
phosphate works, they took full advantage of all the administrative help the government could give them to leave for Britain
(see Chapter Five).

    [9] This observation is based on a general reading of the New Territories
annual reports and on interviews with colonial officials. It is clear that
the government tried to make passports and work permits readily available
to the villagers. A 1958 memo circulated within the New Territories Administration stressed that emigration should have the "fullest encouragement"
because of the high unemployment in parts of rural Hong Kong (Yuen
Long District Office file no. P. S. 412/57 I: *Immigration and Emigration
of New Territories Villagers*).

COMMONWEALTH IMMIGRANTS ACT AND "BEAT-THE-BAN" EMIGRANTS

During the first six months of 1962, thousands of "beat-the-ban" immigrants rushed into the United Kingdom before the July 1 deadline of the first Commonwealth Immigrants Act (Patterson 1969:141). The Act restricted the number of Commonwealth workers who could enter Britain and introduced a voucher system requiring each new employee to have a job waiting for him upon arrival. One result of the Act was that the Hong Kong Government stopped encouraging emigration and greatly restricted the number of passports issued in late 1962 (see Table 7). However, after the full provisions of the Act became known and it was apparent that New Territories emigrants did not constitute a "problem", the rate of passport issues began to rise again.

The conscious urge to beat the Act's deadline is undoubtedly the major reason for the large increase of passports issued to the Mans before July of 1962 (Table 4). Villagers all over the New Territories believed that the new legislation would put an end to further emigration because the most sensational aspects of the parliamentary debates on this issue were well

TABLE 7

Estimated Number of New Territories Emigrants Entering the
United Kingdom before and after the 1 July 1962 Deadline of
the Commonwealth Immigrants Act

1959	900[a]
1960	1250[b]
1961	2270[c]
1962	1138[d]
January–June	869[e]
July–December	269[e]
1963	775[d]

Sources: [a] New Territories Report 1959–60:21.
        [b] New Territories Report 1960–61:27.
        [c] New Territories Report 1961–62:11.
        [d] Immigration Report 1964–65:22.
        [e] Labour Report 1962–63:53.

reported in the Hong Kong newspapers. Almost 900 "beat-the-ban" emigrants from the New Territories entered Britain during the first six months of 1962 (see Table 7). It is ironic that, in the long run, the first Commonwealth Immigrants Act did more to encourage emigration from San Tin than to discourage or curtail it.

PUSH AND PULL IN THREE
NEW TERRITORIES COMMUNITIES

San Tin, of course, is not the only village subjected to the push and pull factors outlined in this chapter, nor is it the only emigrant community in Hong Kong. The interrelations between push and pull can best be illustrated by a comparison of three communities, only one of which eventually made the conversion to large-scale emigration.

The first community is Sheung Shui, a single-lineage village which has been admirably described by Hugh Baker in his *A Chinese Lineage Village: Sheung Shui* (1968). Sheung Shui (1961 population 4,400) is about six miles east of San Tin and is controlled by the Liao lineage, which settled in the New Territories region prior to the arrival of the Mans. Although there are few important differences between the modes of social organization and the elements of peasant culture found in the two villages, the ecological setting of San Tin is strikingly different from that of Sheung Shui.

The second community is Poon Uk Tsuen, a small village on the edge of the Deep Bay marshlands which shares the same brackish-water ecological setting with San Tin. Poon Uk Tsuen ("Poon Home Village") has a population of about 160 people, all members of the small Poon lineage. The Poons were traditionally a client lineage living in the shadow of the more powerful Man lineage, but they owned much of the land they tilled and managed to co-exist with their patrons by paying regular protection fees. In return, the Mans did indeed "protect" the Poons from the other lineages in the New Territories region. Although Poon Uk Tsuen is a single-lineage village, it was too small and too weak to become an important community in the power circles of the New Territories. Freedman has suggested that the best way to compare lineages in Chinese society is to arrange them in an A to Z continuum based on increasing complexity (1958:131). In terms of organization and activities, therefore, the Poon lineage is close to the A type because it is relatively poor and undeveloped; while the Liaos of Sheung Shui and the Mans of San Tin are near the Z end of the continuum.

The third community, of course, is San Tin. These three villages share a great many things that make them suitable for a controlled comparison. All are populated by members of the same Chinese ethnic group (Cantonese-speaking *pen-ti* peasants),[10] and they are all single-lineage villages of varying complexity. The native-born residents of all three are British subjects, and they are all affected equally by the colonial policies toward emigration from the New Territories. However, only San Tin became an emigrant community. The key factor in determining which village was to make the transition to emigration was the way in which each was affected by the push of economic necessity and the pull of opportunity from abroad.

Each village was influenced by a unique combination of factors. Poon Uk Tsuen was traditionally a village of rice farmers, most of whom relied on a brackish-water technology similar to that of their Man neighbors. In the 1950s, the Poons

[10] The Liaos were originally Hakka speakers who had migrated to the Sheung Shui area from Fukien. Over the centuries, however, they have assimilated to the dominant *pen-ti* culture and now speak Cantonese. Their Hakka past is not widely known in the New Territories (see Baker 1968:39ff).

were also adversely affected by the vegetable revolution and the rise of a cash-based economy. Even though the Poons and the Mans were "pushed" by the same basic combination of local developments, Poon Uk Tsuen did not become an emigrant community.[11] The Poons were unable to send their sons abroad because they did not have the money and did not have the connections necessary to negotiate passage arrangements with restaurant owners abroad. Unlike the Mans, the Poon lineage did not have a foothold that provided a source of readily accessible jobs in Europe. In 1955, a government survey undertaken for the Yuen Long District Officer reported that most of the younger Poon males were working outside the village in military camps.[12] The Poons, therefore, managed to find an early alternative to rice farming which did not involve overseas emigration. Many other villagers in the New Territories have found similar jobs as civilian employees of the British armed forces, and this occupation continues to be an important source of rural employment. However, as outlined earlier, few of the Mans ever worked for the military, even though a large contingent of Gurkha troops is stationed nearby at Camp Casino. The camp jobs were generally passed up in favor of the much more attractive opportunities available in the restaurants abroad.

In Poon Uk Tsuen, therefore, the economic conditions acted as a push to stimulate emigration, but the prospective emigrants lacked the necessary connections to facilitate their movement abroad. An opposite state of affairs prevailed in Sheung Shui. By the 1960s, the Liaos were well represented among the restaurant owners in the United Kingdom: the number of Sheung Shui emigrants is estimated by Baker at

[11] A number of Poon Uk Tsuen residents became emigrants at a later date, but not enough to make the village entirely dependent upon their remittances.

[12] Source: Yuen Long District Office file no. P.S. 3/415/48 19 II: *San Tin Rural Committee.*

between 100 and 200 (Baker 1968:207). Although Baker does not discuss the problem of emigration in detail, it is apparent that the Liaos probably could have sustained a much higher rate of emigration if they had been forced to do so. However, the push of economic necessity did not affect the Liaos as heavily as it did the Mans or the Poons. The vegetable revolution had been beneficial to many of the Sheung Shui landowners and the booming market complex of Shek Wu Hui was almost contiguous with the village. The Liaos apparently had a better choice of local occupations and business opportunities than the Mans. Without the push of an economic crisis in the local community, the pull of high paying jobs abroad was not enough to stimulate a high rate of emigration.

Several other powerful, single-lineage villages in the New Territories were affected by the same general combination of push and pull influences that prevailed in Sheung Shui. Potter notes that Ping Shan had a number of sailors who found their way to Europe before the Second World War (1968:37). Representatives of the localized Tang lineages in Ping Shan and Kam Tin (another single-lineage village) were able to gain a fairly early foothold abroad and now own several lucrative restaurants in the United Kingdom (personal observation). However, as outlined in the previous chapter, the Tangs generally benefited from the commercialization of agriculture in the New Territories and did not send many of their sons abroad.

The comparison of San Tin, Poon Uk Tsuen, and Sheung Shui demonstrates that both push and pull factors are important in the creation of an emigrant community. San Tin was the only one of the three villages in which the push of economic necessity combined with an adequate level of encouragement and support (i.e., pull) from abroad to sustain a high rate of emigration. Any attempt to determine the primacy of either the push or the pull factors would probably be unproductive and inconclusive.

OTHER CHINESE EMIGRANT COMMUNITIES

San Tin is not the only village in the Colony that is totally dependent on emigrant remittances. There are a number of smaller emigrant communities scattered throughout the Hakka-speaking regions of the New Territories (Aijmer 1967, Bracey 1967, Pratt 1960). Many of these are single-lineage villages that conform to Freedman's (1958:131) lineage type A because they are small and undeveloped. The Hakkas of the New Territories have a long history of male out-migration since their villages are located in hilly, marginal areas where the land is often poor. The three villages studied by Aijmer never had strong local economies because their rice harvests were too small while their tea, charcoal, and handicraft enterprises were highly susceptible to adverse market fluctuations (Aijmer 1967:44-48). Among Hakkas in this area, therefore, the most salient feature of village life has always been a constant push toward labor out-migration.

The Hakkas were well represented in the early waves of emigration to the Nan Yang and to other regions such as Panama, where they worked on the Canal.[13] Similarly, a great many became sailors before World War Two and jumped ship in Europe. Although I have no first-hand knowledge of what happened to these ex-sailors, they may have been responsible for the extensive Hakka involvement in the British restaurant market. The Hakka emigrant communities, therefore, are not entirely the result of chronic economic depression (i.e., push factors) because the prospective emigrants needed connections abroad.

It should be noted, however, that these Hakka villages are generally quite small, and in some cases a single restaurant owned by a kinsman might constitute a foothold sufficient to

[13] Hakka emigrants from the New Territories village of Kwan Mun Hau Tsuen worked on the Panama Canal (Elizabeth Johnson: personal communication).

stimulate a movement toward Britain. In Chung Pui (population 201), the total number of emigrants is only 17, but this is enough to make the village dependent on overseas remittances and thus qualify as an emigrant community (Bracey 1967).

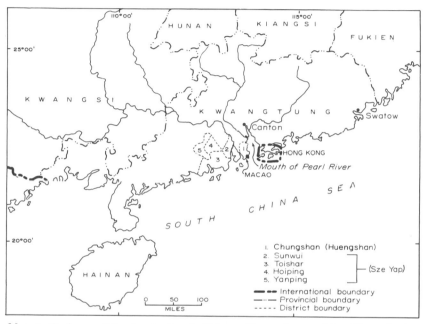

Map 4. Emigrant Districts in South China—Chungshan and Sze Yap Districts

Before the Communist Revolution, there were hundreds of emigrant communities in South China, many of them even larger than San Tin. Certain districts of Kwangtung and Fukien Provinces were particularly noted for their high rates of emigration. For instance, most of the Chinese in Hawaii originally came from Chungshan District, which adjoins the Portuguese colony of Macao (see e.g., Glick 1938). One small county in this district, Lung Tou, contained over twenty emigrant communities at the turn of the century, at least eight of which were single-lineage villages.[14] A similar pattern existed in the

[14] Source: Interviews with Honolulu residents born in Lung Tou county.

Sze Yap Districts (Mandarin, *szu yi*) near Canton and in the region surrounding the city of Amoy in Fukien Province. Emigrants from these communities went mostly to the New World and to the Nan Yang.

Perhaps the best summary of the causes underlying the great nineteenth-century waves of Chinese emigration is found in Skinner's study of the Overseas Chinese community in Thailand (1957). The rural chaos and economic depression following the Taiping Rebellion (1848-1865) "made Fukien and Kwangtung provinces more or less repellent" (Skinner 1957:30-31). While China was entering a period of disorder and depression, Siam was opening up as a relatively stable region with new economic opportunities (Skinner 1957:30). A similar combination of historical circumstances was responsible for the large-scale emigration of Southern Chinese into other regions of the Nan Yang. The replacement of Chinese tea with Indian and Ceylonese tea in the Western markets toward the end of the last century was a major push factor in this movement (Freedman 1958:10). Another was the buildup of population pressure in the South China region which became a severe problem in the mid-nineteenth century (Skinner 1957:29-30). At the same time, the opportunities in the Nan Yang frontier lured the Chinese peasants from their homes.

Chen Ta's *Emigrant Communities in South China* (1939) and Daniel Kulp's *Country Life in South China* (1925) are the most comprehensive sources of information about the home villages of the Nan Yang emigrants. Chen describes three emigrant communities, called X, Y, and Z, which are located in South Fukien and East Kwangtung. Community X had poor quality land near the coast (1939:197) and community Z had "rather swampy", low-yield rice fields (p. 68). Chen states that the rice crops in all three emigrant communities were sufficient only to supply local demands for three or four months of every year (pp. 32, 69). Chen also included a nonemigrant community in his survey to serve as a control. According to his informants, there was no emigration from the control village because the residents could easily find adequate employment in the local region (p. 66). Chen found in one community that 70 percent of the emigrants (from 905 families) left under "economic pressure", while only 20 percent were drawn by "previous connection" in the Nan Yang (see Table 8). Kulp does not present comparable data, but most of the Phenix Village emigrants appear to have left because of "the pressure of living conditions" (Kulp 1925:47).

The major difference between the earlier waves of Chinese emigration (Nan Yang and New World) and the contemporary movement of New Territories restaurant workers to Europe is the increased chance of success. A great many earlier emigrants, like the Man sailors, left with high hopes but returned with empty pockets. As noted earlier, only about 10 percent of the Nan Yang emigrants from Phenix Village returned with enough money to make their ventures a success (Kulp 1925:53). The contemporary restaurant worker, however, is able to save a considerable amount of money if he works hard and does not gamble excessively. The push factors in both the early and the recent waves of emigration are basically the

TABLE 8

Principal Causes of Emigration from One Emigrant Community
near Swatow in 1934

Cause	Number of families	Percent
Economic pressure	633	69.95
Previous connection with the Nan Yang	176	19.45
Losses from natural calamities	31	3.43
Plan to expand specific enterprises	26	2.87
Bad conduct	17	1.88
Local disturbance	7	.77
Family quarrel	7	.77
Other causes	8	.88
Total	905	100.00

Source: Chen Ta 1939:260 Table 26 "Principle Causes of Emigration" (sic).

same kinds of local economic pressures, but the pull of high paying jobs is a much more salient feature of the contemporary movement to Europe.

Chapter Five

ORGANIZATION OF EMIGRATION

WITH the advent of the restaurant boom in Britain during the late 1950s and early 1960s, there was a great demand for reliable emigrant labor. The owners of the Man establishments preferred to hire fellow lineage members to work in their restaurants whenever possible because they were thought to be more trustworthy than other Chinese immigrants. This meant that the Mans had to organize themselves on a scale much larger than anything previously known in the New Territories. Adequate sources of passage money had to be found for hundreds of prospective emigrants who could not afford to buy their own tickets. A system of job introductions and guarantees had to be organized as the restaurants expanded throughout the United Kingdom and Holland. After 1962, the formal paperwork of passport applications and labor vouchers became too complicated for ordinary villagers to comprehend and a system of intermediation was needed. Many of these problems had been dealt with before, but they became more critical as the demand for new emigrants increased.

PASSAGE MONEY

The high cost of transportation between Hong Kong and Europe is the first hurdle a prospective emigrant encounters. Even though the cost has decreased with the advent of charter flights, it is still an investment of major proportions for villagers in the New Territories. Between 1965 and 1970, an emigrant from San Tin needed approximately US$500 to cover his passage, new clothes, and other immediate expenses. If the United Kingdom had not been so far away and the cost so correspondingly high, the rate of emigration from the New Territories undoubtedly would have been much higher. A major characteristic that set the Mans apart from potential competitors in other villages was their ability to find sources of passage money sufficient to sustain a high rate of emigration.

In the earlier stages of emigration from San Tin few of the local people had enough money to cover the cost of a ticket to Europe. Most emigrants had to borrow the money from kinsmen already established abroad; and the usual method was for a restaurant owner to arrange passage for his new employees as an advance on wages. This kind of arrangement is similar to the nineteenth century "credit ticket" system of coolie emigration in which the cost of passage was deducted from the laborer's monthly wages. However, the employers of the Man emigrants are usually close kinsmen, and the relationship is not as exploitative as the earlier "credit ticket" arrangements.

Loans from local people or institutions were also important sources of passage money. In San Tin, the trust funds[1] of the lineage segments were nearly depleted during the conversion period (1957-62) by members who needed money to buy tickets. If the emigrants were lucky enough to belong to one of the segments with surplus funds, they could borrow a maximum of HK$3,000 (US$500) at 3 percent interest per year. Some of the segments required that the borrower put up land as security on the loan, but this was not really necessary in San Tin because the methods of social control are strong enough

---

[1] Ancestral estates in San Tin earned money through commonly-owned property, usually land but sometimes shops and market stalls (see Chapter Ten). Much of this money went to support the annual worship ceremonies of the segment involved. The remaining funds were often kept in a "trust fund" administered by a trustee of the estate.

to insure repayment. Although several loans came overdue, none of the emigrants failed to repay the lineage trust funds. If there had been any cases of refusal, I was told, the offender would have been expelled from the lineage (*ch'u tsu*) and his name removed from the genealogy (*tsu p'u*) until the loan was repaid.

Unfortunately, San Tin was not a very wealthy lineage community, and only a handful of the ancestral estates had sufficient funds to cover the cost of passage to Europe. The majority of the emigrants had to rely upon the advance-on-wages arrangement, or else they had to find loan sources outside the community. Starting in 1960, several modern banking corporations with headquarters in urban Hong Kong began to open branch offices in the New Territories (Freedman 1963:26). Concurrently, a number of travel agencies sprang up in the market towns to take advantage of the commercial possibilities created by the growing rate of emigration. The branch banks handle the remittance trade and the travel agencies arrange inexpensive charter flights to Europe. In order to further encourage business, these institutions also provide passage loans to prospective emigrants.

The banks often accept land as security for the emigration loans (Topley 1964:176), while the travel agencies require a cash deposit and a personal guarantee of future payment for tickets issued on credit. The Mans have shown little interest in the bank loans but have made good use of the agency loans.

After the market potential had been demonstrated in the early 1960s, an enterprising member of the Man lineage started a travel agency to handle charter flights between Hong Kong and Europe. The Mans prefer to use this agency whenever possible because the owner gives his lineage mates small discounts and personalized service. Another attraction of the agency is the ease of obtaining tickets on credit.

The Mans have been quite successful in finding enough money to sustain a high rate of emigration without depending on sources outside the lineage. This is one key to their preeminence among the emigrants from the New Territories. The residents of less fortunate villages have tried other methods of raising passage money for their sons. Freedman found one interesting case in which a wealthy leader of an unnamed New Territories community established a revolving loan fund of HK$7,000 to encourage emigration (Freedman 1963:26). I did not find any of these revolving loans operating in San Tin; but the lineage trust funds served a similar purpose.

In recent years, the Mans have become more affluent as a result of their success abroad and the passage arrangements have changed accordingly. Over half of the emigrants now obtain their passage money directly from fathers or brothers. Loans beyond the sibling network are becoming more infrequent and the number of advance-on-wages passages have declined. However, this is a comparatively new development that is only possible because the Mans were able to organize themselves so effectively during the early stages of emigration.

TRAVEL AGENCIES AND CHARTER FLIGHTS

All of the major market towns in the New Territories now have well-established travel agencies that cater to the specialized needs of the emigrants. The advertisements of these agencies are posted all over the Colony. (A conspicuous sign on the road near San Tin reads: "Universal Travel Service Specializes in Charter Flights, Immigration to Canada and the United States, Student Tickets, Work in Britain. Offices in Yuen Long, Sheung Shui, Kowloon, and London.") Contrary to the impression conveyed by these advertisements, only a small fraction of the local travel agency business is concerned with students or North American immigrants. The primary function of the agencies is to arrange charter flights for restaurant workers destined for Amsterdam and London. Four travel agencies now compete for the emigrants' business in the market town of Yuen Long. One of the most successful is the local branch office of the Man-owned agency referred to above.

The Asia Air Service (pseudonym) was founded in London several years ago by a young restaurant owner of exceptional entrepreneurial ability. He used his restaurant as the original office for the travel agency and convinced eighty of his kinsmen to sign up for the first charter flight. The business has since grown to include over twenty round-trip flights each year on chartered commercial jets. Asia Air Service now has eight branch offices located in London, Birmingham, Liverpool, Brussels, Amsterdam, Utrecht, Yuen Long, and Kowloon. Some of these branches are operated from Man-owned restaurants, but the main offices in London and Yuen Long occupy separate quarters and employ full-time staffs. Two of the owner's elder brothers manage the Hong Kong branch offices, while lineage mates run the others on a profit-sharing basis in the European cities concerned.

In 1970, the Asia Air Service chartered over 40 jets seating 186 persons on each flight. The prices were quoted in a leaflet distributed to restaurant workers all over the United Kingdom and Western Europe, as follows (prices on regularly scheduled, commercial flights in parentheses): Hong Kong to London—adult, one way US$228 (US$694), round-trip US$396 (US$1388); under age 12, one-way US$168 (US$347), round-trip US$336 (US$694); under age 2, 10 percent of adult fare. The charter flights also make intermediate stops in Amsterdam where they pick up and discharge about one fifth of the passengers, charging them the same fares as listed for London.

The agencies cannot always afford to reserve an airplane for a fixed date of departure so most of the "Restaurant Workers' Specials" operate on a flexible schedule. Passengers have to be ready to leave on twelve hours' notice any time within a ten-day period. Sometimes the flights may be delayed three or four times and may actually leave a month later than expected. Although the workers and their employers have learned to accept these delays as inevitable, they still cause a great deal of concern and anguish among the emigrants. The only alternative, however, is to buy a ticket on a regularly scheduled flight, which costs at least twice as much as the average charter.

Villagers are well aware that the agencies make high profits on these irregular flights, but they seldom complain because they feel that the extra services more than compensate for the inconvenience and cost. Asia Air Service takes exceptionally good care of its customers and does more than simply organize cheap charter flights. The cost of the air ticket includes expert help with immigration formalities which sometimes begins several months before the expected date of departure. After the papers are ready and the flight has been scheduled, Asia Air arranges to have the entire flight processed through immigration and customs control as a group, whenever possible. A full-time interpreter travels on every Asia Air flight to handle all details for the emigrants. These services are especially appreciated by the less-seasoned travellers and the village wives who find the experience terrifying. The agency also provides free local transportation to and from the airport at both ends of the flight, as well as an extra baggage allowance for emigrants.

"GREASING THE WHEELS" OF THE EMIGRATION PROCESS

Every subdistrict in the New Territories is represented by a government-sponsored "Rural Committee" that reflects the vested interests of the indigenous villagers in the area. In San Tin, the Rural Committee is controlled by the informal leaders of the Man lineage even though it ostensibly represents the entire San Tin Sub-District, which includes a large number of recently arrived immigrant farmers from China and several smaller, non-Man villages. The local committee has been organized so that its most important functions are directly related to the coordination of large-scale emigration, which again is almost entirely a concern of the Mans. Rural Committees are the only local institutions in the New Territories which the colonial government has endowed with a certain amount of authority and decision-making power. These powers are very restricted and largely ceremonial, but the committees do serve important community functions by providing convenient channels of communication to higher bureaucracies in the colonial administration.

The people of San Tin elect sixteen "Village Representatives" to serve on the committee, and these men in turn select a chairman and two vice-chairmen. The chairman is the most important functionary in the community because he is San Tin's representative in the leadership circles of the New Territories; he is also the key interpersonal link between the village and the colonial administration. He is chosen, therefore, as a kind of liaison officer who must be capable of interacting with intermediate-level Chinese bureaucrats in the Hong Kong Government. The chairman's reputation in the home community is of little concern; and, in fact, it is not uncommon for New Territories villagers to choose unpopular individuals as their representatives to the outside world.

Leaders in San Tin are chosen for their ability to function effectively in the power circles of the New Territories. These circles include both the commercial networks centered in the market towns and the government offices located in Yuen Long. The Rural Committee leaders are often asked by the villagers to serve as intermediaries for transactions with businessmen or government officials outside the village. Besides the ordinary tasks involving land registration, water rights, and business connections, the Man leaders must be capable of meeting the specialized needs of the community. In San Tin, a major qualification for leadership positions is the ability to grease the bureaucratic wheels of the emigration process. Ordinary villagers use the Rural Committee as a buffer in their dealings with the Hong Kong Government's Immigration Department, especially when the transactions become long and incomprehensible.

The emigration procedure requires a number of formal dealings with government bureaucrats in order to procure passports, labor vouchers, entry certificates, or work permits. Most of the villagers believe that all bureaucrats are corrupt and that every transaction must be lubricated with a substantial bribe. These views are exaggerated, but the fear of officialdom is very commonplace throughout the colony of Hong Kong where "squeeze" and "tea money" are well-known facts of life in both government and business (see e.g., Goodstadt 1970, Immigration Report 1966:19). The Mans have seen too many petty officials and policemen accept payoffs and have had too many humiliating experiences in government offices to trust the immigration authorities. They prefer to rely on their Rural Committee intermediaries whenever possible.

Many of the important leaders of the San Tin Rural Committee are well suited to the tasks of expediting the emigration process because they have been emigrants themselves. In 1970, six committee members had active business connections with the restaurant enterprises abroad, and three made regular visits to England every year. These men have also built up a large number of personal contacts in the power circles of the New Territories. The most successful leaders actually spend very little time in San Tin, although they return to the village to sleep. They can usually be found interacting with their peers from other villages in market town tea houses or congregating in the lobbies of the Hong Kong Government building in Yuen Long. It takes many years of intense effort for the Rural Committee leaders to build up an effective network of interpersonal relations. Among the Mans, these networks stretch all over the northern half of the New Territories and throughout many parts of Western Europe wherever concentrations of Chinese restaurants are found.

In San Tin, the Rural Committee performs so many services for the emigrant that he seldom has to leave the village and face hostile bureaucrats in strange government offices. One of the major tasks of the full-time, professional secretary employed by the committee is to explain the often incomprehensible application forms to the emigrants and their families. Although the immigration forms are printed in Chinese, many are bad translations of English originals. The secretary handles most of the petty application details that would ordinarily consume many frustrating hours if the emigrant were forced to fill out the forms alone in an Immigration Department Sub-Station. The Rural Committee leaders are also available to give advice on the maze of laws and regulations governing immigration to various European countries. This kind of information is especially valuable to the prospective emigrants and is not easily obtained in the New Territories. The Mans ordinarily do not share their common fund of emigration experience and expertise with nonlineage outsiders. Local leaders confide that this gives San Tin emigrants a competitive advantage and is an important factor in their continued success.

The Rural Committee also works closely with the "mobile immigration office," which was established by the Hong Kong Government in 1964. Once a week the travelling immigration team sets up a temporary office in San Tin to handle local business. The villagers are able to apply for passports, visas, and entry certificates during these regularly scheduled half-day visits. Several of the committeemen are always in attendance to watch over the proceedings and to assist the immigration officials. The local agent for the Asia Air Service also sets up a table in the Rural Committee building on these critical days. The travel agent, and sometimes the wife of Asia Air's owner, help the prospective emigrants with the paperwork and make arrangements for future charter flights. These weekly immigration team visits are among the most important regular events in village life. A permanent Immigration Department Sub-Station is located only fifteen minutes away in the market town of Shek Wu Hui; but the Mans prefer to wait for the mobile office to visit their Rural Committee, where business is conducted in a more personalized manner and the atmosphere is more congenial.

Even though their official duties are ill defined, the formal leaders of the Rural Committee do much more than provide moral support during the visits of the immigration team. Any duly elected Village Representative may act as sponsor for the passport application of a local resident. Most of the emigrants are processed smoothly with the aid of the Rural Committee and require only routine attention from the secretary or the visiting immigration authorities. Occasionally, however, a prospective emigrant may have difficulty obtaining a British passport because he has no legal proof that he was born in the Colony. In other instances, the emigrant's papers may have been inexplicably held up or misplaced somewhere within the bureaucratic channels. Without the subtle intervention of a well-placed intermediary, these cases might be delayed indefinitely in Hong Kong. The status of Village Representative gives the Man leaders a certain amount of moral authority when dealing with the Hong Kong Government. However, this kind of authority would not get them beyond the lobbies of the government offices if the leaders did not have personal connections in the right places.

LABOR VOUCHERS AND JOB INFORMATION

The 1962 Commonwealth Immigrants Act and subsequent legislation made the formal emigration procedure much more complicated for Chinese emigrants from the New Territories. Every immigrant worker seeking entry to the United Kingdom is now required to obtain a voucher from the Department of Employment and Productivity in London certifying that a job has been guaranteed and reserved for him in advance. The government sets a limit on the number of vouchers each year in an attempt to check the high rate of immigration, which has become a volatile social issue in Britain. Although the new restrictions have had the most effect on the Commonwealth immigrants from India, Pakistan, and the West Indies, the voucher system also applies to the few remaining British Colonies.

Originally, the British government instituted three kinds of labor vouchers for Commonwealth citizens: "A" vouchers, issued to workers with a specific job; "B" vouchers, issued to applicants with "a recognized skill or qualification which is in short supply in Britain"; and "C" vouchers, reserved for all other applicants on a "first come, first served" basis (Patterson 1969:23). The C vouchers were soon abolished because the backlog from the first few months alone became unmanageable (Patterson 1969:25-26). Category B vouchers are issued to skilled workers, teachers, doctors, dentists, nurses, and technicians. Less than 5 percent of the total vouchers granted to applicants from Hong Kong are in this skilled category (from data in Immigration Report 1968-69:4). The vast majority of the Hong Kong Chinese immigrants enter the United Kingdom on A vouchers because they are unskilled restaurant workers. These vouchers are not evenly distributed among the various sectors of Hong Kong's population. In the four-year period between 1963 and 1966, 73 percent of the vouchers for Hong Kong were issued to residents of the New Territories, which includes only about 12 percent of the Colony's population (compare Tables 9 and 10).

Since the inauguration of the first Commonwealth Immigrants Act, the British Government has made it increasingly more difficult for the New Territories workers to obtain A vouchers. In late 1964, a quota system was introduced which

TABLE 9

"A" Labor Vouchers Issued to Hong Kong British Subjects

1962	57[a]
1963	243[b]
1964	720[b]
1965	232[b]
1966	127[c]
1967	197[d]
1968	291[e]

Sources: [a] Labour Report 1963–4:42.
[b] Labour Report 1964–5:50–51.
[c] Labour Report 1966–7:9.
[d] Labour Report 1967–8:9.
[e] Labour Report 1968–9:10.

set a limit on the number of vouchers a restaurant proprietor could legally obtain for new employees. This quota is based on the size of the premises and the volume of business handled by each establishment (Immigration Report 1964-65:22). The immediate impact of this new restriction can be seen in the sudden drop in A vouchers issued to Hong Kong workers in 1965, shown in Table 9. Further restrictions came in 1968 with the passage of additional Commonwealth Immigrants legislation.

The revised Act favored voucher applications for the British manufacturing industries, but certain "dependent territories" were given a special quota of 600 vouchers each year in recognition of their unique problems. Half of these special vouchers were reserved for the Colony of Hong Kong, thus setting an absolute limit of 300 new workers each year (Immigration Report 1967-68:21). The 1968 Act also put an end to the practice of sending village youths to live in Britain just before they turned 16, the legal age limit for free entry (Immigration Report 1967-68:20).

In spite of these restrictions, the overall rate of emigration from San Tin has increased progressively since 1963 (see Table 4, Chapter Four). Not all of the passports indicated in Table 4, of course, were issued to emigrants going to the United

TABLE 10

Labor Vouchers Granted to New Territories Residents

1963	152
1964	512[a]
1965	219[a]
1966	85[b]

Sources: [a] Immigration Report 1965–6:37.
        [b] Immigration Report 1966–7:40.

Kingdom; approximately 30 percent of Mans have found employment in other parts of Western Europe, notably in Holland. Even with these limitations in mind, however, it would appear that the Mans have been highly successful in meeting the challenge of ever increasing immigration restrictions. Again, much of their success is due to the cooperative efforts of individual emigrants working within the framework of the lineage to obtain job introductions and labor vouchers.

An important feature of the voucher system is that the actual application is made by the employer, and not by the prospective employee. If the vacancy is verified, the voucher is issued to the employer who, in turn, must send it to his new employee (Patterson 1969:23). The voucher system eliminates the possibility of entering the United Kingdom with the intention of finding a job after arrival. Instead, the system gives an automatic advantage to emigrants who are able to arrange employment in advance. With their extensive network of lineage mates strategically located in cities all over the United Kingdom, it is relatively easy for new emigrants from San Tin to obtain labor vouchers whenever a vacancy appears in the Man-owned restaurants.

Eighty-three percent of the emigrants surveyed during my village census were introduced to their first jobs abroad by lineage members (detailed job information of this nature is available for fifty-three emigrants). Furthermore, in 1970, 89 percent of these emigrants were either working for a lineage mate or were self-employed. Only a handful of the contemporary Man emigrants are loners who managed to find their way abroad without help from the lineage. One made it to Dallas, Texas, where he works in a bar; three are now working in Denmark; and at least one is employed in Sweden. These are rare individuals, however, and the vast majority rely on their kinship network for job introductions.

The Mans have shown little interest in expanding into commercial endeavors outside the restaurant trade pioneered by their lineage mates. For instance, no more than a dozen of the Mans now living in the London area have found jobs that are not performed inside the confines of a Chinese restaurant. Even these few jobs, however, are service positions dependent on the larger Chinese community of restaurant employees (e.g., gambling attendant, hire-car driver, and travel agent). Like most Chinese emigrants who leave their home villages for overseas destinations, the Mans tend to follow the same occupations as the kinsmen who preceded them (cf., Crissman 1967:186).

THE LINEAGE AS EMIGRATION AGENCY

It is apparent from the foregoing discussion that the bonds of agnatic kinship play a decisive role in the organization of emigration from San Tin. However, a number of questions regarding the role of the lineage must still be considered: Was the lineage the crucial factor in the success of the Mans? If San Tin had been a multilineage village would its residents have been as successful? Is the key institution involved with the emigration process the lineage or the family?

Ultimately the family is responsible for the emigration of most workers because the financial obligations are assumed by the family as a whole. However, the Mans approach emigration as they do most other problems outside the confines of the immediate family. They mobilize the social bonds of agnatic kinship and the formal institutions of the lineage to mediate with the outside world. Job introductions are sought from lineage mates previously established abroad, and passage money can often be obtained from lineage trust funds or from future employers—who are almost invariably lineage members. Charter flights are arranged through a Man-owned travel agency, and the lineage-controlled Rural Committee performs much of the tedious paperwork. Lineage leaders are available to act as intermediaries in difficult negotiations with government bureaucracies. Furthermore, the lineage serves as a pool of dependable employees for the Man restaurant owners in Europe. In effect, then, the Man lineage has become a kind of emigration agency.

There is some evidence that the Mans are not unique in this respect. T'ien notes in his study of the Chinese in Sarawak that the lineage assumed some "collective responsibility" to help finance the emigrants' original passage abroad (1953:80). Even though Amyot found no evidence that the lineages had actively promoted emigration to the Philippines, he does stress that there was a unidirectional flow of new migrants from China, based largely on kinship networks (1960:63-64). Chen Ta also speaks of a continuous chain of migration from a single-lineage village in Kwangtung to the Malaysian city of Penang which lasted for nearly two centuries (1939:163).

Certainly not all of the overseas movements of the Chinese are based on lineage networks, but it seems clear that the lineage is ideally suited to the needs of large-scale *chain migration*. This type of migration is characteristic of Overseas Chinese and is best defined as a "movement in which prospective migrants learn of opportunities, are provided with transportation, and have initial accommodation and employment arranged by means of primary social relationships with previous migrants" (MacDonald and MacDonald 1964:82). San Tin would probably be a very different community today if the local people had not had the bond of common lineage membership upon which to build an elaborate system of chain migration.

The fact that San Tin is a large and powerful single-lineage village gives the Mans an advantage over emigrants from smaller, multilineage communities. The Mans have no difficulty controlling the Rural Committee in their district and using it to serve their own specialized needs. Nor do they have to contend with any other lineages in their efforts to to organize for large-scale emigration. In multilineage villages, the kin groups are often split into rival factions; and, as a consequence, emigration from such villages generally is not organized on a community-wide basis (see, e.g., C. K. Yang 1959:45, 72-73).

The Mans also have internal schisms, but they are better able to present a united front to the outside world. The lineage continues to serve as an effective basis for community organization in spite of the influence of rapid social and economic change in the surrounding countryside. It is too often assumed that kinship groups like the one discussed in this study are so inflexible and tradition-bound that they are incapable of adjusting to the demands of a modern economy. In San Tin, at least, the lineage still functions in a modified form, and it continues to be a guiding influence in the lives of individual members. We will return to these matters in the concluding chapter, but at this point I would like to reemphasize that the lineage played a *central* role in San Tin's successful conversion to emigration.

Chapter Six

THE MANS IN BRITAIN

THE exact number of Chinese immigrants now residing in Britain is unknown, but estimates range from 30,000 to 50,000 (see, e.g., K. Ng 1968:2, note). The majority are directly employed in the "catering industry" (hotel and restaurant work), and only a handful are students, nurses, professionals, and domestics. Ng Kwee-choo, in his short monograph entitled *The Chinese in London* (1968, Institute of Race Relations), outlines the history and much of the social organization of the Overseas Chinese community in Britain. The following comments, therefore, are confined largely to the business operations and the lifestyle of the Mans who work in the United Kingdom.[1]

I was somewhat surprised to find that the villagers have not adjusted to the host culture in Britain and that they have made few efforts to become assimilated. Most of them are oriented toward the New Territories where they hope to retire. Later in this study, I show how the Man restaurant workers are able to maintain close ties to the home community even after years of work abroad. There is some evidence that these attitudes may be changing as the emigrants bring their wives to Europe, but the traditional patterns of long-term savings

[1] This chapter is not a "community study" in the usual sense because it focuses on selected aspects of the economic and social life of one emigrant group (viz., Mans from San Tin). It is based on a three-month follow-up study of Man restaurant workers living in the London metropolitan area. This phase of the research was conducted in late 1970, immediately after I left Hong Kong. Some of the information is also based on conversations with holiday returnees and retired emigrants in San Tin (see also Watson 1974).

and intensive labor continue to be the mainstays of the Man restaurant enterprises. To the Man emigrants, therefore, Britain is not their home; it is simply the country where they work.

CHINESE RESTAURANTS IN BRITAIN

The early Chinese restaurants in Britain began during the 1930s as small noodle shops and cheap diners catering to Chinese seamen in the dock areas of Liverpool and London (Cheung 1970a). The British public did not "discover" Chinese food until the post-World War Two era when the demand grew so quickly that it caused a restaurant boom by the mid-1950s. Three groups of Chinese immigrants have been involved with the restaurant business in Britain: (1) "Northern" Chinese, (2) Singapore Chinese, and (3) Hong Kong Chinese (K. Ng 1968:29). Most of the Northerners are former staff members of the Nationalist Chinese embassy, which was closed down after the Communist Revolution. These Mandarin speakers operate some of the most expensive "Peking-style" restaurants in the greater London area. Ng found only four restaurants in London which are managed and staffed by Singapore Chinese (K. Ng 1968:30). The largest group of owners and workers originate from Hong Kong's New Territories.

According to data made available by the Hong Kong Government Office in London, there are 1,406 Chinese restaurants in the United Kingdom (1970 data).[2] Almost every town in Eng-

[2] Source: Card file maintained by the Hong Kong Government Office in London. This office requests that public health inspectors in the United Kingdom collect data on the name, ownership, and number of employees of all Chinese restaurants in their local districts. Although it is the most comprehensive source available, it is not entirely reliable because many health inspectors do not send in all the data requested. The 1970 figures cited here are based on my own analysis of the card file. The Hong Kong Government Office (HKGO) is a rather unusual agency, which functions

land with a population of 10,000 or more now has at least one Chinese restaurant. The people from San Tin own nearly one hundred restaurants distributed fairly evenly throughout the country. Most of the Man establishments are medium-sized (10-15 tables) and employ between six and ten full-time workers.[3] A standard dinner for two in these places runs over £2, which is somewhat above the average for medium-priced restaurants in Britain. The emigrants categorize their restaurants according to the quality and authenticity of the food served. By their own definition, therefore, the Man establishments are known as "chop suey" restaurants in which the cuisine is adjusted to suit the palate of their British clientele. The more authentic Chinese restaurants, which the Mans themselves patronize on their days off, are found in London's Soho district (see page 116).

The economic setbacks that Britain has suffered in recent years have had a serious impact on the business of the ordinary Chinese restaurants. People are now less inclined to pay high prices when they dine out. In response, many of the New Territories immigrants have opened carry-out Chinese food shops, which are cheaper than restaurants. The carry-out business has become very popular in the London area and reached a peak, according to Man informants, in 1968. These new businesses can be operated by a single family unit and

---

as a branch of the Hong Kong colonial administration. This office helps New Territories immigrants in their dealings with other governmental agencies in London and acts as a kind of consulate to protect the workers' interests while they are living in Britain.

[3] A survey of the card file mentioned in footnote 2 above shows that the Mans own and operate at least eighty-six restaurants (many other Man-owned restaurants are not represented in the file because the health inspectors do not always fill out the cards properly). Most of the Man establishments are located in suburban or provincial areas. There is only one in London's Borough of Westminster (central theatre district), two in Manchester, and none in Liverpool. The card file also shows that the Man restaurants employ an average of 7.2 workers.

require only "hole-in-the-wall" premises, thus saving a great deal on labor and overhead. Other Chinese immigrants have started to operate fish-and-chips diners, especially in Liverpool. Economic stagnation in Britain was also the principal reason that the Mans began to branch over to Continental Europe in the mid-1960s. The new frontier of Chinese restaurant expansion is now in the middle-sized towns of Holland, Belgium, and West Germany.

BANK LOANS AND PARTNERSHIPS: STARTING A RESTAURANT

According to knowledgeable informants, it takes an average of US$15,000 to US$25,000 to open a ten-table Chinese restaurant in the London suburbs. The capital for the new enterprises comes from individual savings, partnerships among friends and kinsmen, and bank loans. In Chapter Four it was shown how smuggling provided an opportunity for the Mans to obtain large amounts of capital for restaurant purchases during the early 1950s. Many of the original owners are wealthy enough to maintain several restaurants as personal investments, shared only with their sons who act as managers or assistants. At the same time, these entrepreneurs may also be part-owners in a number of other restaurants. Before we discuss the important question of partnerships in the formation of new restaurants, the role of bank loans will be considered.

The Hong Kong and Shanghai Banking Corporation, a pillar of Hong Kong's commercial establishment, maintains an important branch office in London. Although this branch is concerned largely with the import-export trade, more than half of its over-the-counter business comes from the Chinese community in the greater London area. The bank employs a full-time "Manager of Chinese Business" to handle the restaurant workers' accounts and to negotiate loans for new establishments. The bank loans are fairly easy to obtain because the Chinese restaurateurs have a very good record of repayment and enjoy excellent credit with a number of catering supply companies. As the manager of a large kitchenware firm put it: "We never have any problems with Chinese customers, and we always accept their checks."

Although the credit ratings of the applicants are generally high, the bank will not cover more than one-third of a new restaurant's total cost. A well-informed Chinese solicitor operating in the West End maintains that approximately 40 percent of all recently established Chinese restaurants in the London area were partially financed by bank loans. It is my impression that these bank loans are generally granted to the larger enterprises opened by the wealthier and more sophisticated restaurateurs. Most of the Chinese emigrants rely upon partnerships to pool the necessary capital for new establishments.

At least half of the Man restaurants are owned and operated as partnerships. The partners are not always close kinsmen, but they usually come from San Tin and share a common membership in the Man lineage. The ideal pattern among San Tin emigrants is to work hard and save diligently until one has enough money to buy into a new restaurant as a partner. Informants both in San Tin and London estimate that it costs US$2,400 to US$3,600 (£1,000-1,500) to join a partnership in Britain and that it takes the average emigrant three to five years to accumulate this much capital. Once they have enough money, the Mans have little trouble finding acceptable investment opportunities because there are always a number of lineage mates in similar positions looking for partners to start a business. The rate of new restaurant openings has slowed down in recent years, but during the late 1950s the market was so good that partners could realize a profit on their initial investments within six months to one year after starting.[4]

There are two types of partnership arrangements in the restaurants I studied: worker-partners and absentee-partners. The first type is the most common among the Mans and also seems to be more prevalent in the restaurants located in the provincial areas. It is not unusual to find Chinese restaurants in which every employee is a partner and has a real interest in the smooth operation of the business. In these establishments, the ownership is divided into shares so that the manager might own three and the head waiter two, with the other cooks or waiters pooling their money to buy the rest. This pattern of shared ownership has worked so well that at least 20 percent of the contemporary emigrants from San Tin are worker-partners.

As the name implies, absentee-partners do not take a direct interest in the day-to-day operation of the restaurants. These men are often entrepreneurs who speculate in other Chinese restaurants in addition to running their own establishments. One speculator from San Tin is reputed to have a share in eleven restaurants located in England, Holland, and Belgium. Only a few of the Mans, however, have enough capital to invest in more than one restaurant. Absentee-partners do not have a controlling voice in the management of the business and do not interfere so long as they receive a reasonable return on their original investments.

Partnership disputes occur often enough among the Mans to be a regular topic of conversation in San Tin's gossip circles. Disputes between the active manager and his absentee partners are common when the business begins to decline or stabilize. The partners suspect the manager of holding back some of the proceeds and juggling the books in their absence. In worker-partner arrangements, the conflict generally arises when partners have equal shares in the business and thus equal voice

[4] Source: Staff members of the Hong Kong Government Office, London.

in management decisions. However, in most cases the manager-owner has controlling interest in the restaurant, while his employees are junior partners. This type of partnership is more stable and long lasting than the absentee type.

Few of the partnerships are formalized by anything other than verbal agreements because the emigrants do not feel the need for a legal document. Any manager or owner attempting to expel his partners from the business without proper compensation would be ostracized by the other members of the Overseas Chinese community, and it is doubtful he would be able to retain his staff. The usual method of dissolving a partnership is for one of the shareholders to take full control of the business by purchasing the other shares. In other cases, the partners may agree to sell to a third party, which is often another group of emigrants who have banded together to form a new partnership themselves. Every Man emigrant dreams of managing his own restaurant, but only a few are ever able to attain this goal. As an alternative, they buy into carefully arranged partnerships with trusted friends and relatives, knowing full well that this trust will be put to the severest tests by the strains inherent in the new relationship.

The most efficient and productive restaurants are managed as family businesses with a father or an elder brother in charge. These establishments have many of the advantages of the "family firm" in which family members can be expected to work longer hours for less salary than paid employees (Benedict 1968:10). Some of the worker-partner arrangements also take on characteristics of the "family firm" because the employees have a stake in the success of the business. Like family members, the worker-partners may be motivated to defer some of their personal income to invest in the expansion of the restaurant. The continued success of all the restaurants, however, depends upon the ability of the emigrants to avoid personal conflicts that interfere with rational management decisions.

EMPLOYEES AND EMPLOYMENT PROBLEMS

Chinese restaurants in Britain have three categories of employees: cooks, kitchen workers, and waiters. The waiters are the highest paid because they must know enough English to help the customers place their orders. Among the emigrants, therefore, waiters have higher prestige than the cooks, who earn less and seldom know more than a few words of English. The Western attitude of holding the cook in higher esteem and granting him more status than the waiters never ceases to amaze the Man emigrants. They find this hard to understand because the cooks are ordinary villagers who have had little training and would never be able to work in a restaurant serving authentic Chinese food. Waiters are often offended when the British customers treat them indifferently and fail to recognize the unusual status distinctions made by the emigrants themselves. There are a number of highly paid, expert cooks in London, but these men work in the more elegant restaurants or in the authentic establishments catering exclusively to the Chinese community (see page 116).

Besides the waiters and the cooks, every restaurant employs unskilled kitchen workers to prepare the food, wash the dishes, and clean the premises. These workers are usually young villagers who have not learned enough English to be waiters. Many will never graduate from the kitchen, but they may pick up enough practical experience to become cooks. Even if they remain in these low-status positions, however, the emigrants are assured of a regular income considerably higher than is paid for most jobs available in the New Territories.

The wages of the restaurant workers have increased steadily since the passage of the 1962 Commonwealth Immigrants Act because it is now more difficult to replace employees who leave. According to newspaper sources in Hong Kong, British restaurant wages almost doubled between 1962 and 1965 (*Wah Kui Yat Bou* 24 Aug. 1965). In 1958, Man emigrants expected to make a weekly average of £8 for "unskilled" work in British restaurants.[5] By 1964 the weekly average had risen to approximately £12 to £15 per week (K. Ng 1968:81). The average income of Man restaurant workers in 1970 was £17 to £20 per week, which was comfortable even by British standards. Store clerks and bus conductors in London were paid a starting wage of about £15 to £18 during the time of this study.

The emigrants' earnings are divided into wages paid directly by the owner and tips left by the customers. In many cases, the wages of waiters may be lower than those of the cooks, but the kitchen-bound employees actually earn less because they do not share in the tips.[6] Most of the Man establishments use a variation of the tip-sharing system described by Ng Kwee-choo in his earlier study of London restaurants (1968:42):

> Gratuities collected by all waiters are put in a common box and at the end of every week are divided among them according to seniority in length of service. The total amount is divided into six shares, each [of the five waiters] being entitled to only one share. The sixth share is subdivided into fifteen portions and the most senior waiter is entitled to five portions; second in seniority, four; third in seniority, three; fourth in seniority, two; and last in seniority, one.

A few of the proprietors have experimented with a new incentive system in which each waiter is responsible for the

[5] Source: Passport application records on file at the Yuen Long District Office, Hong Kong New Territories.

[6] It is difficult to judge the percentage of earnings directly attributable to tips because this is a sensitive issue in all Chinese restaurants. Several Man informants stated that over 50 percent of their total earnings came from tips. Ng Kwee-choo cites one waiter whose wage is £6.4s. per week but who earns a total of £16 each week when tips are included (K. Ng 1968:42). The cooks and kitchen helpers generally do not share in the tips because, according to the waiters, they are not responsible for serving the customers. After a few years of work, however, the Man cooks may be earning over £20 per week if they have proven to be good workers.

tips from a given number of tables. This system was introduced by the management in hopes of improving service (surliness is sometimes a problem), but it has not worked well and has caused some resentment among older waiters who feel that it rewards the younger men who speak better English.

High earnings are not the only advantage of working in the Chinese restaurants, because, in most cases, the proprietor is responsible for providing meals and lodging for his employees. These benefits are not deducted from the standard wages, which means that the restaurant workers are earning significantly more than the average unskilled British worker. The emigrants, however, insist that they deserve higher incomes and argue forcefully, sometimes bitterly, that the British would never tolerate the long hours and poor conditions common in the Chinese restaurant trade. Waiters work ten to twelve hours a day, six days a week; and the kitchen helpers are required to stay even longer to clean up. They also complain that during slack periods most of the staff are confined to the hot, cramped back rooms. With few exceptions, the Man restaurant workers feel that their life abroad is very arduous and that their high earnings come at great human cost.

"SECOND-CLASS" EMIGRANTS

Not all of the Chinese workers in the United Kingdom earn as much as the Man emigrants. In fact, there is some evidence that two classes of Chinese employees are emerging in the restaurant circles of Britain: (1) native-born Hong Kong British subjects, and (2) China-born aliens residing in Hong Kong (i.e., non-Commonwealth citizens). The immigration of Chinese aliens has increased greatly in recent years (see Table 11), partly because these workers are not covered by the voucher system and thus are not restricted by the same quotas that limit the influx of New Territories Chinese.[7]

[7] The immigration regulations on Chinese aliens have changed since this

TABLE 11

Chinese Aliens Entering Britain from Hong Kong

Year	1963	1964	1965	1966	1967	1968	1969
Industry	58	69	68	101	72	77	78
Catering	256	354	380	475	719	720	833
Entertaining ..	10	9	0	23	3	10	6
Nursing	109	132	180	283	290	262	304
Domestics	53	49	81	65	91	71	66
Students	25	48	52	60	52	55	48
Totals	511	661	761	1007	1227	1195	1335

Source: Department of Employment (London), Aliens Section.

To many observers, the Chinese restaurants in Britain seem hopelessly overstaffed, but the proprietors often complain that they are, in fact, short of help and need more workers. One answer to this problem is to hire Chinese aliens living in Hong Kong to work for a prescribed length of time—for wages that are significantly lower than the rate prevailing for New Territories-born workers. The possibilities of exploitation are great in such cases, and the proprietors must be careful to cover up the discrepancies because British law expressly forbids the practice of underpaying alien workers. Unlike the Commonwealth immigrants, these aliens are granted twelve-month permits for a specific, prearranged job and are not allowed to change employers without the permission of the Department of Employment. Furthermore, since they are recruited under the category of skilled workers, they are supposed to have had prior experience working in Hong Kong restaurants for several years. Few of the alien immigrants are able to meet this requirement, but they can purchase certificates of experience

study was conducted. In November, 1971, a quota was placed on the entry of non-Commonwealth immigrants employed in the catering industry; hence, the abuses described here may no longer apply. However, the number of "A" vouchers issued to Hong Kong-born Chinese is still lower than the number of Chinese aliens admitted to the United Kingdom each year (see e.g., Hong Kong Immigration Department Annual Reports for 1970-71 and for 1971-72).

from certain restaurant proprietors in Hong Kong for about HK$600 (US$100). The aliens consider this a necessary expense and do not complain to the British authorities. After the fourth year of service, an alien may apply to have the original restrictions lifted and, if approved, may look for a higher-paying job in another restaurant.

In effect, this system of recruitment has created a new class of Chinese emigrants who are willing to do almost anything to gain a foothold abroad. These aliens generally have few friends and even fewer relatives among the emigrants already established in Britain, so they do not have a protective network of personal contacts. The steady increase of Chinese alien immigration also supports the complaints of New Territories emigrant leaders that the Commonwealth Immigrants Act makes it easier for non-British subjects to enter the United Kingdom than for native-born Hong Kong residents (see, e.g., L. Wong 1967:7).

The Mans feel little sympathy for the exploited aliens, who are regarded simply as "outsiders," the same kind of intruders threatening the dominance of the Man lineage back home in San Tin Sub-District. Even though the Mans have few compunctions about using the alien workers, their restaurants generally are not big enough to accommodate them. Poorly paid aliens are thought to be a disruptive influence in smaller Chinese restaurants, where one or two disgruntled workers might easily upset the smooth operation of the business. Most of the aliens work under close supervision in the back rooms of the larger, more expensive establishments.

PROBLEMS OF LIFE ABROAD: HOUSING AND TRANSPORTATION

The life of the Chinese emigrants in Britain is characterized by hard work and constant stress. All of the Mans hope to

Old style house in San Tin.

Double sterling house, occupying two lots.

Left: Sterling house.

Below: Renovated Empress of Heaven Temple in San Tin.

Emigrants and elders examine list of donors for temple renovation.

Marble plaque inside banquet hall, listing highest donors to re-novation project.

"Double Nine" cere-mony at grave of founding ancestor.

Pigs presented to found-ing ancestor.

Division of ritual pork, shares represent membership in the lineage.

Two of San Tin's five ancestral halls.

San Tin's market.

make enough money to retire in comfort, but in the meantime they must cope with the difficult circumstances of living in an unfamiliar culture. The most pressing problems are finding adequate housing and reliable transportation to and from work. Although housing is now a problem in many parts of Britain, London has suffered a chronic shortage since World War Two. Chinese emigrants face the added burden of racial discrimination when searching for low-cost accommodations and are often forced to pay exorbitant rents for shabby tenement flats. British law forbids sleeping in the restaurants, so the owners must find accommodation for their workers elsewhere. In suburban or provincial areas, the Mans live above or near the restaurants, but in central London the zoning laws and high rents sometimes make it necessary to live a great distance from work. As a result, most of the Man workers I met were living in cramped flats and overcrowded houses. One owner lodged his entire staff of eight male workers, plus his wife and two older children, in two rooms of a tenement building. At least four of the Mans have raised enough money to purchase houses in the London area, but these too are hopelessly overcrowded because the extra rooms are rented to other Chinese emigrants in order to cover the payments.

Urban transportation is another headache for emigrants not lucky enough to live near their restaurants. Since Chinese restaurants in central London normally stay open until at least 1:00 A.M.—well after subway trains have made their last runs and most buses have returned to the garage—private transportation is the only solution. A surprising number of Chinese emigrants in London own automobiles that are used primarily to transport employees. Except for a few wealthy Soho restaurateurs, owners treat their automobiles as business expenses and complain constantly about high maintenance costs.

The need for late-night transportation in the London metropolitan region provided an ideal opening for the entrepreneurs of the Chinese community, and before long two private taxi companies appeared to fill the void. Both companies are operated by New Territories emigrants who hire part-time drivers to chauffeur Chinese workers and restaurateurs around the London area in company-owned cars. The rates are cheaper than those of regular British cabs, and the drivers can be summoned at odd hours when most of London is asleep. Private taxi companies are found in many suburban neighborhoods, but only these two have Cantonese-speaking dispatchers and drivers.

THE EMERGING CHINESE COMMUNITY IN LONDON

In 1965, five Chinese restaurants opened in rapid succession on an obscure street in London's West End theater district (L. Wong 1967:8). Not the usual "chop suey" establishments, these authentic Chinese restaurants serve excellent dishes previously unavailable in Britain and cater almost exclusively to the growing Chinese population. Thus began Gerrard Street's conversion into an incipient Chinatown, known to the emigrants as (c) *Tohng Yahn Gaai* ("Chinese People Street"). Before the Second World War, an earlier Chinatown arose to serve the small Chinese seafaring community in the Limehouse area of London. German bombers obliterated the two streets of that Chinatown, and it never reemerged after the war (K. Ng 1968:18-20). Until recently, Chinese immigration to London had not reached a scale large enough to sustain a Chinatown like the ones in San Francisco or New York. The early sailors were too transient to establish more than a small, service-oriented community, and the contemporary New Territories emigrants are too widely dispersed throughout the country to form a cohesive unit. However, the restaurant workers have nurtured and supported *Tohng Yahn Gaai* as a community focal point. Gerrard Street has become the recreational center of the Chinese all over Britain and, as a result, it has taken on many of the elemental functions of a Chinatown.

Besides the authentic restaurants, a common feature of Chinatowns around the world is the proliferation of gambling houses for the immigrants (see, e.g., Culin 1891:15). Gambling is the main form of recreation for the Chinese restaurant workers in Europe, just as it is for the people back home in the New Territories (see Chapter Nine). Ng Kwee-choo notes (1968:63) that there were seven Chinese gambling houses in London during the time of his 1963-64 study. Today four large gambling establishments are located in basements along Gerrard Street alone, and these appear to have taken over most of the business of the Chinese community. Since they are illegal, the Chinese gambling dens keep a low public profile, with no outside markings to attract business. Gambling in London is legal only in a few private clubs catering mostly to the British. The London police do not disturb the unlicensed Chinese gambling dens on Gerrard Street, even though their presence is widely known and discussed in occasional newspaper articles. The authorities maintain a laissez-faire attitude toward these establishments because they never cause public disturbances and cater exclusively to the Chinese immigrants. Non-Chinese outsiders are actively discouraged by the management and the players from entering the gambling dens. This may be the result of a tacit understanding between the British authorities and the Chinese community.

The gambling dens are staffed by an average of four full-time employees who run the games, watch the premises, and clean up after closing. The salaries of the gambling attendants are on a par with the earnings of the restaurant waiters. One San Tin emigrant working in a Gerrard Street gambling den earns enough to remit an average of HK$450 to his family each month and to return every three years for a visit.

The gambling dens stay open every night until the players decide to leave, which makes them natural places to spend idle hours with friends. In short, Gerrard Street, with its authentic restaurants and recreational facilities, is the center of whatever action or excitement is found in the Chinese community. This is reflected in the local vocabulary of Chinese workers: The London Borough of Westminster, which incorporates Soho and the West End theater district, is called "Imperial City," (c) *wohng sing*; while all the other cities or towns in Britain are referred to as "Little Ports," (c) *fauh jai*. Restaurant workers in the "Little Ports" save their days off for months in order to make extended recreation trips to Gerrard Street.

At first sight Gerrard Street does not appear to be much of a Chinatown. It is only two blocks long, and not all of its stores and shops cater to the Chinese community. One of the oldest Indian restaurants in London, founded in 1915, is located on Gerrard along with a typical British pub and a modern steakhouse. Most of the signs, however, are in Chinese—advertising restaurants, service organizations, and hire-car companies. Four of the authentic restaurants cater exclusively to Chinese, and outsiders are made to feel uncomfortable unless they are accompanied by a Chinese friend. A bookstore sells Cantonese novels, Kuomintang propaganda tracts, and Hong Kong newspapers. Two grocery stores offer a wide range of imported Chinese food, and two Chinese barbershops operate from second-story flats. Three travel agencies, including the Man-owned Asia Air Service, have offices on Gerrard Street, as do the taxi companies discussed earlier. A Chinese solicitor and a Cantonese-speaking Indian doctor have offices nearby, while the Hong Kong Government Office and London branch of the Hong Kong and Shanghai Banking Corporation are both within reasonable walking distance of Gerrard. These and other facilities make *Tohng Yahn Gaai* a Chinatown without a strong residential core.

The growth of London's new Chinatown complex has been limited because zoning laws in the West End exclude most inexpensive housing units. Rents for the few available flats are extremely high. Another important reason is the nature of the restaurant business that employs the vast majority of contemporary Chinese immigrants. The restaurants are scattered all over the United Kingdom, making the Chinese "community" too dispersed to form a localized residential district.

FAMILY EMIGRATION

On Sunday afternoons and holidays, Gerrard Street is crowded with off-duty Chinese restaurant workers who give it the flavor of a small side street in Kowloon. The presence of a surprising number of wives, children, and elderly women makes the setting appear even more like an extension of Hong Kong society. These family members are evidence of an important new development in the emigration of New Territories workers.

Under the regulations of the Commonwealth Immigrants Act, the native-born New Territories emigrants are treated as if they intend to settle permanently in Britain. After they are well established, the Act allows them to bring over their "statutory dependents" without difficulty. This privilege is not shared by the alien Chinese workers, who must stay at least four years before applying for permission to bring their families. In earlier times, however, few of the Chinese restaurant workers

TABLE 12

United Kingdom Entry Certificates Issued to "Dependents and Relatives" from Hong Kong

1962	135[a]
1963	285[a]
1964	659[b]
1965	845[c]
1966	1122
1967	1211[d]
1968	833[e]

Sources: [a] Immigration Report 1963–4:26.
[b] Immigration Report 1964–5:43.
[c] Immigration Report 1965–6:80–1.
[d] Immigration Report 1967–8:53.
[e] Immigration Report 1968–9:57.

ever considered it necessary or feasible to send for their wives and children. Only since 1964 have a significant number of dependents begun to join the New Territories emigrants working in Britain (see Table 12).

The emigrants are allowed to claim their wives and all of their children under age 16 as dependents. These family members are not covered by the labor voucher system and need only obtain Entry Certificates to pass through British immigration control. Prior to 1968, the immigration authorities noticed that Chinese emigrants were using the age limit of 16 years as a loophole to bring over a large number of 15-year-old workers who did not need vouchers (Immigration Report 1966-67:41). This loophole was partially eliminated by subsequent legislation that made it mandatory for both parents to be living in Britain before children could join them abroad (Immigration Report 1967-68:20). The drop in the number of entry certificates issued to dependents in 1968, as shown in Table 12, may be a reflection of this new restriction.

The availability of inexpensive charter flights is primarily responsible for the recent trend toward family emigration. Among the younger Mans, the ideal marriage is one in which the wife of the emigrant lives with him while abroad. The rationale for this new pattern is firmly rooted in financial advantage because the Mans have calculated that a wife is more productive working abroad than staying home in San Tin. Many of the emigrant wives are kitchen helpers or cashiers in the restaurants, while others are housekeepers for the workers' residences. In most cases the children—even infants—are sent back to San Tin, where they are raised by their grandparents, thus freeing the mothers for work. Older children may be brought over to learn English before they are 16, but the essential feature of family emigration is a concern for productivity. The new pattern of emigration, therefore, is selective and does not include all statutory dependents. This selection process is reflected in the fact that 48 percent of the

Hong Kong dependents entering the United Kingdom in 1968 and 1969 were women and only 51 percent were children, a much lower percentage of child entries than found among other Commonwealth immigrant groups (see Table 13).

A small number of the New Territories emigrants are elderly mothers brought over by their sons to help with housework and childrearing. Less than 1 percent of the dependent emigrants have been old men (see Table 13) because, according

TABLE 13

Dependents of Commonwealth Immigrants Admitted to the
United Kingdom in 1968 and 1969

Territory that issued passport	Men		Women		Children	
Hong Kong						
1968*	7		363		405	
		1%		48%		51%
1969	10		519		553	
India						
1968	493		6281		11944	
		2%		36%		62%
1969	179		3389		4718	
Jamaica						
1968	42		266		4168	
		1%		6%		93%
1969	27		177		2350	
Pakistan						
1968	156		4430		7949	
		1%		36%		63%
1969	127		4429		7324	
Trinidad and Tobago						
1968	3		58		211	
		1%		21%		78%
1969	4		42		165	

Sources: *Commonwealth Immigrants Act 1962 and 1968, Statistics 1968* (Cmnd 4029, page 8) and *Statistics 1969* (Cmnd 4327, page 8). London: Her Majesty's Stationery Office.

* Note: Apparently not all of the Entry Certificates issued to dependents in Hong Kong were used. Compare figures for 1968 in Tables 12 and 13.

to Man informants, there is no way for them to be even minimally productive abroad. Between 1964 and 1968, more than a dozen older women from San Tin went to live in Britain, but by 1970 they had returned and this peculiar form of parent emigration had ceased among the Mans. After 1968 it became more difficult to bring over elderly dependents because the British government raised the minimum age requirement for the free entry of parents from 60 to 65 (Immigration Report 1967-68:20).

A more important reason for the decline of parent emigration from San Tin was the circulation of stories about the misery the old women had experienced abroad. Although these women were kept busy, they became lonely and disoriented in the strange British cities, where they were not even capable of venturing alone outside their over-crowded homes. One of these women became so despondent and homesick that she attempted suicide while her son and his family were out working. The older women could not cope with the problems of emigrant life, so they returned to the village, telling their peers about the terrifying flights and the dull months spent confined in crowded flats or houses. One mother in San Tin who had recently turned down her son's request to live with his family in England said: "It makes us happy to know our sons still need us, but none of us will go over there anymore. Britain is no place for an old woman."

Some of the younger wives fare little better than the old emigrants and also have to be sent home to San Tin. The women have great difficulty adjusting to the new life because they rarely see other Chinese women and they understand little English. All of the emigrants complain about the British climate, which they consider unbearably cold during the winter. The women are often lonely because their younger children are sent back to the village. The views of a 26-year-old woman are typical of the Man wives living in England: "Even though I work hard, I feel like I am living in a prison. I can't go

anywhere alone because I am afraid and my husband works
all the time. I just count the months until we can go back
to Hong Kong for the Chinese New Year."

Even among the children there are problems because the
Man parents have devised an unusual system of childrearing.
They insist that the young grow up in the village where they
will learn the elements of Chinese culture, but at the same
time they want them to be fluent in English and capable of
operating comfortably in British society. As a result, many of
the children are shifted back and forth between Hong Kong
and Britain almost as if they were on a shuttle service. These
problems are discussed at length in the section on "grandparent
socialization" in Chapter Nine.

LINEAGE ACTIVITY ABROAD

Although the Mans have greatly increased their numbers
abroad and have started to bring over some of their families,
there is no formal lineage organization in Britain. The Mans
do not have any regularly scheduled gatherings abroad; their
only meetings are organized on an informal, ad hoc basis when
a special need arises, such as a contribution drive for public
works in San Tin (see Chapter Seven). When asked why there
are no formal lineage activities in Britain, the Mans almost
invariably reply: "Why do we need them here? We have a strong
lineage with many ancestral halls back in San Tin." The Mans
see no need for formal gatherings in Britain because the
important ritual and social activities are still directed by the
lineage leaders based in San Tin.

At least two Chinese surname groups, the Cheung and the
Pang, have formed clansmen associations in Britain (*Wah Kui
Yat Bou* 3 March 1970). Unlike lineages, the membership rules
of these associations are not based on strict agnatic descent,
so that unrelated individuals with the same surname may join.

The Cheung Association has over 300 members and holds an annual convention banquet in England every year to appoint new officers who arrange the following year's meeting. Aside from the annual banquets, these surname associations do not appear to have many other important activities and certainly do not function as lineage organizations abroad.

The propensity of Overseas Chinese to organize their communities segmentally according to association membership is well documented (see, e.g., Crissman 1967, W. Willmott 1970:141ff). In Britain, social clubs and welfare associations for restaurant workers are the most common types of associations. In earlier times, when the majority of the Chinese in Britain were sailors, the associations were devoted to fighting discrimination and providing welfare benefits to needy members. The Mans generally show little interest in the Chinese associations except to take advantage of the recreational facilities provided.[8] Most of the restaurant workers are preoccupied with the everyday difficulties of their jobs and are too busy working to devote much time or energy to community activities.

LANGUAGE, INTERMARRIAGE, AND ASSIMILATION

According to Ng (1968:88) and Broady (1955:74, 1958:34), the Chinese are by far the least assimilated of all the immigrant minorities in Britain. Broady's findings are not surprising

[8] The only exception appears to be a recreation club called the Chung Sam Workers' Club, a left-wing organization favoring the Communists over the Kuomintang. According to Ng's 1963-64 study, 109 out of the 250 members of this club are surnamed Man (K. Ng 1968:54). Most of these are residents of the small village of Chau Tau, which is located half a mile from San Tin. Chau Tau branched off from the core lineage many centuries ago, but its residents retain their membership in San Tin's Main Ancestral Hall. Chau Tau is often considered part of the San Tin complex of subvillages, but it has a separate identity and a separate tradition.

because he concentrated on the small, insular Chinese community in the Liverpool docks area. Ng's conclusions, however, are interesting because the restaurant workers he studied were scattered throughout London's twenty-eight metropolitan boroughs and were not cloistered inside a ghetto. Under these circumstances one might expect the restaurant workers to have extensive contacts with the British public. Ng found that this has not happened in the London area because the Chinese make few efforts to participate in the host culture.

This is illustrated in a most elemental way by the low level of English comprehension and speaking ability among the restaurant workers. Fewer than 10 percent are able to carry on a simple conversation with their customers, and most of the waiters learn only enough to handle the menu. The cooks and kitchen helpers have few opportunities to learn or practice English: "It is not uncommon for a Chinese cook to emigrate here [London] to work for several years and then return home to the New Territories without exchanging a word with English people" (K. Ng 1968:89). In his study of three Hakka villages Aijmer discovered that the emigrants could not speak English even after years of work in Britain (1967:76).

I found a similar lack of English-speaking ability among the Man emigrants. Only a handful of the younger Man waiters and three or four of the more successful owners could speak English well enough to operate effectively outside the Chinese community. To overcome this language barrier, the Mans have developed a system in which each restaurant employs at least one waiter or manager who is competent in English and is able to act as a mediator for the others. Most of the Mans seldom venture beyond the security of either the restaurants or the recreation centers where Cantonese is spoken.

The language problem is only one indicator of the low level of assimilation found among Chinese workers living in Britain. The majority of Man emigrants I met in San Tin and in London had absorbed only the most superficial elements of British culture while working abroad. For instance, there is some evidence that the younger restaurant workers from San Tin are attracted to the lifestyle of British youth. On their visits home they antagonize the village elders by wearing modish clothes and listening to Western pop music. They also comment favorably about the amenities of life in London as opposed to the hardships they reencounter during their stay in San Tin. From the perspective of the village, I had interpreted this as evidence of a basic change in traditional values and attitudes. After visiting the same workers in London, however, it was clear that these are only surface adjustments.

Intermarriage is often considered an indicator of assimilation, but only if the migrant is drawn away from his native tradition and chooses to accommodate himself to the culture of his wife. Furthermore, spouses can provide a bridge to the host society only if they have not become outcasts themselves by the very act of marrying an immigrant. Most of the English wives or consorts of contemporary Chinese restaurant workers have cut their family ties and are treated as social misfits by the host culture (K. Ng 1968:76). Both Broady (1955) and K. Ng (1968:76) found that the majority of these intermarriages are with working-class women and that the relationships seldom lead to a higher level of assimilation because the Chinese male ordinarily takes the dominant role. In my own work, I found that the only exception to this general rule is when the worker marries a middle-class girl whose parents and friends accept the union. I discovered only two such cases among the Mans— and these emigrants had effectively "dropped out" of Chinese culture and into British culture. The assimilated workers have histories that make them aberrant from the other Man emigrants.[9] A larger number of San Tin men have married or

[9] Although I made a major effort in San Tin and in London to discover how many sons had "dropped out," I found only two (and one other suspected case). These men are highly educated by village standards (i.e., high school level) and are fluent in English. They also received some of their schooling

consorted with working-class women and have not cut their ties with their home (this problem is taken up in more detail in Chapter Nine). Intermarriage has not yet had a significant effect on the overall assimilation of Man emigrants.

THE RESTAURANT NICHE

The economic niche that the Chinese emigrants have come to dominate allows the Mans to live, work, and prosper without coming into significant contact with the British public and without acculturating to the patterns of life in a Western metropolis. One of the biggest surprises of my entire two-year project was to discover how little the emigrants had actually changed as a result of their urban experience (see Watson 1974). The reason, of course, is that the restaurants are virtual islands of Chinese culture in the larger British society—isolated pockets where the emigrants can interact with the alien outside world on their own terms. Many of the cooks and kitchen workers never have to emerge from the back rooms, except in those unexpected instances when they are presented to appreciative, big-spending customers as the house "chef." Similarly, even the few waiters who speak fluent English may never have contacts with members of the host culture after working hours. The Man emigrants I spoke with stated that they had no English (or Dutch) friends; and, perhaps more significant, none expressed any regret. Except for the two known exceptions who have assimilated, the Man emigrants are not particularly interested in making new friends or in changing their way of life. In their view, Chinese culture is infinitely superior to the European cultures they encounter abroad. They have few illusions, however, about their role as workers in an alien

in England during their early teens, and later married middle-class English girls, who led them to sever their family ties.

society, and they prefer to maintain a low public profile while they accumulate as much money as possible.

The restaurant business is ideally suited to the needs of the Man emigrants because it forms an unobtrusive niche on the fringe of the British economy. Unlike the majority of other Commonwealth immigrants in Britain, the Chinese do not compete with British workers for jobs in commerce or industry. The few Chinese who are not employed in restaurants tend to work as professionals, domestics, or shopkeepers. This is one reason why the Chinese are not perceived as a "problem" in race-conscious Britain. Broady observes that the Chinese in Liverpool of the early 1950s were well treated "precisely because they have not attempted to become assimilated" and did not threaten the livelihood of any British workers (Broady 1958:34). The catering industry is controlled predominantly by immigrants, and few English work in the low to moderately priced London restaurants. The franchised hamburger chains, for instance, employ Spanish and Italian workers, while most neighborhood restaurants are "ethnic" types (e.g., Greek, Italian, French, Indian) employing migrants from the owner's homeland. The Chinese, therefore, are only one of the many immigrant groups working to feed the British public.

Besides being unobtrusive, the restaurant niche does not require a high degree of sophistication or knowledge about the host culture. It is quite simple for an immigrant to start a restaurant once he has found enough capital and a suitable location. Proprietors need only comply with national immigration laws and municipal health regulations, and they are relatively free of outside interference. The restaurant niche lends itself easily to the traditional patterns of intensive labor and long-term savings that have characterized Chinese emigrant enterprises all over the world. It is one of the easiest economic niches for an immigrant to enter in Britain, and it causes the least difficulty to members of the host society.

The only problems that the Mans encounter with the British public are caused by teenage ruffians who occasionally refuse to pay their bills. The ensuing fights are a favorite topic of conversation among the workers and a source of anxiety for the owners.[10] Some of the Man restaurants in tougher neighborhoods have hired British women as waitresses or cashiers because they are thought to have a calming effect on unruly customers. (As one owner put it: "The English have great respect for women because they have a Queen.") These problems, however, are minor and do not threaten the overall success of the business. The Chinese are generally treated with detached reserve by the British public.

TEMPORARY WORKERS OR PERMANENT IMMIGRANTS?

One of the major goals of my London research was to determine whether the Man emigrants have decided to settle in Britain or to return to San Tin after retirement. As I noted in the Introduction, the ideal pattern among Chinese emigrants who left to seek their fortunes in the Nan Yang and the New World was to return to their "native place"[11]

[10] In 1963, several British youths ate in a Chinese restaurant in St. Helen's, Lancashire, and refused to pay the bill. A fight broke out between the youths and the restaurant's six Hakka waiters (all, incidentally, worker-partners) in which a British boy was killed. The local residents were incensed and a protest march began outside the restaurant (K. Ng 1968:58-9). This was perhaps the most explosive incident involving the Chinese community in recent times.

[11] "Native place" (*heung ha* in Cantonese) is a term that refers to an individual's home district or village somewhere in China (or, as in this case, the New Territories). The term has very strong psychological connotations relating to security and kinship. In many cases, especially in the exodus to the Nan Yang, the native place of the emigrant was anything but secure. The economic and social instability of China's southern coastal areas was

in China upon retirement. They did not intend to become permanent immigrants. This pattern of emigration has been true of Man emigrants from the earliest sailors to the present restaurant workers. However, there is growing evidence of a change among some of the most recent emigrants. A major feature of the traditional pattern is that emigrants normally leave their families in the home village, but, as shown above, this is no longer true of an increasing number of Man emigrants.

The precise number of families that have emigrated is hard to determine, but the rate increases every year. Many of the older residents of San Tin are disturbed by this trend toward family emigration because they fear the workers will sever their ties with the village when they no longer have to return to see their families. The Hong Kong Government assumes that the increase of dependent emigration in recent years is evidence that "many men have decided to make Britain their permanent home" and will not return to the New Territories (Immigration Report 1966-67:40). The problem, however, is more complex than it appears, and the rise of dependent emigration does not necessarily support the conclusions of government observers in Hong Kong.

The new pattern of family emigration is highly selective because the Mans are primarily concerned with the productivity of each emigrant, irrespective of age or sex. Emigration is still considered to be strictly an economic venture, and taking along family members does not automatically imply a change in world view. Similarly, the Mans always emphasize that the emigrant life is difficult and trying, and they do not feel secure enough to pull up stakes in their home community. It is too early to determine how many of the Mans will actually decide to settle in Britain because the trend toward family emigration is a recent development. When asked, most uphold the tradi-

a primary cause of earlier waves of emigration. However, despite the contradiction it often implies, the concept of native place as an ideal of warmth and security is a persistent feature of Overseas Chinese culture.

tional ideal by stating that they intend to retire in San Tin. It is my impression after conducting the London follow-up study that few of the Mans have made a conscious decision to become permanent residents of Britain, but this may change if the political equilibrium of Hong Kong is altered significantly.[12] In the meantime, the majority of the Man emigrants consider themselves to be transients in an alien culture, sojourners working only for the day they can retire in comfort to their home village.

[12] Other developments that may affect the pattern of migration described in this chapter are the recent changes in European immigration laws. In late 1973, I made a brief trip to London and found that Hong Kong's quota of "A" vouchers has been decreased from 300 to 200 per year. This change has made it more difficult for the New Territories workers to emigrate and has caused some panic in the Chinese community. One consequence has been a dramatic increase in dependent emigration from Hong Kong (see below), apparently in anticipation of further restrictions. At the same time, more and more New Territories emigrants are choosing to work in continental Europe because they feel the opportunities are better there. Holland has approximately 10,000 Chinese immigrants, mostly from Hong Kong (personal communication: S.A. Webb-Johnson, Hong Kong Government Office, London). It is still uncertain how these changes will affect the Mans, but if Britain, Holland, and Belgium decide to cut off immigration from Hong Kong, San Tin will face a severe crisis (see Chapter Nine, page 195).

U.K. Entry Certificates (Dependents)
British Subjects from Hong Kong
(1969-1972)

1969-70	1970-71	1971-72
1,547 a	1,988 a	2,958 b

Sources:
a. Immigration Report 1970-71:63.
b. Immigration Report 1971-72:5.

Chapter Seven

EMIGRANT TIES
TO THE HOME COMMUNITY

BEFORE the Second World War it was quite difficult for a jumped-ship sailor to keep up with events back in San Tin. There was no system of regular communication with people in the village and return trips before retirement were almost nonexistent. Furthermore, the sailors had few opportunities to demonstrate their allegiance to the community besides sending occasional remittances to their families. As a consequence, the pre-1950 emigrants had little impact on the dominant, agriculture-oriented culture of the village. However, when San Tin's traditional economy changed and the villagers found themselves dependent on remittances, the absentee workers began to influence the community on a scale commensurate with their economic contributions. Man emigrants now play an active role in local affairs, even though they work halfway around the world.

As noted in the previous chapter, the restaurant workers are not committed to settle in Europe and the majority of them still plan to retire in San Tin. This attitude of transience is reflected in the way they dispose of their earnings. The emigrants have poured so much money into San Tin during the last decade that it is gaining a reputation in the New Territories as a center of affluence and leisure. The community's physical appearance is changing rapidly as the emigrants replace their traditional homes with modern-style houses and finance the renovation of important public structures. Return- ing workers always bring expensive gifts for their families and throw elaborate banquets to entertain the villagers. Even the younger emigrants are careful to maintain close community ties that go well beyond the basic requirements of sending regular remittances to their families. It is clear from their actions that the Man workers still consider San Tin to be their primary reference point, no matter how long they have lived abroad.

This chapter deals specifically with family remittances, con- tribution drives, public banquets, and return trips because they are the most common expressions of emigrant concern for the home community. Except for the family remittances, which are not for public scrutiny, the absentee workers have a pen- chant for spending their hard-earned money in the most osten- tatious manner possible. In doing so, they are making invest- ments in future security and laying the foundations for their own retirement. Throwing banquets, donating money, and sending remittances are ways in which emigrants can verify their status in the home community, thus ensuring that they will be welcome when they finally return. Similarly, the materi- al investments in housing and public construction help to make San Tin a more appealing social environment for the workers and their families. The first duty of all emigrants, regardless of age or relative affluence, is to support their dependents in the best possible manner through regular remittances.

FAMILY REMITTANCES

In June, 1964, the Hong Kong Government completed a large post office building on the main highway just outside San Tin. Local leaders had been lobbying for the construction of a post office since the village first began to receive regular remittances. Before this time there was little demand for postal services in San Tin because few people had occasion to send or receive mail. However, by 1963 the Mans had overtaxed the postal services of the nearby market towns by cashing an ever increasing flow of remittances from Europe. The government's decision to build a post office in the village was a recognition that San Tin had become a full-fledged emigrant community.

The San Tin Post Office cashed a *monthly* average of US$12,150 in postal orders from the United Kingdom alone in 1969.[1] During the same year, the village was responsible for 23 percent of the postal remittances for the entire Yuen Long District[2] (and the Mans constitute less than 2 percent of the district's population). Although the postal records are fairly reliable, it is difficult to make an accurate estimate of the total remittances for San Tin because the emigrants use several other methods of sending money to their families. Many of the restaurant employees now prefer to transfer funds through the branch offices of the Hong Kong and Shanghai Banking Corporation in London and Yuen Long rather than depend on the postal services which are sometimes erratic in parts of the New Territories. The records for Tai Po District give some indication of the relative importance of bank remittances compared to postal orders among emigrants. In 1968 and 1969 the Tai Po branch of the Hong Kong and Shanghai Banking Corporation handled approximately HK$26,000,000 in remittances from overseas, while the Tai Po Post Office cashed a total of over HK$50,000,000 during the same period.[3]

Besides the banking and postal services, New Territories emigrants send remittances to their families in cash and travellers' checks. Returnees often carry large amounts of cash to the relatives of fellow workers because some of the Mans

[1] Source: Postal records held at the Yuen Long District Office, "Remittances from Overseas to the New Territories, 1969," *Postal Service Yuen Long*, Y. L. 1/C9.

[2] *Ibid.*

[3] Source: Records held at the Tai Po District Office, "Family Remittances from Overseas," T. P. 1-71-59-11.

still do not trust the mails or the banks. These personal methods are reminiscent of the earlier Nan Yang emigrants who relied on professional currency carriers to send money back to South China (T'ien 1953:84, Wu 1967:29-31). The Mans are quite sophisticated in their knowledge of exchange rates because foreign currency is freely circulated in the village. It is not unusual to see Dutch guldens, British pounds, and Deutsche marks mixed with Hong Kong dollars on the gambling tables in San Tin's tea houses. Some of the old women amuse themselves by hoarding a few pound notes until the exchange rates turn to their advantage.

Although the subject proved difficult to probe, most informants agree that the average remittance for a married man with a family of three living in San Tin is between HK$300 and HK$450 (US$50-75) per month, plus extra amounts for New Year and special occasions. This estimate compares favorably with the remittance figures cited by other field researchers who have worked among Chinese emigrants from Hong Kong.[4] Of course, not all of the emigrant families receive a monthly income of HK$300, but those who do are able to lead a comfortable life by New Territories standards (cf. Potter 1968:136).

A good example of the faithful provider is Man Dak-chuen, a cook who works in London. Every month he sends HK$450 to his wife, who lives with their children in one unit of his father's housing compound. Dak-chuen's father, mother, wife, and two children form a single household that shares a common budget. All of the food and other necessities are paid for out of the regular remittances. Like most other people in San Tin, Dak-chuen's dependents live very well. They eat only the best quality rice and spend an average of HK$5 each day for (c) *sung*

---

[4] Ronald Ng (1964:35) estimates that the Hakka emigrants from the island village he studied in the New Territories sent home up to HK$400 per month. Ng Kwee-choo (1968:81) puts the average remittance for restaurant workers in London between HK$200 and HK$350 per month in 1963-64.

(vegetables, meat, and fish) to vary their diet. The children always go to school in clean, new clothes, while the wife and grandparents own several sets of the standard pants-suit garb worn by all adults. Dak-chuen has already spent thousands of Hong Kong dollars to renovate one section of his father's housing compound and plans to complete the job in future years. Inside the house, the family displays a wide range of modern consumer items, including an electric rice cooker, two fans, a small refrigerator, and a large television set. Less than ten years ago this family was relatively poor, by local standards, and Dak-chuen's father was never able to make a living by farming alone. Now in his late sixties, the father displays his new-found affluence with great pride and radiates the confidence that is characteristic of elders who have no more financial worries.

Nominally, Dak-chuen's father is still the head of the household, but the daughter-in-law controls the regular remittance budget (i.e., she receives the money order and does most of the shopping). This is not an uncommon arrangement in San Tin. The change in the traditional pattern of budget control is a sensitive issue among the emigrants because they realize it undermines the authority of their fathers and can easily lead to domestic conflict.[5] In order to compensate his father and to give symbolic recognition to his status as household head, Dak-chuen sends him a special remittance of HK$600-700 at the end of every year. Ostensibly this money is to repay the father for any expenses he might have incurred while taking care of his grandchildren, but in fact he has no other source of personal income.

Most San Tin households derive only a small proportion of their income from nonemigrant sources. In his 1930s study of

[5] A similar problem has arisen with the change in marriage patterns. Emigrants are now able to arrange their own marriages because they have independent incomes; and this in turn challenges the traditional authority of the parents (see Chapter Nine, page 172).

Nan Yang emigrants, Chen Ta estimates that 81 percent of the average monthly income of one hundred dependent families came from remittances (1939:83). This estimate would also be reasonably accurate for San Tin. For instance, out of thirty-eight households in my village census, twenty-four (63 percent) were totally dependent on remittances and eleven (29 percent) relied on some help from emigrants. Only three of the households operated without any remittance aid, and two of these were barely able to survive.

Since the remittances are so important, some of the most common themes of gossip in the village are rumors of nonremitting sons or husbands. Dependents are always concerned that their bread winners might stop sending money home, but this fear is not a preoccupation in San Tin as it appears to be in some other Chinese emigrant communities (cf. Bracey 1967). The Mans apparently have been able to control the problem because there are enough lineage members scattered throughout the United Kingdom and other parts of Western Europe to enforce sanctions on all but the most unrepentant. Even one of the younger Mans who has effectively "dropped out" of Chinese culture while in England continues to send occasional gifts to his mother in San Tin.

CONTRIBUTION DRIVES AND PUBLIC WORKS

Almost every year the Man emigrants working in Europe are asked to contribute to the construction of a new public building or some other civic project in the village. The response has been overwhelming, and the lineage elders find themselves in command of so much money that they held a special meeting in 1970 to decide what kind of project to initiate next. It was not easy to find an acceptable outlet for emigrant donations because San Tin has a new temple, a renovated ancestral hall, two new banquet halls, and a relatively new school. The meeting ended without a decision when some of the elders began to argue that there had been enough building construction in recent years and that it was time to concentrate on improving the village paths.

Other communities in the New Territories are rarely confronted with this kind of problem because they do not have a source of readily available outside funds. The same might be true of San Tin if the emigrants had cut their ties with their home community. Quite the opposite has happened, however, and in one case (described below) the absentee workers oversubscribed, allowing an even more elaborate hall to be built than was originally planned. Although these contribution drives are voluntary, the emigrants are expected to donate as much as possible (a "respectable" contribution is equivalent to one-half of a week's total earnings). In return the worker has his name, along with the amount donated, posted for public display during the grand opening ceremony. He is also given the satisfaction of knowing that he and his fellow emigrants are indispensable members of the community even though they work abroad.

The Man lineage has used the contribution drive as a basic method of soliciting public funds for centuries. Once a year lineage trustees circulate through the village collecting a subscription fee of HK$5 from each member (males only, of course) to help defray operating expenses of the lineage. This fund drive is not entirely voluntary, although the elders occasionally excuse a destitute member who has paid regularly in the past. Anyone who fails to pay is ostracized and risks being expelled from the lineage. Besides the annual lineage subscription, the Mans had other types of fund-raising drives in traditional times. Many of the older banquet halls were built from membership contributions, and the local Empress of Heaven Temple has been renovated several times during the last 400 years almost entirely from voluntary donations. Fund drives are an integral part of the traditional peasant society in South China, where almost every temple, hall, and bridge bears a marble plaque preserving the names of the donors. Emigrants have always played a significant part in these public works,[6] but in San Tin they have taken the dominant role.

The Mans now have an elaborate and well-organized procedure for soliciting funds from lineage members living in Europe. New projects are devised and approved by the San Tin elders after consulting with emigrants home on vacation. In recent years, project decisions have been influenced by the availability of government funds for the preservation of certain types of historical buildings. After the proper clearance has been obtained from government authorities, the elders appoint a standing committee to take charge of the enterprise. These committees are always divided equally between leaders residing in San Tin and prominent restaurant owners living in Europe. The resident committee manages the everyday affairs of the construction while the emigrant committee handles most of the fund raising. The elders try to choose at least one restaurateur in every European city with large concentrations of Man workers, including London, Brussels, and Amsterdam. One committee member is made responsible for Germany and two or three for the provincial areas of the United Kingdom.

Each of these men receives a formal letter signed by the lineage leaders authorizing him to collect money as their agent. The agents then circulate throughout their prescribed territory, visiting Man-owned restaurants and Chinese recreation clubs. Notices are posted in all the customary gathering places and letters are sent to some of the more isolated lineage members. After the money is collected, it is sent as a bank draft or a postal order to the resident committee in San Tin. Finally,

[6] To cite only a few examples, both Chen Ta (1939:161-166) and T'ien (1953:80) note that Nan Yang emigrants helped to build schools and to renovate ancestral halls in their home communities before the Communist Revolution. Aijmer reports that the Hakka emigrants from Big Stream Village in the New Territories donated about HK$4,000 to build a bridge near their home (1967:68).

the committee sends formal receipts back to the agent for distribution to each contributor acknowledging the exact amount donated and giving assurance that his name will be publically posted on the opening day of the new project.

This method of soliciting funds has proved extremely successful in San Tin because the emigrants are able to see the concrete results on their trips home. A good example is the modern banquet hall built entirely from emigrant contributions in 1962. Yuk Ging Hall was one of the first public works to be initiated after San Tin made the conversion to a remittance economy, and the emigrants were more than willing to demonstrate their new-found affluence to the other villagers. The original building had long since crumbled into ruins, leaving a large section of the community without an adequate banquet hall. When the elders suggested a new building, the emigrants overwhelmed the committee with contributions. Instead of the single-story, traditional structure originally planned, the committee was able to fund San Tin's first two-story, modern-style public building. Over US$12,000 was donated by emigrants living mostly in the United Kingdom at that time. The highest contributors have their photographs transposed on porcelain plates which are affixed to a marble plaque inside the hall.[7] This method of commemoration is an elaboration of traditional patterns and is now common throughout the New Territories.

---

[7] The Cantonese villagers in this part of China distinguish between large and small donations by having two systems of public recognition. The highest donors have their names and the amount contributed carved in a marble plaque, which is preserved for posterity. The rest of the contributors have their names posted on red paper sheets that last only until the next rain. In each case, the project commitee sets a minimum amount required to be included in the group listed in marble. For instance, although there were over 300 original donors for Yuk Ging Hall's renovation, only 98 contributed enough to have their names carved in the plaque mounted inside. Similarly, the committee for the Tin Hau Temple renovation discussed in this chapter placed a "marble limit" of HK$50 for the contributors in 1970.

A VILLAGE EXTRAVAGANZA:
TEMPLE RENOVATION AND OPERA

During my stay in the village, San Tin's 400-year-old Empress of Heaven (Tin Hau) Temple[8] was renovated and an opera troupe was hired to provide entertainment for the reopening. The resulting celebration lasted for over a week, during which the community put on an impressive display of wealth. This extravaganza gave me the opportunity to observe the organization of an elaborate contribution drive that raised large sums of money from Man emigrants working abroad.

In 1969 the lineage elders decided it was time to rebuild the old temple because it was approaching a state of disrepair that made it dangerous to worshippers. The villagers proceeded with plans for a complete renovation and began to solicit contributions from emigrants. When it was finished a year later, the entire enterprise had cost well over HK$100,000. The Hong Kong Government contributed one-third of this total; but, directly or indirectly, the Man emigrants were responsible for the rest. At the grand opening ceremony the names of over 600 emigrant donors were prominently displayed on sheets of red paper outside the temple. Another 200 people (mostly emigrants living in Europe) contributed enough to have their names carved in a marble plaque mounted on the wall. Besides the actual renovation expenses, local residents spent an extra HK$20,000 or more on new furnishings and decorations for the temple. Many absentee workers made special contributions to help pay for these embellishments. Three Man emigrants,

---

[8] "Tin Hau" (Mandarin *t'ien hou*) is often called the "Empress of Heaven." Originally she was the patron goddess of the fishermen along the South China Coast, but she is also worshipped by the *pen-ti* ("native") farmers in the Hong Kong region. She has also taken on many of the attributes of the Buddhist Goddess of Mercy, Kwan Yin. There are many temples dedicated to Tin Hau in the New Territories, and "Tung Shan Old Temple" located in San Tin is thought to be one of the oldest.

including the owner of the Asia Air Service travel agency, shared the honor for the highest contribution to the general renovation fund (HK$1,000 each).

By supporting the renovation, the Man emigrants did more than simply pay for the construction of a new building. They also provided the villagers with a number of diversions to help break up the monotonous pace of life that characterizes emigrant communities during much of the year (see Chapter Nine). The temple renovation involved a series of minor rituals and one major event, the beam raising ceremony, which required the presence of lineage elders. Upon completion, the grand opening was an occasion for celebration that gave everyone in the village a chance to participate in one form or another. As several elders intimated, the religious content of these occasions was of secondary significance compared to the entertainment value provided by the sequence of ceremonial events.

The festive atmosphere of the grand opening was heightened by the presentation of a Cantonese opera. Although the opera was performed in celebration of the temple renovation, it was handled as a self-supporting, profit-making enterprise with a separate budget.[9] A special committee hired a professional opera troupe, contracting with a bamboo-scaffolding company to erect a temporary auditorium on the school soccer field. The normal life of the entire village came to a standstill during the opera, which lasted for five days and nights (over nine hours a day). The combination of renovation ceremonies and opera made this one of the most exciting periods in the recent history of the village. The elders stated nostalgically that it reminded

---

[9] Admission was charged for the 2,000 seats and tenders were accepted for the food and gambling concessions. According to local custom, the balance sheet of the enterprise was posted in the village market for public scrutiny. The Opera Committee made expenditures of HK$92,000 and took in a total of HK$93,000. The profit was donated to the trust fund of the Main Ancestral Hall.

them of the old *ta chiao* ceremonies held by the Mans once every ten years in traditional times to placate the spirits of the dead (cf. Baker 1968:87).

Opera ceremonies still occur in the New Territories (although rarely) and are not confined to emigrant communities. However, in this particular case the episode would never have been possible without the help of the emigrants. Their contributions paid for most of the temple renovation expenses, thus providing the excuse and opportunity to stage an opera. Indirectly, the emigrants also paid for the opera because their families made special requests for additional remittances to cover the price of admission. The ticket prices were high (from HK$80 to HK$200 for a block of four seats lasting the entire series of nine performances), but almost every adult in the village was able to attend. It became a matter of honor among emigrants to make certain their parents, grandparents, and wives had good seats.

Besides the immediate entertainment value of the festival, the renovation and opera had an immense impact on the other villages in the surrounding countryside. The proceedings were colorful, loud, and ostentatious in every detail, making it impossible for outsiders to ignore. The prestige of the lineage and the community depends heavily on the willingness of the emigrants to continue supporting public works and festivities of this nature.

Financial support in the form of remittances and contributions is one measure of the concern emigrants maintain for their families and their home communities. It is clear that the Man emigrants score rather high in this regard. Their families have a relatively high standard of living, and their village projects an affluent image to the outside world. These are not the only indicators of emigrant concern, however, because the workers have other, less tangible methods of demonstrating that San Tin is still their "home."

RETURN TRIPS

As noted in the Introduction, the "classic" pattern of Chinese emigration is often characterized by a tendency on the part of the workers to defer material gratification while abroad. This is especially true of emigrants who have not adjusted to the host culture and are planning to return to China upon retirement. Although there are many variations, the usual pattern is for the worker to deny his immediate needs (food, clothing, lodging, personal comfort, etc.) for years in anticipation of a long-planned trip home, during which he will spend most of his savings in a matter of months. With certain modifications, this pattern of emigration is still characteristic of most restaurant workers from San Tin.

Before the advent of commercial air traffic between Hong Kong and Western Europe, the emigrants travelled by ship. Once they arrived at their destination the workers did not return for at least seven to ten years because the cost was so high and the passage so uncomfortable (Cheung 1970b). The earlier Man emigrants usually did not return at all until they had saved enough money to retire. Under these circumstances it was difficult for the workers to keep abreast of events in San Tin or to have more than a passive influence on village affairs. This has now changed and the contemporary emigrants are able to exercise a direct and active influence on their home community. The availability of frequent, inexpensive charter flights is the primary cause of these changes.

The Man emigrants now return on the average of once every three to five years. The first trip is usually delayed the longest because it takes several years of hard work before the new workers are affluent enough to return in the accepted style. Similarly, the younger emigrants do not return until they have saved enough money to get married. The only exception is an emergency caused by the death of a parent, which requires the worker to fly home immediately, even if it means going deeply into debt.

Married emigrants return whenever possible in order to direct the affairs of their families. Important decisions, such as the education of children and the division of parental estates, are usually postponed until the men are home on vacation. During these trips, the emigrants also play an active role in the life of the community. They attend public meetings and express opinions on any matter that might concern them. The elders always seek out the returnees whenever an important decision is about to be made which will affect the entire community. Although they are absent for years at a time, the emigrants are able to keep up on developments in the village and are capable of voicing dissent if anything displeases them.

The emigrants schedule return trips to coincide with the Lunar New Year festival that occurs in Hong Kong's cool winter season. Traditionally this was the most joyous and entertaining part of the year, but in San Tin the festival has taken on an even more important meaning. The Mans now celebrate an extended New Year holiday that lasts for several weeks to take full advantage of the emigrants' return visits. Most workers prolong their trip for at least three months, arriving before the Lunar New Year and departing after the Ch'ing Ming Festival in early spring. During this period the sleepy central plaza of the village sometimes takes on the incongruous appearance of a bus terminal as large groups of emigrants arrive from the airport.

Every New Year season over 200 restaurant workers return from Europe to visit their families. The patterns of long-term saving and deferred gratification are clearly demonstrated by the actions of these men. Returnees make up for the years of hard work abroad by spending their money at a furious pace as soon as they enter the village, thus creating a festival atmosphere that lasts as long as they stay.

All emigrants are expected to arrive laden with gifts for the entire family. The workers try to bring items that are not available locally, but this is difficult because Hong Kong is a tax-free port where European goods are often cheaper than in the country of origin. Many overcome the problem by selecting materials that are not ordinarily exported to subtropical regions. For instance, English woolens and heavy overcoats are especially prized by the older villagers, who never appear to be warm enough during Hong Kong's mild winters. Some returnees simply wait until they return to the Colony and purchase great quantities of liquor and delicacies in Kowloon's food markets. Unless the emigrant is able to provide elaborate and expensive gifts for his family and other important kinsmen, he might decide to postpone his return until the next Lunar New Year season.

The workers must also have enough money to make their holidays pleasurable and rewarding in a personal sense. It is not uncommon for an unmarried emigrant to buy an automobile during his three-month stay to help in his wife-hunting efforts (see Chapter Nine). The vehicle is then sold before the owner returns to Europe. Although the resale value for used cars is high, this is evidence of conspicuous consumption in its most obvious form because private automobiles are the status symbols par excellence in the Colony. Younger emigrants also spend hundreds of dollars on new clothes during their return trips. The wardrobes of many constitute investments of considerable magnitude. San Tin has one Western-style tailor (a lineage member) who caters to the emigrants and fills as many of their orders as he can handle. During the New Year season he works at a feverish rate turning out suits, sport coats, shirts, and trousers. Even though he takes frequent mail orders from his customers throughout the year, he makes 70 percent of his annual income during the holiday season.

Returnees spare no expense for entertainment while they are home, and the most popular diversion is gambling. During the height of the New Year season, the gambling sessions in the local teahouses last until dawn as the free-spending emigrants play for very high stakes. Some of the older returnees find a more sedate form of entertainment by watching Cantonese television for weeks at a time. Since 1967, San Tin has been able to pick up television broadcasts from urban Hong Kong. The main attraction for the emigrants is a constant run of low-budget movies, Cantonese operas, and dubbed American serials. In Europe, few of the workers are able to understand enough of the host language to follow local television programs. The availability of Cantonese broadcasts is so appealing that the emigrants often buy expensive, wide-screen sets to use for only a few months. When they return to Europe, the sets are left with their families or sold at a loss in the market towns nearby.

BANQUETS

For the nonemigrant population of the village, the most exciting prospect of the New Year season is the continuous round of banquets thrown by returning workers. These feasts have a special significance for the older residents, who seldom leave San Tin except for an occasional visit to a nearby market town. The banquets are almost literally the only thing many elders have to look forward to during the entire year. The emigrants are certainly aware of this—as many of them stated: "We try to bring a time of joy to the village at least once a year."

The banquets are indeed joyful occasions. They are held in the host's branch ancestral hall, or in one of San Tin's "banquet halls" which have kitchen facilities and special equipment (tables, chairs, etc.). Attendance varies from 100 to 800 depending on the generosity of the host and on the occasion. Many returning emigrants hire professional cooks from the nearby market towns to provide nine-course feasts consisting of the best food available in the New Territories. Imported French brandy is consumed by the case, usually mixed with soft drinks "to make it go down faster." Although the men rarely allow themselves to become visibly inebriated, they enjoy themselves immensely and stay as long as possible.

Besides entertaining the villagers, the banquets often serve as a rite of reentry for the older emigrants when they decide it is time to retire to their native village. One restaurant worker in London told me that he had postponed his retirement one more year in order to save enough money for an elaborate reentry banquet. This is not a condition for acceptance back into the community, but the elders have come to expect a banquet from all retiring workers who consider their sojourn to be a success. Although there is no formal ceremony during these occasions, the feast is a way of indicating to the villagers that the emigrant still considers them to be the most important people in his life.

Somewhat similar are the banquets held by emigrants to mark their sons' first year after birth, the age when they are recognized as members of the lineage. Traditionally, an annual banquet was provided for the elders by all of the males who had new sons during the previous year.[10] In recent years,

---

[10] This is the annual *k'ai teng* ceremony, which occurs during the Lunar New Year season (see Baker 1968:48-50). *K'ai teng* literally means "to open lanterns," or "to begin the light" (referring to the spirit of the new son), and the ceremony involves hanging colorful paper-lanterns in the ancestral halls. According to San Tin elders, the *k'ai teng* ceremony was once required of all males who wished to have their sons (or adopted heirs) accepted as legitimate members of the lineage. Besides the lanterns, the new fathers were expected to provide a banquet for the elders. The *k'ai teng* banquet is still a very important part of the ritual cycle in San Tin, even though it is no longer a condition of acceptance into the lineage. In 1970, the Man lineage held its *k'ai teng* banquet in San Tin's largest ancestral hall and it drew an overflow crowd. The individual birthday banquets (discussed in the text above) are usually held during the same holiday season as the *k'ai teng* observance.

however, the emigrants have used the birth observances as opportunities to give elaborate, individual banquets for their new sons. This is especially true if the child was born abroad and presented to the lineage at a later time. Technically, the banquets are not conditional rites of entry into the lineage because not all sons born abroad are made the object of these festivities (often it is only the emigrant's first son). However, if there is even a hint that a question might arise about the boy's legitimacy, the father will be certain to host a banquet for his son (cf. Baker, 1968:50).

This was also true for the earlier, jumped-ship emigrants in San Tin. In one case over sixty years ago, a Man sailor felt it necessary to host a banquet for his half-Jamaican son. During this particular ceremony the father went so far as to ask the elders present to sign a red cloth banner certifying their acceptance of the son as a member of the lineage. This was an extreme precaution because certification of membership in the Man lineage is required only in certain cases of adoption (Watson n.d.). Since the son had Negroid features, his father felt that his position in San Tin might be ambiguous and hoped to preclude any later challenges regarding his legitimacy. Two other sailors returned to the village with foreign-born sons; and, although they both held banquets, neither asked for the certification ceremony. In recent years, a number of Man restaurant workers have married European women, and all their sons have been born abroad (see Chapter Nine). Even though there have been no problems of acceptance in the village, the fathers concerned are always careful to host a large banquet to mark the first birthday of their Eurasian sons.

In San Tin, therefore, the birthday banquets for sons appear to be of vital importance only when the status of the new lineage member is ambiguous. As long as the father is in good standing with the lineage, his son has a legal right to be accepted as a full member. The real test of acceptance, however, is the attitude of the other villagers. Hosting a banquet is one way for the father to symbolize his awareness of the problem and to compensate the villagers for their acceptance. More severe restrictions have been noted in other Chinese emigrant communities. Skinner (1957:246-7) cites one case in which Nan Yang returnees were forced to pay for an expensive feast as part of their efforts to have their half-Thai "barbarian" sons accepted by lineage mates. In San Tin the banquets are never forced and there are no formal restrictions on foreign-born lineage members.

A recent development is the dual banquet celebrated simultaneously in San Tin and in Europe. When an emigrant wishes to mark the birth of a son and is unable to return that year, he may send his father enough money to finance a banquet for the lineage elders. On the appointed day, the emigrant hosts a small gathering of Man workers and other friends in the restaurant where he works and his father acts as host at the larger banquet in the village. Although this arrangement is gaining some popularity, the Mans do not consider it to be an alternative to returning home. Dual banquets do not carry the same prestige as ordinary banquets and do not allow the emigrants to fully enjoy their moments of personal triumph.

These banquets for the "reentry" of retired emigrants and the introduction of new lineage members are not the only festivities that make the New Year season an exciting time in San Tin. Any emigrant with enough money will try to find an excuse to entertain his fellow villagers. In order to accommodate all those who want to give a feast, therefore, the Mans have stretched the traditional banquet categories to include such unorthodox occasions as the birth of a first granddaughter. Another example is the traditional housewarming feast, which has changed its character since San Tin became an emigrant community. Originally this gathering included only the immediate family and a few close kinsmen to mark the opening of a new house, but the emigrants have turned it into an occasion to host large banquets.

By far the most important banquet occasions in San Tin are the emigrants' weddings that occur during the three-month holiday season. In 1970, the Mans celebrated over twenty weddings between the Lunar New Year and the Ch'ing Ming Festival, and none throughout the rest of the year (excluding those of daughters, all of whom marry outside the lineage). Each marriage is marked by at least two banquets in San Tin, one in the morning and one in the evening of the wedding day. The villagers maintain that the wedding is not sealed until the successful completion of both banquets. Five hundred people or more normally attend the morning banquet because a general invitation is posted in the village. The evening banquet is restricted to special guests who receive an invitation card from the groom's family. Both gatherings are held in the groom's branch ancestral hall or in one of the village's many banquet halls. A few of the banquets thrown by the wealthier emigrants are so large that the guests overflow the halls and have to be seated in temporary shelters built especially for the occasion.

Although the wedding gifts brought by invited guests are an important compensation,[11] the emigrants invest a great deal of money in these banquets. An average feast of 40 tables seating approximately 500 people costs about HK$8,000. Wealthier emigrants often spend twice this amount when they have the chance to host a banquet. In 1970, for instance, the vacationing owner of two restaurants in Amsterdam spent HK$32,000 for three banquets (one for a housewarming and two for the wedding of his son).

In recent years the banquets have become more and more elaborate. Some emigrants now hire catering firms based in the nearby market towns to handle all of the arrangements.

[11] Wedding gifts average about HK$7 for each household invited (sometimes two members of the same household may attend but only one gift is presented). These gifts are brought only by guests attending the evening banquet. The morning banquet is by general invitation and there is no obligation to compensate the host.

These firms bring everything they need to San Tin—including the cooks, food, tables, utensils, and even their own stoves. As a result of these changes, it is becoming more difficult for an emigrant to gain high prestige in the village by hosting banquets. Ordinary workers cannot compete with their wealthier kinsmen, but they are still expected to entertain the villagers whenever possible. The older residents have a remarkable ability to remember every banquet thrown in the last decade; and if an emigrant does not find an excuse for hosting one at least every second trip home, he may become the object of community gossip. For the majority of the emigrants, therefore, the banquets have become a way of validating their status as active members of the community.

PLAYING AN ACTIVE ROLE AT A DISTANCE

As shown in this chapter, the emigrant situation does not prevent the restaurant workers from playing an influential role in San Tin's local affairs. Because not all of the workers return at the same time, the lineage has devised ways of gauging emigrant opinion in Europe. A good example is the method of soliciting funds for public works discussed earlier. The delegated agents of the lineage who gather the money and distribute the receipts in Europe also act as informal pollsters of the local emigrant population. These agents are more likely to make regular trips back to Hong Kong and are important sources of information. Both villagers and absentee workers make use of the annual stream of holiday returnees as the primary medium of communication.

The Mans are not the only New Territories emigrants who continue to think of themselves as indispensable members of their home communities. The Hong Kong Government Office in London handles many of the complaints lodged by absentee workers regarding the actions of people back home in the New

Territories. During the first six months of 1970, for example, this office assisted in ninety-four cases involving land disputes and sixteen cases of domestic unrest.[12] In one instance, a group of emigrants became so incensed over the decision of a lineage trustee to rent a small plot of land to outsiders that they banded together to form an "Overseas Village Committee" in order to protest the action. The leader of the committee was a prominent restaurant owner, who, according to several informants, had not returned to his native village for nearly thirty years.

This case demonstrates that many emigrants are not able to exercise the same level of control enjoyed by the Man workers over decisions back home in the New Territories. The Mans normally keep their disputes within the social network of the lineage. Man emigrants do not have to resort to outside mediators because they have their own highly developed communication channels which allow them to influence decisions in the village. Furthermore, unlike many of the earlier sailors, the contemporary Man emigrants are not discriminated against in any way. The villagers think of them as honored and active members of the community who happen to be working in restaurants abroad.

CONCLUSIONS

From their own point of view, it is understandable that the emigrants should be so concerned about retaining close ties to their home community. First, the majority are not interested in putting down roots as permanent residents in Europe. They find it perfectly logical to defer as many of their material needs as possible while working abroad because it is not their "home." When the emigrants return to San Tin, however, they are

[12] Source: "Assistance to Individuals," 1970 mimeo. Liaison Section, Hong Kong Government Office, London.

expected to spend their money in a conspicuous manner to verify their status in the community. In the meantime, the remittances and the public donations are the most tangible ways for the absentee workers to demonstrate their concern for the village. This is one reason why there are never any anonymous contributions to the civic works in San Tin. The names are always on display so that the villagers know exactly how much everyone has donated, and if individual emigrants are missing it may cause embarrassment to their families.

But the fear of gossip does not entirely explain why the emigrants spend such enormous sums of money to support these traditional ventures. Unlike most other peasant societies (cf. Foster 1965:303), conspicuous consumption and ostentatious displays of personal wealth are recognized values among Cantonese peasants. For the Man emigrants, therefore, the conspicuous displays of wealth are thoroughly consistent with their view of the world because they are emulating what they believe to be the highest values of their traditional culture. Rather than helping to modernize the village, the steady flow of money from Europe has made San Tin an outpost of conservatism in the New Territories. This unique pattern of change will be discussed further in the concluding chapter.

Chapter Eight

"STERLING HOUSES" AND THE ECONOMIC
EFFECTS OF EMIGRATION

TEN years ago when the Mans switched to emigration, San Tin was converted from a center of production to a community of consumption. One of the more visible effects of emigration has been a change in the villagers' traditional investment patterns. Land is no longer an important source of income and it has lost its symbolic value as an investment in future security. In its place the Mans have chosen to invest in private housing. These new homes (known as "sterling houses"[1] after the remittances that pay for their construction) have become a preoccupation among the emigrants and, as a consequence, San Tin's physical appearance is changing rapidly.

Some of the other changes are less apparent to the casual visitor. Besides raising the standard of living, emigration has had a leveling effect on the economic differences within the community. The Mans now have access to good incomes regardless of their position in the old lineage hierarchy. The high level of remittances has also made it unnecessary for the emigrants' dependents to work. The resulting change from production to consumption has had a profound impact on the social and economic life of the village.

[1] I first heard the term "sterling house" used by Chinese staff members of the Yuen Long District Office. People in San Tin refer to them simply as "new houses," (c) *san nguk*.

155

CHANGE FROM PRODUCTION TO CONSUMPTION

Except for a few handicraft items, nothing of any real value is produced in San Tin. The village women spend their idle hours assembling plastic flowers and weaving rattan purses, but these activities are not taken very seriously. The money they earn is hardly enough to cover the women's entertainment and tobacco expenses. Besides the home handicrafts, seven cottage industries have operated in the village during the past ten years. The most common are small-scale knitting shops that produce unfinished sweaters and gloves for the textile exporters in urban Hong Kong.[2]

These knitting shops have had little impact on the local economy because they are a marginal source of income. In fact, San Tin has a bad reputation among the entrepreneurs of the handicraft industries in the New Territories because the available workers, mostly unmarried girls, are not highly motivated. One shop owner (an outsider) struggled for seven years in San Tin to make a living but finally gave up in 1970 and moved to another village. During an interview he admitted that he had made a bad choice when he selected an emigrant community as the site of his first shop. At the time he knew only that there was an abundance of idle people in San Tin and he hoped to exploit the situation by introducing a labor-intensive industry. Unexpectedly, however, his most difficult problem turned out to be a chronic labor shortage. The emigrant remittances are sufficient in most cases to support the villagers at a high standard of living, and very few are willing to work for the meager wages offered in the knitting shops.

Several other cottage industries suffered a similar fate as San Tin became more affluent. Two rattan works and an embroidery shop folded during my stay in the village, and the

---

[2] The unfinished knit products are completed by more highly skilled workers in Kowloon. Shops in San Tin usually obtain contracts from the urban factories for bulk orders of sweater-halves and glove parts.

local agent for plastic flower distribution has contemplated moving his business to another community. Even if these handicraft enterprises had been more successful they could not have rivaled emigration as an alternative occupation for the male villagers. These small-scale industries are fundamentally parasitic because the key to success is the maximum exploitation of cheap labor with the least possible capital investment in the community. The village leaders would like to introduce more remunerative forms of employment; but they realize that, politically and economically, the problem is beyond their control. On several occasions the Rural Committee has petitioned to make San Tin one of the sites chosen by the government to be developed as centers of light industry. There is little chance of this happening because, in terms of industrial potential, San Tin has almost everything working against it: isolation from the urban areas, poor access to transportation facilities, limited water supplies, and an unskilled work force. Also, as noted earlier in this study, the Mans have not proven themselves to be receptive to outside industrial enterprises (see Chapter Four, note 2).

EMIGRATION AND THE LEVELING EFFECT

One of the most important effects of emigration has been the equalization of income for the people of San Tin. In traditional times an individual's income depended in large part on the amount of land he owned and on his position in the hierarchy of lineage segments. Members of wealthy segments received a share in the proceeds of large ancestral estates and were given special rates on the land they rented from the lineage. After the decline of San Tin's agricultural economy, however, these traditional advantages became irrelevant and did not produce any extra sources of income.

The rise of large-scale emigration has caused a general leveling of the old economic hierarchy based on differential ownership of land. This does not imply, of course, that some of the Mans are not richer than others because a few of the restaurateurs have become spectacularly wealthy. However, these differences are due in large part to individual efforts; one's position in the lineage hierarchy no longer predetermines success or wealth. Household income in the village now depends more on the number of emigrants in the family than on the amount of land owned. Emigration may not have turned San Tin into an egalitarian community, but the restaurant jobs have given a large number of talented, achievement-oriented men the opportunity to excel and find economic success abroad.

CHANGING INVESTMENT PATTERNS

In recent years the Mans have advertised their new affluence to the world by engaging in an extensive house-building program that is transforming the outward appearance of the village. The new houses are the ultimate status symbols for the emigrants because they offer visible, and enduring, evidence of success. However, there is more behind the housing boom in San Tin than a simple competition for prestige among villagers: The new houses also represent a practical investment in the workers' future security.

The Mans appear to make a clear distinction between *speculative investments* and *security investments*. For instance, while abroad even the most cautious villager may show an uncharacteristic flair for entrepreneurial activity and risk everything in hopes of making a quick fortune. When the emigrant returns home, he reverts to his former mode of behavior and seeks to maximize his security by investing in the safest possible manner. The most common security investments are the sterling houses; speculative investments usually take the form of partnerships in unproven restaurants. Except for a handful of the more experienced leaders, therefore, the Man emigrants leave their business world in Europe when they return to the New Territories.

Chinese peasants who operated within the limitations of their traditional value system ordinarily chose land as the most logical form of security available (see Gallin 1963). Prior to the 1949 revolution, land had the rare advantage of retaining its original investment value, even during times of civil disorder and depression. In emigrant communities a pattern of spiraling land prices was common because the returning emigrants drove up the market value of the most desirable property by outbidding all other potential buyers. Both Chen Han-seng (1936:104-105) and Chen Ta (1939:117) cite cases in Kwangtung where land prices rose as emigration increased.

In earlier times, the Man emigrants invested their savings primarily in land and, if any money remained, secondarily in housing. This pattern of investment was also characteristic of Chinese sojourners who went to the Nan Yang and the New World (see e.g., R. H. Lee 1960:83). Since at least 1960, however, the order of priority has changed for the Mans and they have stopped buying land. The reason, of course, is that the paddy land near San Tin became essentially worthless after the vegetable revolution. Large stretches of old brackish-water fields now lie fallow in San Tin Sub-District. Abandoned land is also found in the Hakka-speaking parts of the New Territories and is a good indicator that the nearby villages have a high rate of emigration (see also Aijmer 1967:63). The Man emigrants are not interested in buying land in other parts of the Colony and have chosen instead to invest in new houses located in their home community.

Investments in personal housing do not have all the advantages of land because, in San Tin at least, houses rapidly depreciate in value and do not produce any further wealth. However, houses do survive during economic depressions and currency devaluations. In traditional times these were important considerations for the peasants of South China. Chen Ta quotes an old emigrant from the Nan Yang on this subject: "As an investment, a house is far more secure than a bank deposit; for, in China a bank sometimes goes bankrupt, but a house is always there. The house cannot be moved away, and *it will be seen by everybody*" (1939:110, emphasis added). Although the above observation was made in Kwangtung during the early 1930s, the contemporary emigrant from San Tin perceives the world of investments in a similar manner.

While the price of paddy land has stabilized or even declined in some cases, house-lot prices inside the village have skyrocketed with the growing demand. There are approximately 900 house-lots in San Tin's nucleated core settlement, one-tenth of which are vacant or in ruins. As in other Chinese villages (Nelson 1969), the local residents have always engaged in a limited amount of buying and selling of houses among themselves. However, the closed nature of the lineage community has never been broken because the Mans do not sell houses or house-lots to outsiders.

The emigrant demand for house-lots has created a seller's market in San Tin. Many of the workers who wish to build a new house have not inherited any property and are forced to buy a lot from another villager. Competition for the available lots is intense because the Mans are hesitant to sell property that might be needed by sons or grandsons in the future. In 1960, before the building boom, a house-lot cost between HK$500 and HK$800. Depending on the location, an emigrant must now pay up to HK$3,000 for a good lot. After purchase, the old house structures are left standing—often in ruins—until the emigrant has saved enough to start the construction of his new home.

STERLING HOUSES

Speaking of South China in the 1930s, Chen Ta notes that "one can without the slightest risk of error recognize an emigrant community by its new houses, and frequently by its foreign-style houses" (1939:110-111). This observation is also true for the New Territories today because the emigrants' "sterling" houses are easily distinguished from the traditional, single-story village homes. The new houses are box shaped, two-story concrete structures with balconies and flat roofs; and their pastel colors set them apart from the surrounding dark brick buildings. Compared to the old housing units, the sterling houses are roomy, airy, and quite comfortable. The most notable change is the large number of windows, which defy the old geomancy beliefs. Traditionally, houses in this part of China had no windows because the villagers believed that unnecessary openings might disrupt the flow of good luck forces and allow bad influences to enter (see Freedman 1966:139).

It is probable that the design for the contemporary sterling house had its origins in China during the early part of this century. Again, the major source is Chen Ta who discusses the *yang lou*, or "foreign-style houses," which were being built in the 1930s (1939:111). One of these houses is described as a "modernistic" structure of concrete design with three stories (1939:108). C. K. Yang makes note of a "foreign-style house" built by a rich emigrant in Nanching village (1959:73), and R. H. Lee reports that Chinese sojourners returning from America commonly invested in "new Western-style two-storied brick houses" (1960:83). The basic design of the sterling house appears to have been evident in the New Territories at least as early as 1935, according to one Hong Kong Government source.[3] There must have been a gradual evolution of the contemporary house model because some of the prototype buildings were designed to accommodate traditional geomantic beliefs. For instance, the interiors of many were dark and damp, like the old-style houses, because they were built without adequate ventilation (Chen Ta 1939:112). The Mans also experimented with a variety of house designs in the late 1950s and

[3] *Hong Kong Administrative Report*, 1936, Report on the New Territories.

early 1960s when the restaurant workers first began to invest in private homes. In 1957, only three modern-style houses existed in the entire village, and many of the successful emigrants were still building traditional-style homes as late as 1962. During the transition period, five or six odd-looking, half-modern houses were built. However, since 1962 all of the new houses in the village have been variations on the same basic sterling model.

In 1970, sterling houses constituted 19.7 percent (i.e., 148 of 752) of the livable[4] homes in the six core subvillages of San Tin (see Table 14). A better indication of the prevalence of new-style homes is the ratio of sterling houses to "households," defined here as the meal-sharing domestic unit (many households occupy more than one housing unit). Thirty percent of the households in Fan Tin subvillage (66 of 218) live in sterling houses.

The costs vary greatly according to the quality of building materials and the amenities added, but most are built for HK$25,000 to HK$30,000 (US$5,000). In some cases, the richer restaurateurs build elaborate houses that are far more expensive. One emigrant from Holland invested over HK$80,000 in a large sterling house that covers two ordinary lots and has three stories. It also has a modern plumbing system, making it the envy of every other home owner in the village.

EMPTY HOUSES

Given the high costs involved, it seems ironic that many of the emigrants or their families are unable to enjoy the sterling houses after they are built. Nearly one-third of the new homes are left unoccupied because the owners have returned to their jobs in Europe. A survey of sterling houses in two subvillages

[4] The Mans have a loose definition of a "livable" house. It is generally applied to any unit which is not in ruins and has not been used for pigs.

TABLE 14

"Sterling Houses" in San Tin*
(1970)

Subvillage	Total houses	Sterling houses	% sterling
Tung Jan Wai...............	110	12	10.9%
San Lung Tsuen	27	5	18.5%
On Lung Tsuen	74	27	36.5%
Fan Tin Tsuen	301	66	21.9%
Wing Ping Tsuen	72	8	11.1%
Yan Shau Wai	168	30	17.9%
Totals	752	148	19.7%

* This 1970 survey includes only the six "core" subvillages in the San Tin complex.

revealed that seventeen out of fifty-seven (30 percent) were closed up in the spring of 1970. The emigrants refuse to rent out these new houses, even though there is a growing demand for rental space in the village. Several outsiders (including this writer and his wife) have tried unsuccessfully to rent the empty sterling houses. The owners also are reluctant to lease their new homes to close agnatic kinsmen, even if the prospective occupant offers to pay high rent. It is common to find relatively new houses in San Tin that have never been occupied and are now in the first stages of deterioration.

The usual explanation for this pattern of restricted occupancy is that a house must be "broken in" by the emigrant who built it. In fact, however, many of the empty homes have been occupied for a time by the emigrant and his family members before they joined him abroad. The owners themselves often maintain that they want their houses to be available for irregular holiday trips spent in the village. In the meantime, the houses might be empty for as long as five years in some cases. Whatever the reason offered, it is evident that the sterling houses are perceived as highly valued family possessions that are too important to share with others. Although the emigrant would gain back some of his initial investment if he leased the empty house, its value as a security object and a status symbol might be dissipated if it were shared.

These attitudes may be characteristic only of certain emigrants in the New Territories. For instance, according to Baker (personal communication), a number of modern-style houses in the nearby village of Sheung Shui are sometimes rented by the owners. In Ping Shan, new houses built primarily for outsider tenants have become an important source of income (Potter 1968:99). Both villages are similar to San Tin, except for the fact that they do not have high rates of emigration. Although the evidence is insufficient, this may suggest that the unusual pattern of building houses exclusively for personal use is a characteristic of emigrant communities in this part of China.

CONCLUSIONS: THE SEARCH FOR SECURITY

For the Mans, therefore, investments in housing differ from the traditional pattern of land investments, which at least had the capacity to generate further wealth. Unlike land or rental housing, the sterling houses in San Tin depreciate in value over time. Furthermore, the Mans do not benefit economically from the building boom because the contractors and the laborers are all outsiders. It is sometimes difficult to understand why the emigrants sink their hard-earned money into nonproductive sterling houses. Although no one in San Tin likes to discuss the problem openly, the uncertain future of British Hong Kong and the 1997 expiration of the New Territories lease make long-range planning difficult at best.

In spite of these limitations, the Mans continue to build in San Tin in anticipation of future retirement. The evidence suggests that the motivating force behind the emigrants' preoccupation with sterling houses is the search for security and status. By building in San Tin, the owner believes he will always be able to return to a comfortable home in a secure social environment. Furthermore, the expensive homes are used by the emigrants as the ultimate proof of their stake in the community of their birth. It should be noted that the private housing boom is not restricted to the older restaurateurs who are approaching retirement. During my stay in the village (1969-70), I witnessed the construction of over twenty new homes, half of which were financed by workers in their late twenties and early thirties. Sterling houses may not be profitable in terms of capital gain, but they are the only security investments available in a village with a nonproductive economy.

Chapter Nine

THE EFFECTS OF EMIGRATION:
SOCIAL CHANGE

ALTHOUGH the Mans enjoy a high standard of living, the social costs of large-scale emigration have been high. Boredom and inactivity have contributed to a general deterioration in the quality of San Tin's social life. As might be expected, the rapid conversion to emigration has had a profound impact on almost every aspect of life in the community. For instance, the traditional patterns of arranged marriage have been abandoned by the younger emigrants in favor of a new system based on free choice. Perhaps even more important are the changes in the traditional childrearing practices. An increasing number of the Man children have been entrusted to their grandparents, who have taken over most of the childrearing duties in the community. Emigration has also caused some unpredictable changes in the villagers' attitude toward formal education, which, together with the new socialization patterns, may have profound consequences for the next generation. These and other social changes are examined at length in this chapter.

BOREDOM, GAMBLING, AND REEMIGRATION

In 1970, an emigrant who had spent fifteen hard years working in England and Holland retired at age 52 and returned to San Tin. Man Gan-tso gave symbolic notice of his retirement by hosting a large banquet for the village elders a week after his return. He then settled into the comfortable sterling house he had built for his family on a previous trip and spent the next three months loafing in the local teahouses. By the fourth month, however, Gan-tso became disillusioned with retirement and decided to reemigrate, even though his son had already taken over the management of his restaurant in Holland. Gan-tso tried to justify the return by telling his wife and friends that he was needed abroad, but everyone knew that he was simply dissatisfied with life in the village.

Reemigration among the recently retired in San Tin is fairly common because the once active workers have to adjust to a social life that has changed a great deal since their youth. To make matters worse, the Mans often build up a very romanticized image of their home community while working abroad. The emigrants tend to forget the hardships and monotony of village life, and they remember only the pleasant aspects of their previous existence. The holiday trips every three or four years simply reinforce the romantic image because the returnees never stay long enough to see the village after the festive season. It is inevitable that many retired emigrants find San Tin to be a letdown.

The retired emigrants are not the only residents who complain that life in the village is boring and uneventful. Older people who have never visited Kowloon—let alone London— maintain that San Tin has become dull only in the last decade. As noted in earlier chapters, emigration has raised the standard of living in San Tin and changed the community into a center of leisure and affluence. In order for this to happen, however, the productive life of the village has come to a complete halt. Except for the Lunar New Year festival and rare celebrations like the temple renovation, the villagers seldom have any break in the daily routine of eating, gambling, gossiping, and napping. The shopkeepers and the market hawkers (mostly outsiders) are the only residents who work on a regular basis. The women are kept reasonably busy with housework, childrearing, and handicrafts, but the men have difficulty keeping themselves occupied. They do not have any avocations besides gambling; they do not read for pleasure. Television is not even an answer for some of the older people because they are unable to relate to the medium as a form of entertainment, or they have difficulty understanding the Cantonese dialect spoken by the actors. Furthermore, many elders in San Tin are unhappy with their family lives since their sons and adult grandsons are absent. There is no one in the community for them to associate with except other men in similarly unhappy circumstances. Consequently, San Tin's older generation suffers from general boredom and ennui.

A high percentage of villagers find diversion by spending all of their spare time playing mahjong and a Chinese version of dominoes. Gambling is undoubtedly the major pastime in the New Territories (see e.g., Potter 1968:148), but in San Tin it has become a way of life. Residents of all ages, including some of the adolescents, have no other form of recreation except gambling. In order to accommodate the players, San Tin has four full-time gambling houses and ten other shops and tea-houses that devote half of their space to gambling tables (see Table 1, Chapter Two). It is not unusual for these establishments to be filled with Man gamblers every day. The attraction is not the money involved, because the stakes are ordinarily low; the games are the only source of excitement in the village.

The high frequency of gambling is not the only indicator of general boredom and dissatisfaction in the community. There were three cases of suicide—one successful, two attempted—during our stay in the village. The Mans consider this disastrous evidence of breakdown and assert that self-destruction was unknown until recently. Some residents also complain that insomnia has become a serious problem in the village. One of the attempted suicide cases involved an overdose of sleeping pills, which now sell briskly in the community. Before the advent of large-scale emigration, the villagers maintain, all of these things were completely unknown. As one elder put it: "Although we were poor our life was satisfying because we worked hard, slept well, and had good appetites. Now everything has changed."

Many of the developments the Mans find so distressing are a reflection of San Tin's changing population. The village contains a disproportionate number of elderly people because the working age men and some of their wives and children are absent. Improved health facilities and the increasing reliance on Western medical clinics in the market towns have also raised the life expectancy in San Tin.[1] The high proportion of elderly people coupled with the absence of any productive activity gives San Tin at times the appearance of a retirement settlement. Were it not for the presence of the young mothers and their children who have not emigrated, the illusion would be complete. Most of San Tin's social problems, therefore, are caused by the prolonged absence of adult men who fill the essential roles of son, father, and husband.

SECURITY AND THE ABSENCE OF MEN

No more than a handful of men between the ages of 18 and 50 now live in the village. In traditional times, it would have been difficult for a community so completely devoid of able-bodied men to survive in the New Territories. The village would have had no protection and probably would have become an easy target for bandits and neighboring lineages. Most of the earlier emigrant communities in South China were never as totally dependent on emigrant labor as San Tin and in general appear to have sent no more than half of their active males

[1] The general health situation is improving in the Colony. According to a recent survey, the expectation of life at birth in Hong Kong is 66.7 years for males, the same as for infants born in the United States. This figure compares with the life expectancy for males in India, approximately 42 years (Podmore 1971:36).

abroad (see e.g., Kulp 1925:50). San Tin's complete reliance
on emigration is, therefore, in part a reflection of British control,
which eliminated the bandits and suppressed interlineage conflict in the New Territories. In their conversations about the
origins of out-migration in San Tin, the lineage leaders emphasize that the emigrants could not have left in such large
numbers if there had been any danger that the village might
become unsafe for their families. To date there have been few
serious problems, and San Tin has had a remarkably low rate
of crime.[2]

Occasionally, however, an incident reminds the residents just
how susceptible the village would be to outside intruders were
it not for the strong governmental control in the New Territories. In 1967, two men invaded one of the sterling houses
on the fringe of the village, tied up the only occupant (an old
woman), and carried off some expensive appliances. This episode is the most serious breach of security since San Tin became
an emigrant community, and the fact that it is still a regular
topic of conversation indicates that the Mans are not unmindful
of their helplessness. Another incident that occurred in 1969
is an even better illustration of the possible consequences of
massive out-migration. One night during our first few weeks
in the village, an aggressive drunk from a nearby squatter
settlement caused a disturbance in the central plaza of the
village. Although he did only minor property damage, he
managed to terrorize the entire subvillage of Fan Tin for well
over two hours. No one went outside to stop him and the five
village guardsmen (average age 63) on duty that evening did
not attempt to intervene. There simply were not enough young
men available to protect the village from the rampaging of a

---

[2] In San Tin Sub-District as a whole, which includes many other settlements besides the village of San Tin, the New Territores police handled
five assaults, fourteen larcenies, two sexual offenses, and a single murder
between 1962 and 1970. (Data provided by the Royal Hong Kong Police
Force, Police Historical Records Committee, letter of 16 November 1970).

single drunk. The next morning some of our neighbors gathered informally to discuss the incident but decided that it was not serious enough to pursue further. The elders maintained that this kind of disturbance had never been a problem when San Tin was an agricultural community because the younger men would have stopped it immediately. Fortunately this was an isolated incident and it did not recur, but it was a vivid illustration of the fragility and basic helplessness of a total emigrant community.

A lack of community security is not the only problem that has arisen as a direct consequence of the absence of San Tin's productive male population. It has become almost impossible for the villagers to find acceptable candidates for the trustee posts of the lineage's minor segments. Except for two or three of the wealthier segments, these are honorary positions that pay very little and consume a great deal of the trustee's time. Trustees must be literate and experienced in handling money, and in San Tin all but a handful of the men thus qualified are abroad. The leaders of the Rural Committee are able to refuse the smaller, unremunerative trusteeships by claiming to be overworked in their official duties, but they always manage to find time to handle the trust funds of the wealthier lineage segments. The situation became so desperate in one case that a Man shopkeeper who had just returned to San Tin after twenty years in a distant market town was pressed into immediate service as the trustee of a small segment. Within a month he was also asked to manage the trust fund of a lineage segment to which he did not even belong in return for a small annual salary. Since the villagers made it clear they expected him to help, the shopkeeper felt obligated to accept both positions. For the next two weeks he could be seen in his shop studying the Man genealogy because, as he put it: "I've been away for twenty years and I never did know very much about the lineage branches in the first place." The elders were appalled by his ignorance of these matters, but there was no one else available who could manage the account books.

CHANGING MARRIAGE PATTERNS

Emigration has had such a profound impact on the social life of the village that it has caused the modification of some of the central features of San Tin's traditional culture. A good example is the change in the system of arranged marriage.

According to most informants, San Tin's marriage patterns were already in a state of flux before the advent of emigration in the 1950s. Only the older villagers claim to have had "blind" marriages in which the bride and groom saw each other for the first time on their wedding day. After the Second World War, the arranged patterns were modified in many cases to allow the grooms to view their prospective wives in a public setting some time before the negotiations were completed.[3] Although the son was thus given a certain amount of veto power over the bride, his feelings were always subordinate to the interests of the family. Marriage was considered too important to allow the young people a free choice, because there was more at stake than their personal happiness. In the traditional view, marriages were contracted between families; the very term for marriage translates roughly as "to bring in a daughter-in-law." The new daughter-in-law's primary functions were to produce sons for the patriline and to serve as a domestic worker in her father-in-law's household. In most cases, the bride's abilities to fill the roles of sexual partner and companion were irrelevant considerations.

Since the rise of emigration the younger workers have assumed more control over their own marriage arrangements. The new pattern of individual choice in marriage is gaining popularity all over the Colony of Hong Kong and is not limited to emigrant communities such as San Tin (see e.g., Baker 1968:208, Potter 1969:24-26). The major impetus for change is

[3] This modification of the traditional Chinese arrangement is similar to the one that has become popular in Taiwanese villages since the Japanese occupation (Diamond 1969:52-53, Gallin 1966:205-6).

the growth of wage-labor occupations in commerce and industry which have freed a large proportion of the younger people from the financial control of their parents. In San Tin the massive conversion to restaurant jobs has given the youth an independent source of income, and the new "Western" model of marriage choice is now the norm among the Man workers.

The young, unmarried emigrants expect to be treated as autonomous adults because they control the family budget. Most villagers still pay lip service to the fiction that the father is responsible for his son's wedding expenses, but few are able to assume this obligation unless they happen to be successful emigrants themselves. Wealthy restaurateurs take great pride in the elaborate weddings they sometimes provide for their sons; however, this does not give the father enough leverage to dictate the choice of brides. The high wages available to the younger emigrants make it possible for nearly everyone to pay for his own wedding, if necessary. Restaurant workers now base their marriage selections largely on personal considerations, which means that the needs of the groom are no longer subordinate to the demands of the family.

Occasionally, parents proceed with the preliminary marriage negotiations in the absence of the intended grooms, who learn of the impending match only after their return. In most cases the emigrant simply refuses to cooperate if the bride does not meet his expectations. The groom and his parents differ because the emigrants look for wives who will make desirable sexual partners and good companions. The parents, on the other hand, search for daughters-in-law who will be satisfied with domestic life in the village. As a consequence, emigrants often reject the brides chosen by their elders and initiate their own search when they return for their first holiday.

Even though the Mans have embraced the free choice concept of marriage, they have had difficulty finding acceptable wives. The type of young women sought after by the restaurant workers will not always accept the mundane position of daughter-in-law in an emigrant community. San Tin is gaining a bad reputation among the eligible girls in the New Territories; they have heard about its dull social life and they do not savor the prospects of marrying a man who will be absent for years at a time. Prospective brides tend to drive hard bargains before they will accept an emigrant husband. Increasingly, the girls are demanding that they be taken abroad after the wedding, not left at home in the village with their husband's parents. This new development is reflected in the marriage data from my village census: In a sample of thirty-five emigrant marriages, nineteen of the wives (54 percent) were living abroad in 1970, and at least ten of these were recent brides (married two years or less). The older parents, of course, find this new pattern distressing, but there is little they can do as long as the emigrant controls the family budget.

The other difficulty in wife-hunting is the limited time returnees have to devote to their courtship. The average home visit for the Man emigrants is three months, but the unmarried workers sometimes stretch this to as many as five or six months. Yet, even with this extension, the emigrants often complain that they do not have enough time to find acceptable women. The young wife-hunters conduct their search in a very forthright and determined manner. The pace is intense, almost frantic, as the returnees rush around the Colony following up leads and introductions given to them by friends or relatives. Since San Tin is a single-lineage village and surname exogamy is strictly enforced, they spend little time in their home community.

Not all of the emigrants are successful in their search for a bride. In 1970, one young worker had to return to his job in Holland without a wife, even though he had prolonged his stay for seven months. His case is somewhat unusual, but at least five other emigrants were also unsuccessful during the 1970 Lunar New Year holidays and had to postpone their wife-hunting efforts until the next trip home. The older villagers consider the problem so serious that they speak of it only among themselves. They take it as a humiliating reflection on the stature of the Man lineage that the emigrants have difficulty finding suitable spouses.

MAIL-ORDER BRIDES

One method of overcoming the wife-hunting problem is to stay abroad and place the search in the hands of an intermediary. The villagers do not have a term for the arrangement, but in many ways it resembles the "mail-order bride" system common in the popular literature about the American frontier (it is sometimes referred to as the "picture bride" system). The basic elements of the system are that the groom selects his bride on the basis of photographs and does not meet her until they are committed to marriage. This might appear to be only a slight variation of the traditional Chinese arranged marriage pattern because the groom's agent (usually his father) is asked to select the eligible brides. However, there is one critical difference: The young emigrant still retains the power of choice, and the father is unable to impose his will on the son. Even though the worker does not return home, he still pays for the banquets and all the other expenses associated with the wedding. The following case illustrates how the mail-order bride system operates in San Tin.

In December 1969, a 50-year-old retired farmer began to search for a suitable wife for his son. After two months an eligible girl was located through the intermediation of affinal relatives living in Kowloon. The father immediately mailed two photographs of the girl, one close-up and one full-length portrait, to his son in Germany. In two weeks an affirmative reply arrived, stating that the son approved of the girl's appearance and that he trusted the judgment of his two older sisters who had helped in the search. Six months later the wedding took place in the village, but the groom did not return for the occasion. Instead, a live cock was used as his substitute during the ceremonial banquet. The day after the wedding banquet in San Tin the bride flew directly to Europe to meet her new husband for the first time. The marriage was also sealed by a civil ceremony in Germany, but as far as the Mans were concerned the village banquet was enough to make it legal and binding.

Absentee weddings of this type are rare in San Tin because the emigrants and their elders consider it to be a low-status alternative to the standard marriage arrangement. The father in the case presented above justified the actions of his son by pointing out that the arrangement had saved a great deal of money. Although the absentee marriage complied with the lineage tradition of providing a banquet on the wedding day, the villagers made it quite clear to everyone involved that they thought it would have been better if the groom had been present. Any emigrant hoping to gain recognition and prestige from his marriage must return to San Tin and serve as the host at his own wedding banquet. Another reason why the mail-order bride arrangement has not become popular among the Man emigrants is that the workers prefer to meet their prospective wives before they make a final decision. To my knowledge, only three cases of absentee marriage have taken place in the Man lineage since the early 1960s.

INTERMEDIATION SYSTEM

In order to expedite the wife-hunting, the Mans have devised a system of intermediation that allows the returnees to take maximum advantage of the limited time available for their holidays. The emigrants write to their relatives and friends who might be in a position to help as soon as they make the decision to return. They also notify fellow workers from other villages that they are looking for a bride and would appreciate introductions to eligible girls. By the time the emigrant arrives home he usually has two or three leads to follow up during the first weeks of vacation. There do not appear to be any individuals in San Tin who specialize as matchmakers for the emigrants, even though the two old women who performed this service for the villagers in the past are still living. The restaurant workers prefer the intermediation of their personal friends and close relatives because they do not trust the judgment of the older women. Furthermore, the role of contemporary intermediary does not involve matchmaking in the traditional sense. Friends and relatives simply help the emigrant by locating eligible mates and arranging introductions in the nearby market towns. It is up to the worker to initiate the courtship and to handle the negotiations after the formal introduction. Although the concept of romantic love before marriage is relatively alien to the Mans, many of the younger emigrants have started to emulate Western dating patterns by taking the girl out alone to cinemas and restaurants in the urban areas. A few have even adopted the engagement system, complete with the promissory diamond ring, before holding the final wedding banquets to seal the union.

The marriage system of the Man emigrants, therefore, is based on an unusual combination of traditional and modern patterns. The logistical problems that limit the time an emigrant can spend hunting for a wife make it necessary to rely on a variation of the traditional intermediation system. Using this criterion alone, one might be tempted to characterize the marriage patterns in San Tin as more conservative than those of other communities in the New Territories. However, this would be an unrealistic view, because the grooms exercise a great deal of independence and individual choice, in spite of the limitations involved. The wide range of choice is shown in the surname distribution of recent brides taken by the emigrants. Traditionally the Mans restricted their marriage

network to a well-defined area roughly equivalent to the intermediate marketing community surrounding the market town
of Sham Chun (cf. Skinner 1964:36). An analysis of marriage
entries in the Man genealogy shows that twelve surname groups
within this region provided most of the wives for the Mans
up until the Second World War.[4] The emigrants now marry
women from all over the Colony, many with surnames that
are not in the genealogy. Some of these women are recent
immigrants from more distant regions in South China. In one
case, a restaurateur's son chose a bride who was born in
Singapore and educated in England. Other evidence for the
breakdown of the old marriage patterns and the concurrent
rise of individual choice are the European wives taken by the
emigrants while working abroad.

EUROPEAN WIVES

One of the most alarming consequences of emigration, according to the older people of San Tin, is the "loss" of younger
men who choose to marry European women. Considering the
numbers involved, however, this problem is exaggerated. Lineage members in London estimate that approximately twelve
to fifteen Mans have taken European (British, Dutch, and
German) wives. They add that only five of these cases are
known to have been legalized by a civil ceremony. Furthermore,
as noted in Chapter Six, only two of these dozen or more unions
have resulted in the true "loss" of the emigrants involved. Most
of the workers who take European wives or consorts continue

---

[4] The version of the Man genealogy used here is a handwritten one I
was able to photograph toward the end of my research. Over half of the
1,600 entries include the surname of the wife which is sufficient to give
a general idea of the marriage region of the lineage. Rubie S. Watson has
done an analysis of these marriage entries (unpublished paper) and has
found that the genealogy lists approximately seventy surnames, but only
twelve are mentioned regularly.

to send remittances to their families in the village and still consider themselves to be active members of the Man lineage. At least three emigrants have wives in both Europe and Hong Kong; but this is not a cause for alarm because they support their village-based families quite comfortably.

The parents of the emigrants are willing to extend grudging acceptance of the mixed marriages as long as the remittances arrive every month on schedule. Villagers prefer that their sons choose Dutch wives rather than British wives if they must marry abroad. As one old woman put it: "English girls always want to control the money. They don't like second-hand goods and they demand that everything be new. The worst thing about them, though, is that they do not want their men to send remittances back to their families here in San Tin." There are many stories circulating in the village about extravagant British girls who have taken advantage of the young emigrants and made off with their money. Stories about Dutch wives, on the other hand, tend to be more positive because few have encouraged their emigrant husbands to withhold family remittances. Village women are fond of relating how one Dutch wife sent some of her own money when her husband was ill and unable to work.

As noted in Chapter Six, most of the European wives come from working class backgrounds and are often outcasts in their own society. The marriages are seldom legitimized by a civil ceremony, but this makes little difference to the emigrants and their families back home in San Tin. In the San Tin view, a "wife" is any woman who lives with a Man emigrant and is a potential mother of his children. The offspring of these unions are often sent to live with their grandparents in San Tin, where they become thoroughly Sinified and are distinguishable from their peers only by their Eurasian features (see also Aijmer 1967:72). On rare occasions the European wives may even accompany their husbands on a visit to Hong Kong over the Lunar New Year. These infrequent visits are the subject of a growing body of folklore about the difficulties the women encounter in their husbands' village. The most common stories relate how the European wives take one look at the run-down village and demand to be taken back to Kowloon hotels immediately. However, one or two have adapted so well that they have won the admiration of the villagers.

During the 1970 Lunar New Year festival, a German woman (approximate age 35) flew back to Hong Kong with her husband to celebrate the wedding of his younger brother. She stayed in San Tin for nearly a week, living in one of the uncomfortable, traditional-style houses owned by her father-in-law. Although she could not speak Cantonese, she was polite to her in-laws and treated them with respect. She also helped with the household chores and did some of the cooking (the father-in-law later informed his incredulous friends that her Cantonese-style dishes were quite good). Toward the end of the short visit, the woman amazed and delighted the elders by accompanying her husband to the Main Ancestral Hall and offering incense at the altar. This ritual is one of the most important elements of the traditional marriage ceremony because it introduces the wife to her new lineage ancestors. The villagers could think of only one other case in which a European woman (apparently Dutch) had stayed so long and had adjusted so well to conditions in the community.

Although the older villagers are gratified by these exceptional cases, many still resent the fact that the younger emigrants would even consider taking European wives. The protests usually are not framed in racial terms, although some residents do harbor prejudices against Caucasians as a group. The main objection to European wives is that they constitute a potential threat to the economic prosperity of the workers' dependents in San Tin. At another level, the objections are part of a generalized protest against the new marriage patterns of the younger emigrants. The village-bound parents do not like to be deprived of the services of their daughters-in-law. Life is difficult enough for the older people of an emigrant community without the added aggravation of losing some of the potential daughters-in-law.

THE REGULATION OF SEXUAL BEHAVIOR

As mentioned earlier, the recent brides of the Man emigrants do not relish the prospects of living alone with their in-laws in San Tin. Their reluctance is based on more than the normal hesitation common among all Chinese brides about to join a strange, new family (see e.g., Fei 1939:45-50). As a consequence of the prolonged absence of men, the residents of San Tin observe a strict set of customs to regulate the behavior of women and to prevent extramarital affairs. These customs, together with the ordinary hardships imposed by the new mothers-in-law, make the life of the younger wives in San Tin especially difficult.

Chen Ta notes that women in Chinese emigrant communities tend to be more sheltered than their counterparts in ordinary villages. He also found that sexual prohibitions were more rigorously defined in communities with a high percentage of absentee workers (Chen Ta 1939:192). This is certainly true in San Tin, where the Mans teach daughters-in-law to observe a set of rules designed to protect their virtue and to limit contacts with males outside the family. These rules are not codified but are understood implicitly by everyone in the community. For instance, a new bride soon learns that she is expected to retreat into the safety of her house when any male approaches who is not a member of her household or an immediate neighbor. The women are not kept in actual seclusion as in some Arab cultures, but they are sheltered from activities that might bring them into contact with men. The Mans openly encourage their women to be suspicious of strangers, even though outsiders rarely venture beyond the central path leading through the village. To my knowledge there has never been a rape in San Tin, but the older women instruct their daughters-in-law to treat every unknown male as a potential assailant.

The Mans do not allow unmarried outsiders to live in the village unless they are elderly and do not represent any potential sexual threat to the women. My own efforts to find a home in San Tin were fruitless until the villagers had seen my wife and were satisfied that she would live with me during our stay. The elders also made it clear that they did not want our unmarried research assistant to live in the village (he commuted from Kowloon). After these conditions were met an empty house miraculously appeared and we were allowed to take up residence in San Tin.

Because of the high rate of emigration, there are many households in San Tin that do not have any adult males present. It is an unwritten law that no male is allowed to enter these households after dark. If the woman involved has adult children living with her or if her husband is home for a visit, the rule does not apply. In all other cases the woman must be called outside when a male visitor wishes to speak with her. The rules also place severe restrictions on the nocturnal movements of women. Ordinarily women are not to leave their houses after dusk unless they have a pressing errand and are accompanied by a responsible chaperone.

Potter reports that some of the rules outlined above apply in the nonemigrant community of Ping Shan (personal communication). It should also be noted that many of these restrictions on female activity were known in San Tin before the rise of large-scale emigration. However, according to the older women, the rules are now enforced much more rigorously than in the past. The reason they give for the change is that in earlier times the husbands were present to watch over their own wives. After San Tin became an emigrant community the rules were tightened up, partly for the protection of the women and partly to reassure the absent husbands.

The Man workers actually have little reason to be concerned about the conduct of their wives because the vast majority of the women follow the rules willingly. This would be a disappointment in many New Territories circles where a myth has developed about the sex-starved women of San Tin. Frequently in my travels around the New Territories I picked up hints that men from other villages imagine the San Tin women to be free and promiscuous because it is common knowledge that their husbands are working abroad. In fact, San Tin has an almost puritanical air about it. Although a double standard allows the men to indulge in exploits with women outside the community, sexual transgressions by the Man wives are among the most serious offenses conceivable in an emigrant community like San Tin. Similarly, adultery within the lineage (i.e., between a lineage member and the wife of another) is even more serious and could result in the death of both parties if discovered.

This nearly happened in one case that occurred in the early 1960s. The male offender was a lineage member who, while waiting to emigrate to the United Kingdom, seduced the wife of an absent neighbor. After the woman admitted the act, the male was captured by the village guard and forced into a rattan pig-basket (used to transport hogs) which was thrown into a pond behind the village. Had it not been for the timely intervention of the border police, the man would have drowned. But he was able to escape and has never returned to San Tin. Soon after the episode the offender was formally expelled from the lineage (*ch'u tsu*) and his name was removed from the genealogy. I was unable to determine what happened to the woman in this case because no one was willing to discuss the outcome; but I assume she was thrown out of the village in disgrace (in earlier times, she probably would have been killed outright).

Toward the end of my stay in the village some of the elders finally opened up on the problem of sexual frustration and suspected adultery in San Tin. Prior to this time the topics had never been discussed because the sexual problems of the emigrants' wives are taboo subjects. The informants intimated that there had been two and perhaps three other cases of suspected adultery by emigrant wives in recent years, but these could not be substantiated. In each suspected case, they continued, the woman is rumored to have committed the offense with an outsider during trips to one of the nearby market towns. As long as there is no clear evidence of transgression, however, the villagers are reluctant to interfere because they do not like to become involved in unpleasant disputes that could cause serious trouble in the community.

Wives are expected to defer sexual gratification until their husbands' holiday trips, which on the average occur once every three or four years. The children resulting from these infrequent encounters ordinarily become the central focus of the women's lives. Since they have few other outlets, the children are the only source of comfort for the village-bound wives. However, even here the daughters-in-law are sometimes frustrated because they do not have complete control over their children.

GRANDPARENT SOCIALIZATION

In San Tin more and more of the grandparents have assumed primary responsibility for the socialization of the emigrants' children. "Grandparent socialization," as I have chosen to call this pattern, has several basic characteristics that distinguish it from other forms of childrearing. The most important feature is a preoccupation with the child's needs and a tendency to smother him with lavish affection. Since San Tin has few sources of entertainment, many of the old people regard their grandchildren as their only "fun" in life. The grandparents are so indulgent that the children are seldom punished or disciplined, no matter how unruly they become. The best image of grandparent socialization is that of a worried grandmother with rice bowl and chop sticks in hand, running after her three-year-old grandson, begging him to eat.

At this point a clarification should be made about Chinese childrearing in general. Critical readers with a knowledge of Chinese culture are apt to reply to the above description: "What is different about San Tin?" Grandparents often take charge of the childrearing in Chinese families and, as many observers have noted, they are usually more permissive than parents (see e.g., Wolf 1970:47-51, 1972:72-73; M. Yang 1945:66). However, in most of the families so described, there is always a father figure to serve as disciplinarian. In San Tin the fathers are usually working abroad, and the role of disciplinarian falls to the mother, teacher, or grandparent—none of whom seems willing to accept the responsibility. Grandparent socialization, therefore, is a form of childrearing in which the children are indulged and pampered by the elders in the absence of an authoritarian figure who periodically enforces discipline.

Grandparent socialization takes its full form in San Tin when both the father and the mother are working abroad and the children are left in the care of their grandparents. My village census shows that approximately one-third of the children in the village are raised exclusively by their grandparents. Another one-third of the children are shifted back and forth between Europe and Hong Kong so that they are intermittently in the sole charge of their grandparents. The remaining children are raised by their nonemigrant mothers with the help of the grandparents (see Table 15). The full extent of grandparent socialization in San Tin is concealed by these census figures, however, because they do not show the socialization process over time. Most of the children residing abroad with their emigrant parents have at one time been in the care of their grandparents. Furthermore, many of the daughters-in-law now living in San Tin have spent at least two years abroad without their children. A more accurate estimate of grandparent sociali-

TABLE 15

Residential Arrangements for a Sample of 87 Man Children, 1970
(Ages 0 to 13, All Children of Emigrants)

Abroad with parents............................	30	(34%)
San Tin with mother and grandparents..............	33	(38%)
San Tin with grandparents, no mother	24	(28%)
Total children	87	(100%)

zation in San Tin is that approximately one-half of the Man emigrants' children have spent two or more of their formative years alone with their grandparents.

When asked about childrearing, the emigrants generally agree that the best arrangement is to leave the children in the care of their grandparents. This allows the wife to join her husband abroad, where she can become a productive worker in the restaurants. As one emigrant explained: "It is best for my wife to be free to work and earn money if she is able. It is also best to leave our children in San Tin because my mother knows more about childrearing and it gives the old people something to do besides gamble all the time." It appears that the Mans are not the only Chinese emigrants in Europe who have come to the same conclusion. Ng Kwee-choo (1968:86) found that "several babies" born in London were sent back to the New Territories because both parents were actively employed in the restaurant trade.

Another reason for leaving the children in San Tin is to ensure that they become thoroughly embued with the variety of Chinese culture found in the village. The Mans want their children to speak the local dialect of Cantonese and to grow up with a peer group consisting of fellow lineage mates. After nearly ten years of experience, the emigrants have learned that they cannot expect to raise their children in the European host societies without sacrificing some of the essential features of their own cultural heritage. The Mans believe that the best way for the children to be socialized as "proper" Chinese is to leave them in the village.

There are many variations of the grandparent socialization arrangement in San Tin, but the grandmother, or a surrogate grandmother, always plays the central role. The grandfathers normally take only a passive interest in the everyday affairs of childrearing, although they spend a great deal of time playing with the children and serving as indulgent baby-sitters when the women are busy. Grandmothers are rarely expected to handle more than two young children at a time because the work is difficult and trying. If his own mother is overburdened or deceased, the emigrant will try to find another older woman who is willing to take care of his children for a small monthly salary. The surrogate grandmothers are usually widows who live alone in the village and derive great pleasure from taking care of infants. They are given complete authority over their charges, just as if they were the true grandparents and, to date, there have not been any complaints or bad rumors about their conduct. One surrogate grandmother takes care of three children from three separate emigrant families, but ordinarily the surrogates keep only one child.

TWO CASE STUDIES: GRANDMOTHERS IN CHARGE

Some of the problems associated with grandparent socialization are illustrated in the following case studies. The first involves a 66-year-old widow, Lao Mei, who has three emigrant sons working in the United Kingdom. During the past ten years this woman has been responsible at one time or another for six of her eight grandchildren. Her daughters-in-law have spent most of their married lives abroad and have not been expected to raise their own children. In 1969-70, Lao Mei was occupied with two of her youngest grandsons, ages three and five. During the New Year festival one of her sons returned to San Tin with another three-year-old and tried to convince his mother to accept one more charge. Lao Mei was unwilling to comply, however, because she had once fallen ill while managing three grandchildren. Although the emigrant was unhappy with this decision, he was able to find a surrogate grandmother for his son within a few days. Occasionally Lao Mei visits the surrogate, who lives in another part of the village, but does not attempt to interfere with the woman's childrearing methods.

Many of Lao Mei's neighbors believe that her emigrant sons have taken advantage of their mother's good nature and have used her home as a convenient nursery for their children. There may be some truth to these charges, but Lao Mei never complains. Instead she maintains that she enjoys looking after the children because it keeps her busy and makes her feel useful. Her situation is unusual only because she has three emigrant sons who have all decided to leave their children in the village at one time or another. Some of the villagers, like the elderly couple in the next case, would consider themselves fortunate to have Lao Mei's problems.

Man Yan-sau and his wife have never been very successful in anything they have tried. In his youth, Yan-sau attempted to break the cycle of poverty that had plagued his family for three generations by setting up a small shop in one of the nearby market towns. The shop failed after only one year and he spent the rest of his productive life as a poor farmer in San Tin. To make matters worse, Yan-sau's only son had been ritually adopted by his older brother, who had no heirs of his own. Although he and his wife were still able to raise the boy, they knew that eventually their son would be expected to serve two fathers.[5] The couple's feelings of insecurity increased, according

[5] According to the rules of adoption in the Man lineage, the sonless elder brother in this case had the right to claim Yan-sau's only son as his own (see Watson n.d.). The son then inherits from two "fathers" and is responsible for "lighting the lamps of both houses" (i.e., he must worship the ancestral spirits and carry on the patriline of both men).

to their own testimony, after the son emigrated to England and took his new bride along with him. If the son had decided to cut his ties with his parents for any reason, Yan-sau and his wife would have been completely alone in their old age—a prospect the villagers find terrifying.

In 1969 the couple happily announced that their first grand-child had been born in London, but they were even more elated when they learned that the baby would be sent to live with them in the village. Eight months later their daughter-in-law brought the infant home with her on one of the Lunar New Year charter flights from London. The new mother stayed with her son for two months to ensure that he was well integrated into his grandparent's household before she returned to Lon-don. Although the baby was frightened by the strange setting at first, it did not take long before he was happy and contented with his new home. According to a prearranged plan that is common in emigrant households, the daughter-in-law gradually withdrew from the everyday childrearing activities over a six-week period until Yan-sau's wife had complete charge of the baby. Everything seemed to be progressing smoothly as the daughter-in-law's departure date drew near and there was no indication of the problems that were to develop in the following months.

Soon after her arrival back in London the mother became very depressed by the absence of her only child. She began to write long letters (an unusual development in itself) in which she inquired about the health of the baby and expressed her desire to see him again. In one of these letters she asked Yan-sau to send her some color photographs of her baby. Since I had already taken one set of family portraits for Yan-sau earlier that year, he asked me to be the photographer. At the appointed time two days later I arrived at his house with my camera equipment only to discover that the grandmother had taken the baby "for a walk." Yan-sau was greatly embarrassed and promised to rearrange the session for another day. As I was leaving and trying to imagine what breach of etiquette I had committed, the neighbors opined that the woman simply did not want any photographs of the baby sent to her daughter-in-law. The baby had become the center of the grandmother's life, they said, and she did not want to risk losing him. She feared that if the young mother saw a set of baby pictures it would depress her even more and make it more difficult for her to accept the separation. Later I was to see that the neighbors were correct.

Yan-sau was upset by the behavior of his wife, but he was also worried that the baby might be taken back to London. As long as the grandson stayed in San Tin it was clear that the old couple had a secure link to their son and did not have to be concerned about disruptions of remittances or abandonment. Economic considerations of this type may have been important, but Yan-sau and his wife had other reasons for wanting to keep their grandchild. The baby was their only source of joy and they spent most of their time watching and talking about him. When another letter arrived from the daughter-in-law, hinting that she was pressuring her husband to allow the child to be raised in Britain, Yan-sau decided he had to act. Because he is functionally illiterate (he cannot read well and is unable to write) he went to the market town of Shek Wu Hui and hired one of the professional letter writers to record his message. According to his own account later, the letter urged his son not to listen to the pleas of his young wife because she would soon recover from her depression. Yan-sau couched most of his argument in economic terms and detailed how much extra it would cost to raise the child abroad. Furthermore, he added, if the baby were not left in San Tin he would not learn to speak proper Cantonese and might abandon his lineage heritage when he reached adult age. Yan-sau's message apparently worked because the son wrote back that he had decided to leave the baby in the village until he had finished his primary education. The grandparents relaxed after receiving this news—and the photographic session was rescheduled the next day.

GRANDCHILDREN AND DOMESTIC CONFLICT

The case presented above gives an indication of the conflicts that sometimes develop between the daughter-in-law and the grandparents in emigrant households. The problems become even more critical when the daughters-in-law reside in the village and the grandmothers do not have complete control of the children. As Margery Wolf notes, Chinese grandmothers generally have no qualms about interfering with the childrearing practices of their daughters-in-law (1970:49). The child's father is able to mediate between his mother and his wife in most families, so the conflicts do not become too serious. However, in emigrant households the critical male arbiter is absent and this can lead to open domestic conflict. Most daughters-in-law in San Tin are too busy to watch their children all the time because they have the responsibility of cooking, cleaning, and washing for the household. The grandmothers are expected to assume many of the the ordinary childrearing tasks, but they often go beyond this and try to replace their daughters-in-law as the primary agent of socialization.

Conflicts usually arise when the daughter-in-law attempts to punish the child and the grandmother interferes. Many of these domestic quarrels rage on for hours, with half the village listening, as the two women argue about the proper methods of discipline. The grandmothers invariably maintain that the children should not be punished as severely as the mothers believe necessary. Although the relationships between the women in these households may be very tense, they seldom split up into separate domestic units. Unlike some other Chinese emigrants,[6] the Mans will not allow their wives to do this because it would mean supporting two autonomous households and it might make the old people feel unwanted. As a result, the grandmothers play a major part in the socialization of the children even when their daughters-in-law are resident in San Tin. In time, the daughters-in-law learn that it is best not to punish their children unless absolutely necessary because it will only agitate the older women and lead to more domestic conflict. The majority of Man children, therefore, are raised in a very lenient manner.

The absence of the disciplinarians means that there is now a large number of unruly children in San Tin who have no reason to fear the consequences of their actions. This has caused many problems for the community, but none so serious as the breakdown of discipline in the village school.

EDUCATIONAL CRISIS

One afternoon while watching his grandchild scratch out row after row of Chinese characters, an old farmer observed: "It is harder to make a child study than to make a water buffalo work." The analogy captures an essential feature of the traditional Chinese educational system. It implies that the student will not study unless he is under the constant threat of punishment. The elder who made this observation was referring to his own education, which was based on the Confucian ideals of strict obedience, absolute discipline, and hard work. Many of these values are still important in Hong Kong's primary and secondary schools because students are induced to study and to keep up with their lessons primarily by negative sanctions in the home.

[6] In Big Stream Village, a New Territories emigrant community, the wives of six Hakka emigrants did not live with their husbands' parents. Instead they stayed with their own parents and joined their husbands only during infrequent holiday trips (Aijmer 1967:72).

San Tin's large primary school has been shaken in recent years by a general breakdown in discipline. The permissiveness of childrearing in the emigrant households invariably affects the study habits of the children. Man students have learned that they do not have to keep up with their tedious lessons because they are rarely punished for scholastic failure. The school's sixteen teachers are empowered to punish their students; but, being nonresident outsiders who commute to work, they consider the problem an internal lineage matter and prefer not to become involved. They are paid as government civil servants and have little concern for the local community. Even when their classes are disrupted by rowdy students, the teachers hesitate to use physical punishment. They fear that the grandparents of the students may take offense and report the matter to the school board (which, incidentally, is made up exclusively of lineage members). As a result, the morale of the teachers is very low in San Tin's primary school, and the quality of education has suffered accordingly. But the problem is more complex than a simple breakdown of discipline in the classrooms.

In striking contrast to other parts of Hong Kong, academic achievement motivation is low in San Tin. The children are not convinced that education is a necessity because they see semiliterate returnees building sterling houses and driving automobiles. They also realize that the only qualification needed for employment in the high-paying restaurants abroad is membership in the Man lineage. Many of the adolescents drop out before they finish the six forms (grades) of primary school and wait idly, sometimes for years, until they are old enough to obtain vouchers or work permits. When I once asked a youth loafing in one of the village teahouses if he attended school, his friends replied uproariously: "Yes! He goes to Gambling University!"

The headmaster of San Tin's school maintains that the decline of enrollment over the last ten years is due primarily to the growing dropout rate. There are, of course, many other explanations for the enrollment change, including a decline in the birth rate and an exodus of emigrant families, but in 1961 the primary school had a total enrollment of 545 students, and by 1970 the total had dropped to 490.[7] The older villagers are concerned about the dropout problem, but they cannot answer the questions of the younger generation. As one of these youths put it: "What good are history and geography to me? How will it help me work in a restaurant? I know how to read and how to use an abacus (manual calculator), and that's enough for anyone."

Formal instruction has not come to a standstill in San Tin; but the combination of an undisciplined, unmotivated student body and a disinterested faculty has had a devastating effect of the quality of education. Returning emigrants are furious when they find that their sons can hardly read or write after years in the village school. However, only a few of the villagers have felt it necessary to send their children to other primary schools with better reputations in the New Territories. Nor do the Mans encourage their children to attend middle school (high school) after they have completed their primary education in San Tin. Like their children, most of the adults are not convinced that a high level of education is a necessity for the prospective restaurant workers.

According to a knowledgeable informant who has had over twenty years of experience in the local community, these attitudes are a relatively recent development in San Tin. Before the advent of emigration, he maintains, the Mans were like most other Hong Kong people, who value formal education as a means to attain prestige and wealth. But after the restaurant boom in the early 1960s, they could no longer see a direct

---

[7] According to the records of San Tin's primary school, enrollment has declined steadily in the last decade:

1961:545	1963:542	1965:543	1967:513	1969:494
1962:544	1964:537	1966:521	1968:499	1970:490

correlation between educational achievement and monetary reward. There is some evidence that other Chinese emigrants have undergone similar attitude changes. Chen Ta notes that, although most Nan Yang emigrants in his sample had a "profound faith in education" (1939:153), a "strong minority" was skeptical about the value of formal schooling for success in the business world (1939:156).

San Tin has become such a specialized community that the Mans no longer socialize their children to be competitive in the ·local society. As long as the emigrants are able to find opportunities abroad, their children will not have to compete for jobs in Hong Kong's constrained economy. High educational attainment is no longer valued because it is not clear that it gives the emigrant a competitive advantage in the restaurant business. The Mans originally made the conversion to emigration in response to a crisis in the local economy. There is now a real danger that they may face another crisis if the British or the Dutch government decides to cut off immigration from Hong Kong. If this happens the emigrants' children will be "stranded" in their own society, ill-prepared to compete with their better educated and better trained counterparts from other villages.

CHANGING WORLD VIEW

The devaluation of education in San Tin does not mean that the Mans have become more parochial or have withdrawn from the world around them. In fact, quite the opposite has happened. When the Mans are asked what they consider to be the greatest change in the recent history of the village, they often reply that emigration has "opened up" their minds and given them a broader perspective on the world. The villagers now have reason to read newspapers and listen closely to the news on the radio. They take a keen interest in any international development that might have an effect on the immigration policies of European countries.

A good example is the 1970 British general election. Speculations about the outcome of the election were a major topic of conversation in the local teahouses because the Mans were afraid that the Conservatives would put even more severe restrictions on Commonwealth immigration if they won. Rumors circulated in the village about impending controls on the outflow of British currency and the imminent nationalization of Chinese restaurants in England. Most of the men in the village were aware of the issues as the election approached and some knew the names of the major political figures involved (e.g., Heath, Wilson, and Powell). After the Conservative victory the Mans were alarmed when they heard that the new government planned to introduce a revised Commonwealth Immigrants Act later in the year. The new legislation did not have an immediate impact on the immigration of Chinese workers from Hong Kong, but the villagers are constantly on the alert for changes in the European political climate. During my stay in San Tin, the men were also concerned about the plight of the Kenyan Indians, who at that time had only recently been excluded from free entry into the United Kingdom. They asked to have the background of the dispute explained to them and wanted to know if these developments would have any effect on the entry of British subjects from Hong Kong. Similarly, the villagers kept a close watch on Britain's efforts to join the European Common Market because a newspaper editorial had warned that this might have an adverse effect on British Commonwealth laborers living in England, Holland, Germany, and Belgium—the four countries where 99 percent of the Man emigrants work.

The Mans are certainly aware of major world events, but they do not ordinarily respond with interest unless it has a direct effect on their own lives. The moon walks of 1969 registered little more than a passing acknowledgment from the villagers, even though the events were broadcast on the Colony's television station. This reaction was in striking contrast to the response of the urban population in Hong Kong. During the telecasts huge crowds gathered in front of the radio-television stores on the streets of Kowloon to watch the astronauts. The lack of interest in San Tin was not entirely due to the fact that it was an American event. In April, 1970, China launched its first satellite, and Chinese people all over the world—Communist and non-Communist—heralded the feat as evidence of China's technological independence of the more advanced Western nations. In urban Hong Kong it was clear that the launching had aroused the admiration of people in all walks of life, and it became an occasion for displays of cultural nationalism. But in San Tin the satellite caused hardly a ripple. It did not become a topic of conversation in the village teahouses and no one mentioned the launching until I brought up the subject. The men were aware of the event because they had heard about it on the radio, but they were not interested in discussing it.

Emigration may have "opened up" the minds of the men in San Tin and broadened their horizons but it has not really changed the way they look at the world. The villagers still maintain the traditional, lineage-specific attitudes that the world is divided between the Mans and the outsiders. The outsider category has simply been expanded to include more people. The villagers' interest in a specific international event can be gauged in direct proportion to the immediate consequences the event is judged to have on the Man immigrants working in Europe. In some areas, the village men display a remarkable sophistication about the world beyond the New Territories, especially when they talk of travel regulations, currency fluctuations, and immigration laws. However, the same individuals may think that Holland, Germany, and Belgium are colonies of Britain and insist that their London-based sons drove to Canada for a weekend holiday last year. The majority of the villagers see no reason to expand their knowledge of larger issues that do not have a direct bearing on their own economic self-interest and the continued success of their emigrant sons.

Chapter Ten

CONCLUSIONS:
EMIGRATION AND THE PRESERVATION
OF TRADITION

THE Man lineage is examined more closely in this concluding chapter to determine what effects emigration and land devaluation have had on its structure and functions. I argue that, contrary to all expectations, the lineage still survives in San Tin and that its preservation is part of a trend toward "conservative change" in the village. The discussion then turns to a more general consideration of emigration as an agent of social change in traditional societies. Rather than helping to "modernize" the village, emigration has allowed the Mans to remain relatively aloof from the progressive changes that have swept the New Territories in the last two decades. Furthermore, the villagers have used their new sources of income to express themselves in traditional ways and to preserve a way of life that is rapidly disappearing in other parts of the New Territories.

These conclusions may appear to be incongruous with some of the findings reported in earlier chapters. It is true that emigration has had a dramatic impact on San Tin's productive economy and that certain aspects of the traditional culture, most notably the marriage patterns and the childrearing practices, have changed very rapidly in the last decade. However, the basic attitudes of the Man emigrants and their village-based kinsmen have not changed accordingly. In fact, judging from the way the Mans interact with outsiders both at home and

199

abroad, their perceptions of the world have changed very little.

Anthropologists often have difficulty dealing with the kind of change discussed in this study. The very term "change" invariably carries the connotation of "progress" (which is usually defined as forward movement or gradual advance); and it is often assumed that social change is a unidirectional process. As I demonstrate here, the changes that massive emigration has brought to San Tin and to the members of the Man lineage are not uniformly progressive. I use the term "conservative change" to characterize the reassertion of tradition in San Tin because the process involved is not simply an ossification of the old way of life. Conservative change is a dynamic process by which traditional institutions are modified or given a new form, but their functions remain essentially the same. San Tin has also undergone a number of "progressive" or "modernizing" changes (see page 214), but the most salient trend has been toward conservative change. In order to illustrate the principles involved, the fate of the Man lineage will be examined in detail because this is one of the best examples of the preservation and dynamic modification of a traditional institution in San Tin.

It is my contention that the Chinese lineage is considerably more flexible and adaptable as a social institution than earlier observers have assumed. San Tin is the only large, single-lineage village in the New Territories which no longer has even the vestige of an agricultural economy. Furthermore, it has the highest rate of international emigration among the Colony's Cantonese-speaking lineage communities. Even though the Man lineage has been subjected to a wide variety of "modernizing" influences and has undergone a series of structural modifications, it still plays the central role in the life of the community. The findings of this study, therefore, have a direct bearing on the growing body of literature about the Chinese lineage.[1]

[1] See for example: Ahern 1973; Anderson 1970; Baker 1966, 1968; Brim

LAND AND LINEAGE IN CHINA

Freedman (1958, 1966), Potter (1968, 1970a), Baker (1968), and Brim (1970) all demonstrate convincingly that the lineage system developed to its present extent in South China with the common ownership of property, specifically land, as a bond to retain the allegiance of members. Freedman's view is representative of these studies: "In order to explain why some lineages rather than others managed to hold their members together I have adduced the factor of common property" (1958:128). Landed ancestral estates formed the foci of the lineage segments, and the more land a segment owned in common, the wealthier it became in relation to the others. The profits from the corporately-owned land were used to support the activities of the lineage. These included the maintenance of ancestral halls and lesser "study room" halls, the upkeep of lineage schools, welfare benefits for indigent members, plus a wide range of other activities. The wealthier lineage segments also distributed some of the annual profits to individual members and gave them special rates on segment-owned rental lands. It is little wonder, therefore, that previous field workers in the New Territories have found a correlation between high concentrations of corporately-owned land and strong lineages. As Potter notes, "[c]ommon property was the most important single element maintaining the traditional lineage organization [in China]" (1970a:130).

Perhaps the strongest statement on the relationship between land ownership and lineage maintenance is one made by Anderson, an anthropologist who has worked among the Hong Kong boat people: "Once the keystone of the [lineage] system—the rice paddy—is removed, the system fails. When the more radical step of removing *all* land and agriculture is taken, the system disappears" (Anderson 1970:364, emphasis original). Anderson

1970; Cohen 1969; Freedman 1958, 1966; Fried 1966, 1970; Hu 1948; Kulp 1925; Liu 1959; Pasternak 1968a, 1969, 1972a, 1973; and Potter 1968, 1970a.

goes on to single out the absence of land ownership to explain why the boat people do not possess anything that resembles a lineage system. This is one factor that distinguishes the caste-like boat people from the land-owning *pen-ti* farmers in the Hong Kong region (Anderson 1970:364).

Although the Man lineage did not possess high quality land, it was similar to the other *pen-ti* lineages of the New Territories until the late 1950s. At that crucial point in San Tin's history, the brackish-water paddy land owned by the lineage lost its value and fell into disuse. Consequently, when I first chose San Tin as a research site, I assumed that the decline of land as a major factor in the local economy would be reflected in a simultaneous decline of lineage solidarity and influence. All of the previous research on lineage development in China pointed to this seemingly obvious conclusion. The longer I stayed in San Tin, however, the more evident it became that the Man lineage was not conforming to any preconceived models of change.

THE PROBLEM OF ALLEGIANCE:
LAND SHARES AND SOCIAL TIES

One measure of a kinship organization's "strength" is its ability to retain and command the allegiance of individual members. Over the centuries, the Man lineage has maintained its strength in this regard even though there have always been divisive tendencies within the group. Highly-developed Chinese lineages are characterized by structural tension because of the unequal distribution of power and wealth along segment lines. Unless there are strong moderating forces, these tensions might lead to the dissolution of the lineage into openly hostile groups. San Tin's oral history abounds with stories of fights between the larger segments.[2] In spite of these problems, however, the

[2] For instance, two lineage segments are said to have had a *feng shui*

Man lineage did not dissolve and members of mutually antagonistic segments continued to live together in the same localized
community.

There are two basic reasons for this: First, the lineage was
the most effective unit of protection in a hostile social environment. Ordinary peasants were always better off as members
of strong and populous lineages, no matter how much segmentary tension was involved. The lineage served as the primary
buffer institution between the peasant and the outside world
(see e.g., Freedman 1958:130-131). Besides the necessity of
belonging to a strong protective group, there was an equally
important reason for retaining one's membership in the lineage:
Powerful lineages gave their members economic advantages
that most peasants in Southeastern China did not enjoy.

The economic value of membership in the lineage lay in the
individual shares of various ancestral estates that served as
the focal points of the segments. In some lineages, such as the
one described by Potter (1968:110-112), the annual shares from
ancestral estates constituted an income of considerable proportions for certain members. The amount depended upon one's
position in the segmentary system of the lineage. Segments
with the wealthiest estates and the fewest surviving members
distributed the highest shares. Stronger lineages were able to
provide shares of money that were substantial enough to
constitute an additional incentive for ordinary members to
remain in good standing. Without the promise of some form
of economic advantage, weak lineages could not always control
the actions of their members.

The close relationship between personal profit and lineage
maintenance is demonstrated very effectively by Potter in his
study of the Tang lineage at Ping Shan (1968). Potter shows

---

dispute that lasted until the end of the last century. At one time, these
segments lived in two adjoining subvillages, and it was reportedly unwise
for residents of one to venture beyond the walls of the other (see also Chapter
Two, page 22).

how the Tang lineage is preserved in spite of its members who cannot agree on how to divide up their ancestral estates. Because of its proximity to the booming market town of Yuen Long, the land around Ping Shan has become extremely valuable. If the larger ancestral estates were sold to land speculators, the segments involved would make huge profits. However, in most cases the membership is deadlocked on the decision to sell because certain individuals would make higher profits than others if the segmentary divisions are observed. Those who are members of more populous branches opt for a *per capita* division of profits while the few who are survivors of depleted segments argue that the traditional *per stirpes* pattern of division must be observed (i.e., according to one's segmentary position). Were it not for this disagreement, the ancestral estates in question probably would have been sold and the Tang lineage would no longer have an economic hold on the majority of its members (see Potter 1968:109-116, 168). Based partly on these data from his Ping Shan study, Potter concludes that "the economic attractions of collectively owned ancestral property were necessary and primary factors in maintaining a strong lineage organization" (1970a:129).

DECLINE OF THE MAN ANCESTRAL ESTATES

As noted in Chapter Three, San Tin is less fortunate than Ping Shan because the Man land is not close to any of the booming market towns in the New Territories. This, coupled with the demise of rice farming on the brackish-water fields, means that a large proportion of the land owned by the people of San Tin is no longer profitable. The ancestral estates of the Man lineage have declined accordingly and they do not generate enough income to pay for all of the traditional activities associated with the ancestral cult. Furthermore, even the few segments that retain significant sources of income (e.g., vegetable fields and shops) do not distribute annual shares to members.

The decline of San Tin's agricultural economy has had some unusual effects on the segmentary system of the Man lineage. Wealthier segments lost their independent sources of income when the ancestral estates became worthless and they were no longer able to control the village. The most spectacular example of the changes that occurred is the downfall of a small but wealthy segment known locally as the "Eight Family Branch." Nearly two centuries ago a wealthy merchant purchased a large plot of paddy land, which was held in trust by his descendants. By the early part of this century there were only eight males left in the segment, each receiving one-eighth of the profits from the ancestral estate. The Eight Family Branch became a very wealthy and powerful group in the local community. Since the cessation of rice farming, however, the eight families have not received any income from their estate and they have lost their preeminent position in the community.

The Man lineage is no longer held together by the economic bonds of common interest in the ancestral estates. Similarly, the lineage does not play its traditional role of protecting the villagers from bandits and hostile neighbors. Under these circumstances, one might predict that members would begin to lose interest in the lineage and that it would cease to operate as a significant social institution. This might have happened if San Tin had not become an emigrant community.

EMIGRATION AND THE PRESERVATION OF THE MAN LINEAGE

Even though the ancestral estates have declined, the Man lineage continues to play a central role in the economic life of the village. Indeed, the lineage may now be of even greater value to a higher proportion of ordinary members than it was in the past. Earlier in this study I outlined in some detail how the lineage has become a kind of emigration agency. After the British restaurant boom in the early 1960s, all available resources of the lineage, material and nonmaterial, were mobilized to facilitate the emigration process. Prospective emigrants used lineage leaders as intermediaries in their dealings with the immigration authorities. They travelled on charter flights arranged by a fellow lineage member, and found jobs through their lineage contacts abroad. In effect, membership in the Man lineage became a valuable economic asset because it virtually guaranteed one's employment in the high paying, Man-owned restaurants in Europe.

Instead of causing the anticipated decline of individual allegiance, the recent changes have preserved and strengthened traditional lineage bonds in San Tin. Theoretically, emigration might be seen as a way in which the "traditional" mode of personalistic interaction is replaced by a "modern" trend toward universalistic interpersonal relations. In other words, the old lineage-specific attitudes of "Man versus outsider" would be expected to break down as the emigrants gain experience abroad and learn to interact with a wider range of people. This has not happened among the Man emigrants, however, because they retain their insular ties abroad and have only limited contacts with members of the European host societies. Similarly, the nonemigrant residents of San Tin have not changed their basic attitudes of distrust toward outsiders (in fact, there is good evidence that the feelings of lineage superiority have intensified). The common bonds of lineage membership are still of primary importance to the Mans.

In other New Territories communities, the lineage system is losing much of its control over the lives of individual members. As noted above, Potter found that the Tang lineage of Ping Shan is preserved largely in spite of its members who cannot agree on the proper method of estate division (1968:168). Although the Tang lineage continues to be an important ceremonial organization, it is no longer the primary reference group for the residents of Ping Shan (1968:169-172). Potter maintains that "the villagers have become increasingly involved in groups outside the village, with the result that village society as a reference group for confirming social status has declined in importance" (1968:171). Furthermore, he adds, "Status in the social networks outside the village is now more important than status in the village" (1968:172).

Other single-lineage villages in the New Territories have experienced similar patterns of lineage decline. Speaking of Sheung Shui, Baker observes that: "Material prosperity, the influence of the West, and the swamping effect of immigration [refugees from China] have combined to set in motion a process of deterioration which threatens to annihilate the [Liao] lineage as an effective unit of social organization" (1968:207).

Unlike the Mans, the Tangs and the Liaos appear not to have made use of their lineage contacts outside their own communities. *While San Tin was becoming a specialized community focused on a single economic niche, the other lineage villages were diversifying their occupational structures.* Many of the Ping Shan residents, for instance, branched out into trades and occupations in which the Tang lineage had no previous connections (see Potter 1968: Tables 4 and 5). *The Man lineage is the only kinship organization of its kind in the New Territories which has retained a virtual monopoly on the livelihood of its members.* By using their traditional lineage contacts, the emigrants are able to find better jobs abroad than they could locate on their own in the Colony.

Besides the economic advantages outlined above, the lineage serves as an important security mechanism for the Man emigrants. The uncertain nature of emigrant work in alien cultures reinforces the need for a secure and significant group at home. Unlike the residents of Ping Shan, the majority of the Mans consider their status within the lineage to be more important than any status they might derive from outside social networks. Their primary reference group is still the Man lineage and their membership in it is extremely important to them. Furthermore, as demonstrated in Chapter Seven, the prolonged absence of the emigrants does not prevent them from playing an active role in lineage affairs. They also spend a great deal of money to help finance public works sponsored by the lineage. It is clear from their actions that the emigrants and their village-based kinsmen are strongly motivated to uphold the honor and prestige of the lineage.

CHANGES IN LINEAGE STRUCTURE

As a consequence of its unique situation, therefore, the Man lineage continues to be an active and influential social institution. This is not to imply, of course, that the lineage has been preserved in its original form without any structural changes. In fact, San Tin is being converted into a new kind of lineage community, one in which the internal segments have ceased to be of primary importance to the members.[3] As noted earlier,

[3] This raises a fundamental question about the nature of the lineage in San Tin. One of the defining characteristics of powerful lineage systems in South China is the presence of strong, active segments (see e.g., Freedman 1958:131-133). The Man lineage no longer fits this kind of definition, but by many other measures of "strength" it continues to function like a traditional lineage of considerable power and influence. San Tin has certainly not become an amorphous community, loosely organized around the bonds of common residence. As long as members find their lineage to be economically and socially advantageous, San Tin will continue to be one of the most cohesive "localized lineage communities" in the New Territories.

In speaking of the recent changes in rural Hong Kong, Freedman notes that: "None of this means that all, or most, lineages in the New Territories are dead or moribund. They are being transformed, and the point at which we shall no longer be able to recognize them as versions of the 'traditional' southeastern Chinese lineage is yet far off" (1966:172-173). The modification of the Man lineage discussed in this case study is only one of the changes the traditional lineage system has undergone in recent years.

the segmentary system of the lineage has been drastically altered by the decline of the ancestral estates and by the general availability of high paying jobs abroad. Most of the segments in the Man lineage have lost their sources of income and may cease to operate as closely knit organizations based on the ties of shared property.

It is too early to determine if the restaurateurs or their sons will continue the traditional practice of establishing ancestral estates. To do so, the emigrant would have to convert the restaurant wealth into some form of permanent (and profitable) property and set it aside for the exclusive benefit of his descendants. The property would then become the material focus of an incipient segment within the lineage. To my knowledge, none of the restaurateurs has made a conscious effort to found new estates; and unless this happens, it is doubtful that the segmentary divisions of the lineage will continue to be of major importance to the villagers.

However, at the highest level, the localized lineage of San Tin retains much of its traditional power and influence over individual members. The lineage continues to act in unison as a highly organized kinship group in its dealings with the outside world. It also sponsors a wide range of communal activities which are the hallmarks of a strong lineage system in China. Although the brackish-water fields no longer provide a source of income, the Man lineage as a whole (symbolized by the Main Ancestral Hall) owns a number of lucrative shops and commercial lots that help support its activities. The Main Ancestral Hall also levies an individual tax of between HK$5 and HK$10 on all males in the lineage whenever there is need for a large sum of money (see page 138). As a consequence, the lineage is able to maintain its traditional activities at the highest level of agnation while the once powerful segments are gradually becoming inactive.

From an outsider's perspective, the Man lineage might appear to be operating much as it did during traditional times. The lineage still conducts the highly visible rituals associated with the worship of the first ancestor to settle in the New Territories region. Every year on Double Nine (the ninth day of the ninth lunar month) the Mans gather at the grave of the founder, which is located in the hills near Castle Peak Bay, approximately twenty miles away from San Tin. This is an occasion for the ostentatious display of lineage wealth because the long procession of trucks, minibuses, private automobiles, and taxis passes two market towns and several rival villages on the way to the grave. In traditional times, the graves of the larger segment founders were also visited with similar fanfare by their descendants; now all but two are barely noticed.[4] The visit to the grave of the main founder, however, still draws nearly one thousand people and is a very impressive spectacle indeed (see Baker 1968:69-70 and Potter 1970a:126-127 for good descriptions of the same event in other lineages). This commemorative gathering is an important communal act which reinforces the solidarity of the group and symbolizes to outsiders that the Man lineage is still a powerful institution.

Other evidence of lineage activity at the highest level is not hard to find in San Tin. In 1968, the Mans raised over HK$24,000 in a membership subscription drive to help defray the costs of a major renovation of their Main Ancestral Hall. The reconstructed hall is a physical monument to the members' continuing concern for the lineage. It stands out in striking

---

[4] These segments have retained some valuable units of property (e.g., shops and plots of land rented as poultry farms) that continue to produce enough income to support the expensive worship ceremonies. But even these segments have been drastically reduced by the devaluation of land around San Tin. Part of the worship ceremony at the grave is a division of ritual pork. In the past, one of these segments gave each member up to three catties of pork twice a year, plus double shares for elders (*fu lao*, age 61 or older) and newly-born males (*hsin ting*). The same segment now has only enough funds to provide one-half catty for each elder once a year. The pork shares are especially important because they symbolize membership in the group and a communion with lineage ancestors. When a segment ceases to distribute pork, it is indeed in serious financial trouble.

contrast to the rundown appearance of San Tin's four branch ancestral halls that represent the major segmentary divisions. The lineage is also directly responsible for the expensive renovation of San Tin's Empress of Heaven Temple discussed in Chapter Seven. The temple, which is owned and managed by the estate of the Main Ancestral Hall, probably would not have been rebuilt if it had been independent of the lineage. Besides the renovation activities, the lineage supports San Tin's primary school by paying for approximately half of its operating expenses through a special fund (the government handles the rest, plus most of the teachers' salaries). The lineage also hires a caretaker for the Main Ancestral Hall and provides an independent income for the lineage master (*tsu chang*), who is the ceremonial leader of the entire community.

THE CHINESE LINEAGE:
AN ADAPTABLE SOCIAL INSTITUTION

It is clear that the Man lineage continues to operate as an effective social institution at the highest level of agnation, even though its internal segmentation is rapidly breaking down. This finding suggests that the Chinese lineage system itself is more flexible and adaptable than ordinarily assumed. The San Tin data show that as long as members derive some significant form of economic or social advantage from lineage membership, they will continue to pay primary allegiance to the lineage. In most cases the motivating force has been an interest in the ancestral estates owned in common by the segments. The lineage, of course, could not have developed in Southeastern China to its present extent without the bonds of shared property to hold the members together. This point is not disputed. However, once the system is well established, the property bonds may not be essential to the maintenance of the localized lineage in all cases.

This may help explain why the lineage and vestiges of lineage activity continue to be subjects of criticism in China, even after twenty years of land reform.[5] Although the attacks in the mass media should not be construed as evidence that the lineage is still functioning in traditional form in China, one might expect it to have subsided as an issue of concern after so many years. In general, most observers have maintained that land reform was the critical point at which the lineage began to dissolve in China. For instance, according to Potter, "the fate of lineage organization in Communist China suggests that the confiscation of lineage property during the land reform was probably crucial in the destruction of lineage organization there" (1970a:130). C. K. Yang notes in his book *A Chinese Village in Early Communist Transition* that land reform and the class struggles associated with it "seriously weakened the solidarity of the [lineage]" in Nanching Village (1959:179). He continues (1959:180):

> Our observations in Nanching confirmed the impression that the clan [lineage] was unlikely ever to recover its traditional importance in the operation of village life, and that the whole kinship framework of collective action, supported by its traditional status system, would diminish in strength while the universalistic type of political and social order would increase its influence.

I agree with these views of land reform in China, but it is my contention that the key factor is economic and social advantage—not just land. As Yang and others point out, land reform involved much more than the confiscation and redistribution of land concentrations. It was a systematic attack on the central features of the traditional rural society (see also

[5] Criticisms of the lineage, or its remnants, continue to appear in the Chinese press (see, e.g., *People's Daily*, Peking, 21 January 1970; *SCMP* 4589).

Vogel 1969:91-124). In contemporary China, therefore, it is unlikely that the lineage is capable of maintaining itself in even a modified form,[6] but it is possible that the social bonds of common lineage membership may still function to give certain peasants advantages over others.

The Man lineage has proven to be a remarkably adaptable social institution. It continues to thrive as an emigration agency without offering the traditional shared property incentive to members. It is too early to speculate whether the lineage will survive in its present form because the conversion to emigration in San Tin occurred less than two decades ago. The evidence is sufficient, however, to conclude that the *social bonds* of the lineage are strong enough to withstand a considerable amount of economic change and social pressure.

EMIGRATION AND SOCIAL CHANGE

It is apparent from this study that emigration is a very complex, if not paradoxical, agent of social change. Instead of contributing to the demise of the Man lineage, emigration has had the reverse effect of preserving the traditional organization in a modified form. As I hope to demonstrate, emigration has helped maintain many other aspects of San Tin's traditional culture besides the lineage.

These findings run counter to the widely accepted view that emigration is a force for "modernizing" change in peasant societies. For instance, according to Chen Ta in his *Emigrant Communities in South China*, returning workers often become

---

[6] Freedman postulates that certain production teams or brigades could have been composed of small lineage fragments after land reform, but he questions how "lineage-like" these units might be (1966:176-177). He argues in a very convincing way that the lineage *organization* itself would probably not survive because "it is unlikely that [the members] would be able for long to escape the sanctions of a vigilant political apparatus designed to repress unwanted social differentiation and dangerous local power" (Freedman 1966:177).

agents of progressive change who bring new ways of life to their home villages (1939:128). Most of Chen's discussion of change relates to the impact these returnees have had on the material culture (pp. 195ff), but he also maintains that emigration has changed "the central features of the social system" in the communities under investigation (p. 143). He implies throughout the book that the traditional way of life in parts of South China has been positively influenced by Western concepts of education, communication, and social welfare brought back by the more enlightened emigrants.

Chen's views of emigration as a force for progressive change may in part be due to the nature of his sample, which appears to have been largely upper-class, Nan Yang merchants of considerable wealth. Whatever the reason, his conclusions are difficult to support. Several years after the book was published, Francis L. K. Hsu reviewed Chen's original data and came to opposite conclusions. Hsu held that "South-Seas emigration has. . . .not only had no effects opposed to the traditional ways of life, but has caused them to be expressed with greater clarity and force" (1945:48). The present case study of San Tin lends further support to Hsu's critical position, and it shows that emigration is often overrated as an agent of modernizing change.

It is undeniable that San Tin has undergone some changes in recent years which have had a "modernizing" effect on the community. These are basically the same kinds of changes that Chen Ta outlined in his earlier study of South China. They include an introduction of modern consumer items, a change in clothing and styles, an interest in modern health methods, and a growing knowledge of the world beyond the New Territories. Although these changes are important, they are characteristic of many nonemigrant communities in the Colony as well. It should *not* be assumed that emigration has brought San Tin into the realm of the cosmopolitan, Western-oriented culture that is evident in parts of urban Hong Kong. Most of the Mans still interpret these changes and amenities in terms of their traditional culture.

One of the best examples is the change in world view discussed in Chapter Nine. The Mans are now conscious of major world events and they take an interest in developments beyond their intermediate marketing region. Ordinarily, a change of this nature might be interpreted as evidence of modernization and growing sophistication. Both Amyot (1960:29-30) and Chen Ta (1939:143-194) maintain that emigrant communities are more progressive and sophisticated than nonemigrant communities in China. My own research in the New Territories does not support this conclusion. The Mans may be wealthier than many of their neighbors and they certainly know more about immigration policies, but it does not follow that they are necessarily more sophisticated than residents of nearby villages. In fact, the people of San Tin are notorious for their conservatism and for their "backward" views about outsiders. The expanding knowledge of the outside world has not altered the fundamental insularity of the Man lineage.

The emigrants themselves are not particularly interested in changing San Tin into a "progressive" community because they have had enough of the modern world abroad. When they retire, the restaurant workers are concerned primarily about personal security and they do everything in their power to recreate the idealized village of their youth. One way to do this, they believe, is to invest in traditional ventures such as the renovation projects and the public celebrations. Few of them choose to invest their money in productive enterprises that might have a modernizing impact on the village (e.g., local transportation facilities, capital-intensive industries, or service institutions). Rather than acting as *change agents*, the retired emigrants are often among the most enthusiastic proponents of traditional values in San Tin (see also, Newell 1962:21).

CONSERVATIVE CHANGE

The outside sources of money and the steady remittance incomes have allowed the Mans to emulate some of the highest ideals of their cultural heritage. In traditional times, a community in this part of South China validated its status in the local region by sponsoring ostentatious celebrations and public displays of wealth. The temple renovation extravaganza and the other celebrations discussed in Chapter Seven are expressions of traditional values, which continue to have meaning in San Tin. With the financial support of the emigrants, the Mans are now able to produce bigger and more elaborate public displays than they ever dreamed possible in the past. The villagers could use some of these funds for less conspicuous public endeavors, such as the extension of running water into every home, but they prefer to invest in large public buildings and celebrations.

The Mans are also preserving elements of the traditional culture that are no longer found in other parts of the Colony. San Tin is one of the few communities in the New Territories which still follows the traditional "rocket ceremony" during its annual celebration of the Empress of Heaven's birthday.[7] Even though the rocket ceremony is dangerous and illegal, the Mans have refused to change this part of the celebration. As

[7] Every year in San Tin, small voluntary associations known as *hua p'ao hui* ("Flower Cannon Society") gather at the local Tin Hau Temple to celebrate the patron goddess's birthday in the fourth lunar month. The highlight of the festivities is a competition during which the members of the societies fight over coins fired from specially constructed, ritual rockets (actually small cannon). The youth who catches the coin (one per rocket) receives a prize and a *hua p'ao* altar made of colorful paper which becomes the focus of a new association for the forthcoming year. In San Tin there are ten such associations, ten *hua p'ao* altars, and hence ten rockets each year. Since the rocket ceremony is dangerous and leads to many fights, it is outlawed in the Colony. Most other Tin Hau birthday celebrations in Hong Kong substitute a lottery for the old competition (see also Johnson 1971:141-142).

a result, San Tin has become a minor tourist attraction for some of the Colony's urban Chinese middle class who want their children to see the observances in the full traditional form. (During the 1970 celebration, I overheard a stranger explaining the proceedings to his urbanite son: "Now watch closely, this is how your grandfather did it.") The elaborate celebrations associated with the temple renovation discussed in Chapter Seven also drew a number of Chinese tourists from the city of Kowloon.

These developments have a special irony because the large festivals and public displays are meant to attract the attention of the other New Territories villagers, not the handful of urban visitors that happen to pass by. The Mans still consider themselves to be in competition with their traditional lineage rivals in nearby villages. Their old rivals are certainly impressed by ostentatious celebrations like the 1970 opera and temple renovation, but they are less inclined to treat these displays as threats to their own status, as they might have in the past. The Mans, in effect, are competing for status in terms of the traditional culture, but they are playing the game alone.

This kind of conservatism appears to be characteristic of emigrant communities all over the world, not just in China. Perhaps the best statement on this matter is made by Gonzalez in her study of Black Carib household structure: "[The patterns of migratory wage labor] may ... be viewed as mechanisms for *maintaining* a traditional society with only slight modifications long after the initial impact of industrialization has hit the larger system of which that society is a part" (Gonzalez 1969:xv, emphasis original). In Lebanon, another country with a long tradition of international emigration, the increasing wealth of emigrant communities reinforces the ideal patterns of female seclusion (Sweet 1967:183). Furthermore, "apart from drawing the interest of the stay-at-homes beyond their immediate locality," the Lebanese emigrants studied by Gulick did not introduce significant modernizing changes to their home communities (Gulick 1955:62). In a recent study of a Lebanese emigrant community, Ralph Lewis found a pattern of cultural persistence: "In spite of sustained permanent emigration, [the home village] remains strongly conservative, traditional, and still uses the old mechanisms of individual integration" (R. Lewis 1968:4855-B).

A similar pattern is found in the emigrant communities on Montserrat, an island in the West Indies that sends a large number of emigrants to Britain (Philpott 1970:18, 1973). According to Philpott, "returned migrants produce very little social or economic innovation" in Montserrat (1973:190). The conservatism of many rural-urban migrants in Africa is well known (see e.g., Plotnicov 1970, Van Velsen 1960:265); and in pre-Revolution Russia, labor out-migration "led to the preservation of the traditional structure, even when its agricultural base had largely disappeared" (Dunn and Dunn 1967:38).

Other examples could be cited, but it is enough to note that the pattern of conservatism discussed in this study is not unique to San Tin. While the rest of the New Territories has undergone a great deal of modernizing change in recent years, the Mans have been able to keep themselves relatively aloof. Instead of modernizing, the villagers cling to the shadows of their past history. The result is a pattern of lagging emulation in which the Mans seek to attain high status for themselves and for their community by upholding a way of life that is no longer meaningful or important to large numbers of New Territories residents. The festivals, operas, public work projects, and conspicuous displays of wealth have indeed given the community a new measure of prestige, but San Tin is most admired by the people of Hong Kong as an anacronistic holdout in a rapidly changing social system.

GLOSSARY I

Mandarin Terms

ch'u tsu	出族	Nan Yang	南洋
Chungshan	中山	pen-ti	本地
fang	房	Szu Yi	四邑
feng shui	風水	shu fang	書房
fu lao	父老(佬)	su po hsiung ti	叔伯兄弟
hsi min	細民	ta chiao	打醮
hsin t'ien	新田	*ta fu ti	大夫弟
hsin ting	新丁	ta tsu t'ang	大祖堂
hua ch'iao	華僑	tou	斗
hua p'ao	花炮	t'ien hou	天后
hua p'ao hui	花炮會	tsu chang	族長
k'ai teng	開燈	tsu p'u	族譜
k'e chia (Hakka)	客家	tsu t'ang	祖堂
Lung Tou	隆都	yang lou	洋樓

*Alternative pronunciation, *tai fu ti*.

219

GLOSSARY II

Cantonese Terms

fauh jai	埠仔	san nguk	新屋
ha fu	下伕	san tin*	新田
haahm mun	鹹滿	san tin* yahn	新田人
haahm tin*	鹹田	sung	餸
heung ha	鄉下	Tin Hau (hauh)	天后
huhng mai	紅米	Tohng Yahn Gaai	唐人街
ngoi leih yahn	外來人	wohng sing	皇城

*According to the Yale romanization system, the term
for "field" should be *tihn*, indicating a low tone.
However, in order to avoid confusion, it is romanized
to be consistent with standard place-name usage in
Hong Kong (hence it is *san tin*, not *san tihn*).

GLOSSARY III

Surnames Used

Cheung	張	Man (Wen)	文
Hau	侯	Pang	彭
Lam	林	Poon	潘
Liao	廖	Tang	鄧

BIBLIOGRAPHY

Ahern, Emily M.
  1973 *The Cult of the Dead in a Chinese Village.* Stanford: Stanford University Press.
Aijmer, L. G.
  1967 Expansion and extension in Hakka society. *Journal of the Hong Kong Branch of the Royal Asiatic Society* 7:42-79.
Akers-Jones, David
  1964 Report on a visit to San Tin village complex. IN *Aspects of Social Organization in the New Territories,* pp. 43-44. Royal Asiatic Society, Hong Kong Branch.
Amyot, Jacques
  1960 *The Chinese Community of Manila: A Study of Adaptation of Chinese Familism to the Philippine Environment.* Philippine Studies Program Research Series, no. 2. University of Chicago.
Anderson, Eugene N., Jr.
  1970 Lineage atrophy in Chinese society. *American Anthropologist* 72:363-365.
  1972 *Essays on South China's Boat People.* Asian Folklore and Social Life Monographs, no. 29. Taipei: Orient Cultural Service.
Baker, Hugh D. R.
  1966 The five great clans of the New Territories. *Journal of the Hong Kong Branch of the Royal Asiatic Society* 6:25-47.
  1968 *A Chinese Lineage Village: Sheung Shui.* Stanford: Stanford University Press.
Barnett, K. M. A.
  1964 Hong Kong before the Chinese. *Journal of the Hong Kong Branch of the Royal Asiatic Society* 4:42-67.

Benedict, Burton
  1968 Family firms and economic development. *Southwestern Journal of Anthropology* 24:1-19.
Bose, Ashish
  1971 The urbanization process in South and Southeast Asia. IN *Urbanization and National Development*, ed. by Leo Jakobson and Ved Prakash. Beverly Hills: Sage Publications.
Bracey, Dorothy
  1967 *The Effects of Emigration on a Hakka Village*. Ph.D. Dissertation in Anthropology, Harvard University.
Brim, John A.
  1970 *Local Systems and Modernizing Change in the New Territories of Hong Kong*. Ph.D. Dissertation in Anthropology, Stanford University. Ann Arbor:University Microfilms, no. 71-12,862.
Broady, Maurice
  1955 The social adjustment of Chinese immigrants in Liverpool. *The Sociological Review* 3:65-75.
  1958 The Chinese in Great Britain. IN *Colloquium on Overseas Chinese*, ed. by Morton H. Fried. New York: Institute of Pacific Relations.
Campbell, Persia Crawford
  1923 *Chinese Coolie Emigration*. London: P. S. King and Son, Ltd.
Census and Statistics Department
  1972 *Hong Kong Population and Housing Census: 1971 Main Report*. Hong Kong Government Press.
Chen Han-seng
  1936 *Agrarian Problems in Southernmost China*. Shanghai: Kelly and Walsh, Ltd.
Chen Ta
  1923 *Chinese Migrations, with Special Reference to Labor Conditions*. Bulletin of the United States Bureau of Labor Statistics, Miscellaneous Series, no. 340.
  1939 *Emigrant Communities in South China*. Shanghai: Kelly and Walsh, Ltd.
Cheng Huan
  1972 For Overseas Chinese, a return to the "good life." *Far Eastern Economic Review* 75 (3):14-15.

Cheung Kam-ch'uen
1970a History of the first Chinese emigrants: notes. (In Chinese). *Wah Kiu Yat Bou*, Hong Kong, 21 July 1970.
1970b Historical background of Chinese emigrants in England. (In Chinese). *Wah Kiu Yat Bou*, Hong Kong, 22 July 1970.

Chiu Tze-nang
1964 Land use problems in the extreme east of the New Territories. IN *Land Use Problems in Hong Kong*, ed. by S. G. Davis. Hong Kong: Hong Kong University Press.

Cohen, Myron L.
1968 The Hakka or "guest people": Dialect as a sociocultural variable in Southeastern China. *Ethnohistory* 15:237-292.
1969 Agnatic kinship in South Taiwan. *Ethnology* 8:167-182.

Coughlin, Richard J.
1960 *Double Identity: The Chinese in Modern Thailand*. Hong Kong: Hong Kong University Press.

Crissman, Lawrence W.
1967 The segmentary structure of urban Overseas Chinese communities. *Man* 2:185-204.

Culin, Stewart
1891 *The Gambling Games of the Chinese in America*. Publications of the University of Pennsylvania. Series in Philology, Literature, and Archaeology, vol. I, no. 4.

da Silva, Armando
1972 *Tai Yu Shan: Traditional Ecological Adaptation in a South Chinese Island*. Asian Folklore and Social Life Monographs, no. 32. Taipei: Orient Cultural Service.

Davis, S. G.
1964 Rural-urban migration in Hong Kong and the New Territories. IN *Land Use Problems in Hong Kong*, ed. by S. G. Davis. Hong Kong: Hong Kong University Press.

Diamond, Norma
1969 *K'un Shen: A Taiwanese Village*. New York: Holt, Rinehart and Winston.

Douglass, William A.
1970 Peasant emigrants: Reactors or actors. IN *Migration and Anthropology*, ed. by Robert F. Spencer. Proceedings of the 1970 Annual Spring Meeting of the American Ethnological

Society. Seattle: University of Washington Press.

Dunn, Stephen P., and Ethel Dunn

1967 *The Peasants of Central Russia*. New York: Holt, Rinehart and Winston.

Elliott, Alan J. A.

1955 *Chinese Spirit-Medium Cults in Singapore*. London School of Economics Monographs on Social Anthroplogy, no. 14.

Endacott, G. B.

1964 *A History of Hong Kong*. London: Oxford University Press.

Fei Hsiao-t'ung.

1939 *Peasant Life in China: A Field Study of Country Life in the Yangtze Valley*. London: Routledge & Kegan Paul, Ltd.

Fei Hsiao-t'ung, and Chang Chih-i

1948 *Earthbound China: A Study of Rural Economy in Yunnan*. London: Routledge & Kegan Paul, Ltd.

Feng Rui, and Yung Ping-hang

1931 A general descriptive survey of the Honan Island village community. *Lingnan Science Journal* (Canton) 10(2-3). (Cited in Freedman 1966:188).

FitzGerald, C. P.

1972 *The Southern Expansion of the Chinese People*. New York: Praeger Publishers.

Foster, George M.

1964 Treasure tales and the image of the static economy in a Mexican peasant community. *Journal of American Folklore* 77:39-44.

1965 Peasant society and the image of limited good. *American Anthropologist* 67:293-315.

1967 *Tzintzuntzan: Mexican Peasants in a Changing World*. Boston: Little, Brown and Company.

Freedman, Maurice

1957 *Chinese Family and Marriage in Singapore*. Colonial Research Studies, no. 20. London: Her Majesty's Stationery Office.

1958 *Lineage Organization in Southeastern China*. London School of Economics Monographs on Social Anthropology, no. 18. London: Athlone Press.

1959   The handling of money: A note on the background to the economic sophistication of Overseas Chinese. *Man* 59:64-65.

1960   Immigrants and associations: Chinese in nineteenth century Singapore. *Comparative Studies in Society and History* 3:25-48.

1963   *A Report on Social Research in the New Territories*. Privately published in Hong Kong (mimeo).

1966   *Chinese Lineage and Society: Fukien and Kwangtung*. London School of Economics Monographs on Social Anthropology, no. 33. London: Athlone Press.

Freedman, Maurice, and Marjorie Topley

1961   Religion and social realignment among the Chinese in Singapore. *British Journal of Sociology* 14:3-23.

Fried, Morton H.

1954   Community studies in China. *Far Eastern Quarterly* 14:11-36.

1966   Some political aspects of clanship in a modern Chinese city. IN *Political Anthropology*, ed. by Marc J. Swartz, Victor W. Turner, and Arthur Tuden. Chicago: Aldine.

1970   Clans and lineages: How to tell them apart and why—with special reference to Chinese society. *Bulletin of the Institute of Ethnology, Academia Sinica* (Taiwan) 29(1):11-36.

Fried, Morton H. (Editor)

1958   *Colloquium on Overseas Chinese*. New York: Institute of Pacific Relations.

Gallin, Bernard

1963   Chinese peasant values toward the land. IN *Proceedings of the 1963 Annual Spring Meeting of the American Ethnological Society*. Seattle: University of Washington Press.

1966   *Hsin Hsing, Taiwan: A Chinese Village in Change*. Berkeley: University of California Press.

Geddes, W. R.

1963   *Peasant Life in Communist China*. Society for Applied Anthropology, Monograph no. 6.

Geertz, Clifford

1963   *Agricultural Involution: The Process of Ecological Change in Indonesia*. Berkeley: University of California Press.

Glick, Clarence E.
   1938 *The Chinese Migrant in Hawaii*. Ph.D. Dissertation in Sociology, University of Chicago. (Microfilm).
Gonzalez, Nancie L. Solien
   1961 Family organization in five types of migratory wage labor. *American Anthropologist* 63:1264-1280.
   1969 *Black Carib Household Structure: A Study of Migration and Modernization*. American Ethnological Society Monograph no. 48. Seattle: University of Washington Press.
Goodstadt, Leo F.
   1970 The fixers. *Far Eastern Economic Review*, 30 July 1970, pp. 21-23.
Grant, Charles J.
   1960 *The Soils and Agriculture of Hong Kong*. Hong Kong: Hong Kong Government Press.
   1964 The extension of the arable area in Hong Kong. IN *Land Use Problems in Hong Kong*, ed. by S. G. Davis. Hong Kong: Hong Kong University Press.
Grist, D. H.
   1959 *Rice*. New York: John Wiley and Sons, Inc.
Groves, R. G.
   1969 Militia, market and lineage: Chinese resistance to the occupation of Hong Kong's New Territories in 1899. *Journal of the Hong Kong Branch of the Royal Asiatic Society* 9:31-64.
Gulick, John
   1955 *Social Structure and Culture Change in a Lebanese Village*. Viking Fund Publications in Anthropology, no. 21.
Hanks, Lucien M.
   1972 *Rice and Man: Agricultural Ecology in Southeast Asia*. Chicago: Aldine.
Hayes, James
   1970 A casualty of the Cultural Revolution. *Journal of the Hong Kong Branch of the Royal Asiatic Society* 10:196-197.
Hsiao Kung-chuan
   1960 *Rural China: Imperial Control in the Nineteenth Century*. Seattle: University of Washington Press.

Hsu, Francis L. K.

 1945 The influence of South-Seas emigration on certain Chinese
       provinces. *Far Eastern Quarterly* 5:47-59.

Hu Hsien-chin

 1948 *The Common Descent Group in China and its Functions.*
       Viking Fund Publications in Anthropology, no. 10.

Immigration Report

       Annual Departmental Reports. Director of Immigration,
       Hong Kong Government Press.

Jansen, Clifford J.

 1970 Migration: A sociological problem. IN *Readings in the
       Sociology of Migration,* ed. by C. J. Jansen. Oxford: Perga-
       mon Press.

Johnson, Graham E.

 1971 From rural committee to spirit medium cult: Voluntary
       associations in the development of a Chinese town. *Contribu-
       tions to Asian Studies* 1:123-143.

Jordan, David K.

 1972 *Gods, Ghosts, and Ancestors: The Folk Religion of a
       Taiwanese Village.* Berkeley: University of California Press.

Kulp, Daniel M.

 1925 *Country Life in South China.* New York: Columbia Universi-
       ty Press.

Labour and Mines Report

       Annual Departmental Reports. Commissioner of Labour and
       Mines, Hong Kong Government Press.

Labour Report

       Annual Departmental Reports. Commissioner of Labour,
       Hong Kong Government Press. (Supersedes Labour and
       Mines Report).

Lai Chuen-yan

 1964 Rice cultivation, distribution and production in Hong Kong.
       IN *Land Use Problems in Hong Kong,* ed. by S. G. Davis.
       Hong Kong: Hong Kong University Press.

Land Use

 1968 *Land Utilization in Hong Kong as at 31st March 1966.* Hong
       Kong: Hong Kong Government Press.

Lee, Rose Hum
1960 *The Chinese in the United States of America.* Hong Kong: Hong Kong University Press.

Lewis, Oscar
1951 *Life in a Mexican Village: Tepoztlan Restudied.* Urbana: University of Illinois Press.

Lewis, Ralph K.
1968 (Abstract of:) Hadchite: A Study of Emigration in a Lebanese Village. Ph.D. Dissertation in Anthropology, Columbia University. *Dissertation Abstracts International* 28:4854-B. (Ann Arbor: University Microfilms, no. 68-8593.)

Lin, D. Y.
1957 *Report of a Trial Survey of the Economic Conditions of Sixty Families in the New Territories of Hong Kong.* Mimeo. Chung Chi College, Chinese University of Hong Kong.

Liu Hui-chen Wang
1959 *The Traditional Chinese Clan Rules.* Association for Asian Studies Monograph no. 7. Locust Valley, New York: J. J. Augustin, Inc.

Lockhart, Stewart
1900 Report on the New Territory at Hong Kong, 1900; Appendix III, Memorandum on land. IN *Hong Kong Sessional Papers.* Hong Kong Government Press.

Ma, Ronald A., and Edward F. Szczepanik
1955 *The National Income of Hong Kong, 1947-1950.* Hong Kong: Hong Kong University Press.

MacDonald, J. S.
1956 Italy's rural social structure and emigration. *Occidente* 12(5):437-455.

MacDonald, John S., and Beatrice K. MacDonald
1964 Migration, ethnic neighborhood formation and social networks. *Milbank Memorial Fund Quarterly* 42(1):82-97.

Mak Shui-hung
1964 The fish ponds and oyster beds in the Wang Chau area, Hong Kong. IN *Land Use Problems in Hong Kong*, ed. by S. G. Davis. Hong Kong: Hong Kong University Press.

McGee, T. G.
  1971 Catalysts or cancers? The role of cities in Asian society. IN
         Urbanization and National Development, ed. by Leo Jakob-
         son and Ved Prakash. Beverly Hills: Sage Publications.
Myrdal, Jan
  1965 *Report from a Chinese Village.* New York: Pantheon Books.
Nelson, H. G. H.
  1969 The Chinese descent system and the occupancy level of
         village houses. *Journal of the Hong Kong Branch of the
         Royal Asiatic Society* 9:113-123.
Newell, William H.
  1962 *Treacherous River, A Study of Rural Chinese in North
         Malaya.* Kuala Lumpur: University of Malaya Press.
New Territories Report
         Annual Departmental Reports. District Commissioner of the
         New Territories, Hong Kong Government Press.
Ng Kwee-choo
  1968 *The Chinese in London.* Monograph of the Institute of Race
         Relations. London: Oxford University Press.
Ng, Ronald
  1964 Economic life and the family. IN *Aspects of Social Organi-
         zation in the New Territories.* Royal Asiatic Society, Hong
         Kong Branch.
Owen, Nicholas C.
  1971 Economic policy in Hong Kong. IN *Hong Kong: The Indus-
         trial Colony,* ed. by Keith Hopkins. London: Oxford Univer-
         sity Press.
Pasternak, Burton
  1968a Agnatic atrophy in a Formosan village. *American Anthro-
         pologist* 70:93-96.
  1968b Social consequences of equalizing irrigation access. *Human
         Organization* 27:332-343.
  1969 The role of the frontier in Chinese lineage development.
         Journal of Asian Studies 28:551-561.
  1972a *Kinship and Community in Two Chinese Villages.* Stanford:
         Stanford University Press.

1972b The sociology of irrigation: Two Chinese villages. IN *Economic Organization in Chinese Society*, ed. by W. E. Willmott. Stanford: Stanford University Press.

1973 Chinese tale-telling tombs. *Ethnology* 12:259-273.

Patterson, Sheila
1969 *Immigration and Race Relations in Britain, 1960-1967*. London: Oxford University Press.

Pearson, George A. and Alvin D. Ayers
1960 *Rice as a Crop for Salt-affected Soil in Process of Reclamation*. United States Department of Agriculture, Agriculture Research Service, Production Research Report no. 43.

Peterson, I.
1957 Co-operatives and marketing. IN *Hong Kong Business Symposium*, ed. by J. M. Braga. Hong Kong: South China Morning Post, Ltd.

Philpott, Stuart B.
1970 The implications of migration for sending societies: Some theoretical considerations. IN *Migration and Anthropology*, ed. by Robert F. Spencer. Proceedings of the 1970 Annual Spring Meeting of the American Ethnological Society. Seattle: University of Washington Press.

1973 *West Indian Migration: The Montserrat Case*. London School of Economics Monographs on Social Anthropology, no. 47. London: Athlone Press.

Plotnicov, Leonard
1970 Rural-urban communications in contemporary Nigeria: The persistence of traditional social institutions. *Journal of Asian and African Studies* 5:66-82.

Podmore, David
1971 The population of Hong Kong. IN *Hong Kong: The Industrial Colony*, ed. by Keith Hopkins. London: Oxford University Press.

Police Report
Annual Departmental Report. Commissioner of Police, Hong Kong Government Press.

Potter, Jack M.
   1968   *Capitalism and the Chinese Peasant: Social and Economic Change in a Hong Kong Village.* Berkeley: University of California Press.
   1969   The structure of rural Chinese society in the New Territories. IN *Hong Kong: A Society in Transition,* ed. by Ian C. Jarvie and Joseph Agassi. New York: Praeger Publishers.
   1970a Land and Lineage in traditional China. IN *Family and Kinship in Chinese Society,* ed. by Maurice Freedman. Stanford: Stanford University Press.
   1970b Wind, water, bones, and souls: The religious world of the Cantonese peasant. *Journal of Oriental Studies* 8:139-153.

Pratt, Jean A.
   1960   Emigration and unilineal descent groups: A study of marriage in a Hakka village in the New Territories, Hong Kong. *Eastern Anthropologist* 13:147-158.

Purcell, Victor
   1965   *The Chinese in Southeast Asia.* Second edition. London: Oxford University Press.

SCMP
   1970   *Survey of the China Mainland Press.* American Consulate Translation Service, Hong Kong.

Siu, Paul C. F.
   1952   The sojourner. *American Journal of Sociology* 58:34-44.

Skinner, G. William
   1957   *Chinese Society in Thailand: An Analytical History.* Ithaca: Cornell University Press.
   1958   *Leadership and Power in the Chinese Community of Thailand.* Ithaca: Cornell University Press.
   1964   Marketing and social structure in rural China, Part I. *Journal of Asian Studies* 24:3-43.

Speare, Alden, Jr.
   1971   A cost-benefit model of rural to urban migration in Taiwan. *Population Studies* 25:117-130.

Sweet, Louise E.
  1967 The women of 'Ain ad Dayr. *Anthropological Quarterly* 40:167-183.
Tannous, Arif I.
  1942 Emigration in an Arab village. *Rural Sociology* 7:62-74.
T'ien Ju-k'ang
  1953 *The Chinese of Sarawak: A Study of Social Structure.* London School of Economics Monographs on Social Anthropology, no. 12. London: Lund Humphries.
Topley, Marjorie
  1955 Ghost marriage among the Singapore Chinese. *Man* 55:29-30.
  1959 Immigrant Chinese female servants and their hostels in Singapore. *Man* 59:213-215.
  1961 The emergence and social function of Chinese religious associations in Singapore. *Comparative Studies in Society and History* 3:289-314.
  1964 Capital, saving and credit among indigenous rice farmers and immigrant vegetable farmers in Hong Kong's New Territories. IN *Capital, Saving and Credit in Peasant Societies*, ed. by Raymond Firth and B. S. Yamey. Chicago: Aldine.
Topley, Marjorie (Compiler)
  1969 *Anthropology and Sociology in Hong Kong: Field Projects and Problems of Overseas Scholars.* Centre of Asian Studies, Hong Kong University Press.
Tregear, T. R.
  1958 *Land Use in Hong Kong and the New Territories.* Hong Kong: Hong Kong University Press.
Van Velsen, J.
  1960 Labor migration as a positive factor in the continuity of Tonga tribal society. *Economic Development and Cultural Change* 8:265-278.
Vogel, Ezra F.
  1969 *Canton Under Communism: Programs and Politics in a Provincial Capital, 1949-1968.* Cambridge: Harvard University Press.

Ward, Barbara E.
  1954a A Hakka Kongsi in Borneo. *Journal of Oriental Studies* 1:358-370.
  1954b A Hong Kong fishing village. *Journal of Oriental Studies* 1:195-214.
  1959 Floating villages: Chinese fishermen in Hong Kong. *Man* 59:44-45.
Watson, James L.
  1974 Restaurants and remittances: Chinese emigrant workers in London. IN *Anthropologists in Cities*, ed. by George M. Foster and Robert V. Kemper. Boston: Little, Brown and Company.
  n.d. Agnates and outsiders: Adoption in a Chinese lineage. Forthcoming in *Man*, 1975.
Wickberg, Edgar
  1965 *The Chinese in Philippine Life, 1850-1898*. New Haven: Yale University Press.
Willmott, Donald E.
  1960 *The Chinese of Semarang: A Changing Minority Community in Indonesia*. Ithaca: Cornell University Press.
Willmott, W. E.
  1964 Chinese clan associations in Vancouver. *Man* 64:33-37.
  1967 *The Chinese in Cambodia*. Vancouver: University of British Columbia Press.
  1970 *The Political Structure of the Chinese Community in Cambodia*. London School of Economics Monographs on Social Anthropology, no. 42. London: Athlone Press.
Wittfogel, Karl A.
  1957 *Oriental Despotism: A Comparative Study of Total Power*. New Haven: Yale University Press.
Wolf, Margery
  1970 Child training and the Chinese family. IN *Family and Kinship in Chinese Society*, ed. by Maurice Freedman. Stanford: Stanford University Press.
  1972 *Women and the Family in Rural Taiwan*. Stanford: Stanford University Press.

Wong, C. T.
  1964 Changes in agricultural land use in Hong Kong. IN *Land Use Problems in Hong Kong*, ed. by S. G. Davis. Hong Kong: Hong Kong University Press.

Wong, Leslie
  1967 *Overseas Chinese in Britain Yearbook: 1967*. London: Overseas Chinese Service.

Wrong, Dennis H.
  1961 *Population and Society*. New York: Random House.

Wu Chun-hsi
  1967 *Dollars, Dependents, and Dogma: Overseas Chinese Remittances to Communist China*. Stanford: The Hoover Institution.

Yang, C. K.
  1959 *A Chinese Village in Early Communist Transition*. Cambridge: MIT Press.

Yang, Martin C.
  1945 *A Chinese Village: Taitou, Shantung Province*. New York: Columbia University Press.

INDEX

Adoption, 149, 188n
Adultery. *See* Sexual relations
Affines, 175, 178
Aijmer, L. G., 82
Alcohol, consumption of, 148
"Alien" Chinese (non-Commonwealth immigrants), 6, 112-114
Amsterdam, jumped-ship sailors in, 62, 64
Ancestor worship cult: financial support of, 21, 36; and marriage ritual, 180; grave ceremonies, 210
Ancestral halls: in San Tin, 14, 21-22, 36; and geomancy, 19-20; as banquet sites, 147, 148n, 151; marriage ritual in, 180; renovation of, 210; caretakers of, 211
Ancestral tablets, 22
Anderson, E. N., Jr., 201-202
Assimilation of Chinese in U.K., 124ff
Australia, New Territories emigrants to, 66

Baker, Hugh D. R., 5, 78, 207
Bandits, 23
Banks: in New Territories, 89; in London, 106-107; and remittances, 134
Banquet halls: in San Tin, 22, 36, 147; construction in past, 138; modern renovation of, 140
Banquets: as rites of reentry, 148; as birth observances, 148-150; wedding, 151-152, 176; housewarming, 150

Belgium, Mans in, 28, 106
Boat people: as ethnic group, 11; and landownership, 202
Boredom in San Tin, 142, 147, 166-169
Brackish-water paddy: and history of Man lineage, 31ff; ecological limits of, 37; operation of, 38ff; conversion to fresh-water paddy, 45n; effects of demise, 50, 204ff; conversion to fish ponds, 52-53; near other villages, 78-80; fallow land, 159
Britain: Hakka immigrants in, 82-83; Mans in, 103ff; Chinese "aliens" (non-Commonwealth immigrants) in, 112-114. *See also* Commonwealth Immigrants Act, London
Brunei, New Territories emigrants to, 76
Bureaucracies, lineage intermediation with, 23, 92ff

Cantonese (*pen-ti*) as ethnic group, 11-12, 79n. *See also* Language
Chain migration, 101
Ch'ao Chou (Teochin) as ethnic group, 47
Charter flights, 75, 90-92, 120, 144-145
Chen Ta, 1, 4, 84-85, 160-161, 181, 213-214
Childrearing. *See* Grandparent socialization
China. *See* People's Republic of China
"Chinatown." *See* Gerrard Street